"Good Night, Chet"

"Good Night, Chet"

A Biography of Chet Huntley

LYLE JOHNSTON

McFarland & Company, Inc., Publishers

Jefferson, North Carolina, and London

Library of Congress Cataloguing-in-Publication Data

Johnston, Lyle, 1948–
   "Good night, Chet" : a biography of Chet Huntley / Lyle Johnston.
     p.   cm.
   Includes bibliographical references and index.

   ISBN 0-7864-1502-9 (softcover binding : 50# alkaline paper) ∞

   1. Huntley, Chet, 1911–1974.   2. Television journalists— United
States— Biography.   I. Title.
   PN4874.H834J64   2003
   070.92 — dc21   2003004121

British Library cataloguing data are available

Cover photograph: Chet Huntley in his NBC News office (Museum of the
Rockies Archives, Bozeman, MT)

Manufactured in the United States of America

McFarland & Company, Inc., Publishers
  Box 611, Jefferson, North Carolina 28640
  www.mcfarlandpub.com

To my wife, Paulette,
with all my love

Acknowledgments

In writing this book, I was helped by a number of people, to whom I offer my gratitude.

First, my wife, Paulette, for putting up with my Montana trips the last several years, and the evenings, weekends and vacations spent researching and writing. She saw me through the painful and all but overwhelming process of getting permissions for needed quotes. What an education!

To the Gallatin County Historical Society staff, Bozeman, Montana; the Bozeman Public Library personnel, the Montana Historical Society, Helena; and Chris Mullin, Jennifer Rusk, Laura Rouch, and Jennifer Horsley, at K. Ross Toole Archives at the University of Montana, Missoula; to Amy McKune, Jenny Bocksnick and Steve Jackson at the Museum of the Rockies, Bozeman (the last two archive Chet Huntley's collections); to Bruce Landis of Cardwell, Montana, for helping me find the former Northern Pacific Railroad depot, now a private home, in Cardwell; to Vivie Portnell and Ray Ring at the *Bozeman Daily Chronicle*; to Vonnie Cutler, Belgrade, Mont.; and to Bill Merrick, Bozeman.

To the Northern Arizona University Library, Flagstaff, for having nearly all the books, the *New York Times* microfilms and index and magazines listed in the bibliography and endnotes; to Williams public librarian Andrea Dunn for her interlibrary loan skills and the use of the library computers for Internet research; to Flagstaff City–Coconino County library personnel for their help; to Whitehall, Montana, High School librarian Jeff Vial for information on Chet's high school years; to Roy Millegan and the Jefferson Valley Museum, Whitehall, Montana; and to the Harris Group, Williams, Arizona, for fax machine use. Chet would be envious of what we have today in writing and visual aids, compared with what he worked with at NBC from the 1950s to 1970.

To Bill and Madge Davis, Bea Nothdurft, and our daughter, Celesta, my special gratitude for reading, correcting and making additional comments on this manuscript.

To the following publishers and others for permission to use text and photographs reproduced in this book: *Bozeman* [Mont.] *Daily Chronicle, Billings* [Mont.] *Gazette, Great Falls* [Mont.] *Tribune, Denver* [Col.] *Post, Big Timber* [Mont.] Pioneer, Whitehall [Mont.] *Ledger,* H. W. Wilson Company, University of Illinois Press, New York University Press, University of Washington Press, Oxford University Press, MIT Press, ABC News, New York, University of Missouri Press, University of North Carolina Press/American Film Institute, Iowa State Press, Author: Jonathan Wiesel for his "Big Sky" article quotes, Westview Press/Perseus Books Group, University of Michigan Press, Bantam Books, Publishers, Roy Millegan/Jefferson Valley Museum/*Jefferson Valley News*/Montana Historical Society (Whitehall, Mont. High School pictures/prose; Cardwell Railroad depot photo; newspaper articles), Author: Allen Matusow, Warner Books, Publishers, Author: Rick Graetz, *National Review,* University of Montana, Missoula: K. Ross Toole Archives, Chet Huntley Collection (speeches/photos), Binford & Mort Publishing, Mountain View Publishing Co., *New Republic,* University of Nebraska Press, Wadsworth Publishing Co., *Montana Farmer-Stockman,* Princeton University Press, Random House, Inc., Publishers, Wisconsin Historical Society Press, *Independent-Record* [Helena, Mont.], Hastings House, Publishers, Montana State University: *Exponent,* Houghton-Mifflin Company, Publishers, *McCall's* (magazine), International Creative Management, Inc.: authors: John Chancellor/Walter Mears, *New York Times,* Greenwood/Praeger Publishers, HarperCollins, Publishers, Big Sky [Mont.] Chamber of Commerce (map), Alfred A. Knopf, a Division of Random House, Inc.: David Brinkley, University of Chicago Press/author: Kathleen Turner, Penguin-Putnam/H. R. Haldeman, Sterling Lord Literistic, Inc./author: Edward Epstein, *Time* (magazine), *Life* (magazine), *Broadcasting and Cable* magazine, Gallatin County Historical Society/Pioneer Museum, Bozeman, Mont. (photo), *Variety* (magazine), *Newsweek* (magazine), Nixon Presidential Material Staff (Mar. 21, 1974), Facts on File News Service, CBS News, New York, a division of CBS Broadcasting, Inc., Museum of the Rockies, Bozeman, Mont.—

photos, Richard Nixon Library, Yorba Linda, Cal., TV Guide Magazine Group, Inc., New York, *Washington* [D.C.] *Post* / Writers Group, Reuven Frank, William Whitworth, National Broadcasting Co., Inc. (NBC), New York.

Finally, thank you readers, for buying this volume. I hope it gives Chet Huntley a balanced and definitive biography.

Contents

Preface

Presidential historian Theodore White wrote: "Historians are schol-ars who tell us later what it all means, after time has burned off passing detail, and left the ridges of change bare; their job is to make us aware of [humanity], by dividing the past into periods, or epochs, or eras."

Maybe this biography of Chet Huntley had to wait over twenty-five years to be written. Some who worked parallel careers with him, and those who mention his work, have written their books. Some comments were negative; many others were positive. During the 2000 presidential elec-tion, I heard Chet Huntley and David Brinkley mentioned several times, relating to the 1960 presidential election. On NBC's 75th Anniversary spe-cial, May 5, 2002, NBC remembered Huntley-Brinkley in several video clips from conventions to death announcements.

Like millions of others, I grew up on NBC-TV's nightly newscast, *The Huntley-Brinkley Report*. It ran from 1956 to 1970. I did not know and never had the opportunity to meet Mr. Huntley or Mr. Brinkley person-ally.

Mr. Huntley wrote two books. The first, published in 1966, was *Chet Huntley's News Analysis*, an essay on world politics in 1965. In 1968, Hunt-ley published his second book, *The Generous Years*. It was a biography of his first 18 years in Montana. I wish he had written about the other 44 years but it was not to be.

This biography was created after I visited Bozeman, Montana, in

August 2000. I was surprised by the information that the Montana Historical Society in Helena and the Gallatin County Museum in Bozeman had on Huntley. His papers and artifacts are in the University of Montana library in Missoula, which surpised me, since he was never a student there. Other artifacts are in the Museum of the Rockies in Bozeman. Copies of his NBC newscasts are at the University of Wisconsin, Madison, Vanderbilt University television archives, Nashville, and NBC.

Chet Huntley is quoted often in this biography. A person's biography needs that person's thoughts and words, so wherever possible, Chet comments. The reader will notice, too, that I have put Huntley's life and work in context with American and regional historical events.

When Chet retired as a news anchor in 1970 to oversee building and promoting the Big Sky Resort and ski area south of Bozeman, he did not totally leave broadcasting. He continued to provide commentary on various subjects both in documentaries, in other news and voice-overs on commercials for such clients as American Airlines and the Big Sky Resort. Big Sky produced controversy, and Chet dealt with it. Whether Big Sky might have stayed within his grasp had he lived is unknown. It took another company to take up the torch and become a part of Big Sky's future.

Chet Huntley was a "Westerner" (although the phrase was never fully defined) and a Montanan. He never forgot his roots, and he came home to build something he deeply believed would bring Montana a financial boost and a recreational name. Sadly, he did not finish it. His parents, a sister and Chet are buried in the Sunset Cemetery in Bozeman.

This author found Mr. Huntley to be an interesting human being. I have no tabloid material to offer. This is a simple, straightforward biography.

Now, here is Chet Huntley.

Lyle Johnston
Williams, Arizona
February 2003

I. Chet Huntley:
The Man

Chet Huntley was six feet, one inch in height, about 190 pounds, handsome, brown-haired, blue-eyed. *TV Guide*'s Edith Efron described him as "world-weary faced and soberly dramatic." He had a "dark intensity, with just the slightest touch of pugnacity."[1]

He was often characterized as a serious and well-spoken person. Huntley could read "cold copy" flawlessly.

His career ethic could have been classified as workaholism. One story is told that when he was scheduled to go on vacation, he would write and tape as many as ten "Emphasis" radio commentaries ahead so he would not lose any money (sponsorships) while he was gone![2]

Huntley objected to labels as a "crusader" or a "commentator." He summed up his understanding as a newscaster:

> If a judgment were ever rendered on all the multi-million words I have spoken into microphones, I hope something like this could be said: 'He [Huntley] had a great respect, almost an awe, of the medium in which he worked. He regarded it as a privilege, not a license. He acknowledged, with regret, that for some reason or other he was not endowed with sufficient wisdom to permit him to tell others how to vote, whom to hate, whom to trust, or in what to invest....' Perhaps the best I might hope is that by some accident of voice tone or arrangement of words I did, on a few occasions, excite,

3

exhort, annoy, or provoke a few of my fellow human beings to think with their heads, not the viscera."[3]

On controversial issues, he always insisted on giving background information on *both* sides. His work about the 1950s Communist scare in the United States brought disapproval from American West Coast pressure groups that tried to drive him off the air (see Chapter III). From the Boy Scouts to the United Nations, farming in New Jersey, raising Hereford cattle in Montana, he was interested in many civic and philanthropic groups. An "insufferable do-gooder," Huntley did not think it was a "severe indictment" to be labeled that way.[4]

Professional organizations he belonged to, to name a few, included Overseas Press Club, Association of Radio News Analysts and the San Francisco Press Club.[5]

His wife, Tippy, said: "he had a real affection for rural, usable things: natural textures, no tinsel. Everything had to be good of itself, and sturdy."[6]

Co-anchor David Brinkley said of him,

> Sometimes he was too nice for his own good. Long after we both became, shall I say, household words, he kept his phone listed. And on a Sunday afternoon, the phone would ring and somebody he had never heard of would say, 'Chet, this is Sam Williams. My wife and I are here from Tulsa. You know my cousin so-and-so, and he told us to look you up.' So Chet would end up going to some restaurant with this couple from Tulsa or wherever they came from."[7]

He was described as a "warm, unaffected Westerner." One way to describe this term is mentioned above; another, is while at NBC, Huntley worked from an "old-fashioned roll-top desk," with a painting of "Custer's Last Stand" on his office wall, a brass spittoon in the corner and a Winchester rifle above the desk. The desk was his father's. Concerning the rifle, Huntley stated, he "picked it up in an old junk shop in Billings. Paid $15 for it. Imagine it was used to hit a few buffalo in its day."[8] On a stand nearby was his 1950 Royal typewriter where he wrote thousands of words of commentary.

His evenings involved visits with friends, television viewing, or items newscasters should read: newspapers, magazines and nonfiction books.[9] He did not like New York nightclubs. An occasional outing at a restaurant was not ruled out (see "Tippy" Chapter VII below).

As news anchors, he and Brinkley were "the target of considerable amorous attention. Female admirers phoned both men, stormed their hotel rooms at convention time, pounced on them in the street," and wrote letters. "Love letters, Lots! Some of them even think I can see them from the TV screen," Chet said. NBC producer Reuven Frank added, "He's a pushover for flattery." Chet stated he "did not want to be a celebrity. What business does a reporter have signing autographs?" Nevertheless, he did.[10] He enjoyed signing autographs with "the utmost humor. He really liked people; it was no act."[11] A genuinely nice man, Huntley was an unspoiled, friendly, open person.

Fellow newsman Edwin Newman said, "No other newsman personified NBC News in a way Chet Huntley did." He was "calm, equable, friendly. You could disagree with him but you could not be angry with him — he was too full of good will." Huntley was "big and strong, with an impressive voice and a delivery that could deal with any script." At the national political conventions, "he was a

Chet Huntley. Photograph in Chet Huntley Collection, by permission of K. Ross Toole Archives, Maureen and Mike Mansfield Library, University of Montana, Missoula.

rock. We would see him at his best — easy, relaxed, humorous but on top of the news. He considered all the other broadcasters as equals. Nobody was patronized, nobody was put down."[12]

Another NBC News correspondent and later "NBC Nightly News" anchor John Chancellor said Chet enjoyed "comradeship, practical jokes and good drink." He "worked like a demon and had an outdoorsman-like grace." Huntley was "honest, warm, patriotic and decent."[13]

NBC "Today" show and later ABC-News' "20/20" co-host Hugh Downs stated Huntley "was a consummate reporter and audiences tended to believe him."[14]

Finally, Chet appraised himself in a 1961 *Newsweek* interview: "He's a solemn, frozen, horse face that some people seem to like. He thinks he's awfully lucky to be where he is and sometimes feels it's all transitory, fleeting. He's aware of all the incredible things he does not know. He can't stand ignoramuses or stuffed shirts."[15]

II. The Early Years: 1911–1933

The state of Montana was twenty-two years old at the time of the birth of Chet Huntley. Montana's population in 1910 was 376,053. He was born during the Progressive Era (1900-1916). Thoughtful Americans were concerned with social problems: business abuses, the exploitation of women and children, alcohol traffic, and political corruption.

During the first two decades of the twentieth century, Montana saw a tremendous increase in immigrant farmers from many foreign countries. The Great Northern Railroad's James Hill made plans for this. Glacier National Park was created by a 1910 act of the U. S. Congress. By 1910, agriculture had replaced mining as Montana's major source of income. The 1911 Montana Legislature approved the Everett Bill that allowed Montanans to vote for their U. S. senators directly. In 1914, a constitutional amendment was approved by Montana voters granting women the right to vote in everything. America's first congresswoman and one of Montana's two representatives, Jeannette Rankin, was elected from Montana in 1916. She served two terms (1917–1919 and 1941–1943). Montanans, in 1916, approved the prohibition of alcoholic beverages. Montana went "dry" in 1918. Into this Montana, one half of America's most famous news team was born.[1]

This author is grateful that Chet wrote about those first 18 years. Some

7

Northern Pacific Railway Depot, Cardwell, Mont. Living quarters were on the far end. (The identity of the man is not known.) The building was removed at an unknown date and replaced by the private home pictured opposite. Photograph courtesy of Jefferson Valley Museum, Whitehall, Mont.

of that writing is quoted below. The book in its entirety is recommended to the reader. It can be found in city and college libraries or by interlibrary loan, or in used book stores.

Chester Robert Huntley was born in Cardwell, Jefferson County, Montana, in the Northern Pacific Railroad depot living quarters on Sunday, December 10, 1911. (When he retired from NBC and would visit in the Cardwell and Whitehall area, and wanted to purchase and move the depot to Big Sky, he found that it was privately owned.) Cardwell is today still a small town about 30 miles east of Butte in the southwestern part of the state. A then unincorporated community with a population of 100 in 1910, Cardwell was founded in 1889 when the railroad built in that direction from Bozeman. The community is between the Bull Mountains on the north and the Tobacco Root Mountains on the south. Southeast of Cardwell is the confluence of the Boulder and Jefferson Rivers. The area is very picturesque with its mountain scenery and quietness. Five miles west of Cardwell is Whitehall where the Huntleys would settle when Chet was 15. Today, U. S. Interstate 90 passes on the north edge of both communities. The Northern Pacific Railroad is now the Burlington Northern and its trains are still required to sound their warning horn as they pass on the north edge of Cardwell.

The Huntley ancestry originated in Scotland. Since 1624, the Huntleys have lived in America, starting in Connecticut. Chet was a descendant of the second United States President, John Adams. The Huntley men were veterans of the Revolutionary War, the War of 1812 and the Civil War. Chet, in a tribute to his father, said "Pat" was very proud of his Adams heritage.[2]

Chet's great-grandfather, Reuben Huntley (1824–1862), a corporal in Company K, 6th Wisconsin Infantry, died at the Battle of South Mountain in Maryland. Chet presented his great-grandfather's Civil War letters to the Wisconsin State Historical Society in 1971. The letters between Reuben and his wife, Sarah, have interesting reflections. One letter mentioned a battle: "It last[ed] til dark and then we fell back of the field but we could he[ar] the screams of the wounded awl nite. O Sarah it was awful

Former Northern Pacific Railroad Depot where Huntley was born in 1911. Now a private residence. Lyle Johnston photograph, 2001.

to think of...." He offered another observation: "We have marched 100 miles in one weke when we cum here it was dark and we expected to fi[gh]te in the morning but the rebs run of[f] in the ni[gh]t." Chet mentioned his mother "was horrified when she found that his younger sister [Margaret] had removed all the stamps from the envelopes for a school project."[3]

Sarah Dawes (1825–1898) married Reuben in 1844. One of their children was Albert, Chet's grandfather. Albert Huntley (1846–1925) was a skilled craftsman: woodworker, furniture and carriage maker. Albert married Alice Morris. They would have eight children; the sixth, Percy — "Pat"— was Chet's father.

An older sister of Chet's father had married a Montana Northern Pacific Railway telegrapher. The Northern Pacific Railroad had entered Montana from North Dakota at Glendive in 1881 and completed laying its primary tracks in 1883. Following the Yellowstone River valley, the railroad laid its tracks west across Montana first through Billings, Bozeman, Helena and Missoula then into Idaho and beyond. By 1887 the railroad had received two million-plus acres of Montana from the federal government,[4] a few of which would play a part in Huntley's later life. In 1889, the railroad arrived in the Cardwell-Whitehall area.

Chet's parents were Blanche Wadine Tatham, a former schoolteacher, and Percy Adams "Pat" Huntley, a railway telegrapher. Chet said his father had problems with his name, Percy. If his mother had named him "Adam" he would have been happy. However, his father in later years, when asked his name, would simply say, "Purse." The senior Huntley ultimately became "Pat" for some unknown reason.[5] Pat was born on January 10, 1889, in Necedah, Juneau County, Wisconsin, the sixth child of Albert and Alice (Morris) Huntley. Alice was born in Lemonmeir, Wisconsin, in May 1855 and died in Bozeman, on September 15, 1920. Blanche was born on June 7, 1892, in Wakenda, Carroll County, Missouri, the second daughter of William Robert "Bob" Tatham (1868–1959) and Frances N. Walden (1868–1921). Wakenda is on the north shore of the Missouri River about 50 miles east of Kansas City. The Tathams' lineage can be traced through Kentucky to Virginia; then arrived in Missouri in the 1820s. The Tatham and the Walden families owned several farms and were considered "well off."[6] According to genealogy information, the Tathams came to Montana through Colorado in 1900. Blanche said in a tribute written by her daughter-in-law, Tippy, "My father was always interested in being some place new. We left for Colorado in a covered wagon, with 17 horses ... my mother, my little sister, my father and I. We even camped at Pike's Peak." They returned to Missouri in 1902. John Tatham, an uncle, talked

Blanche's father Bob, into moving to Montana.[7] According to one article, the Tathams lived around Belt, Armington and Great Falls, Montana.[8]

At age 19 Pat came west to visit his sister and her husband. Pat's brother-in-law taught him telegraphy that eventually brought Pat employment on the Northern Pacific. Telegraphy included taking or passing on company messages, emergency information and Western Union telegrams. His salary, in 1912, was $80 a month.[9] Pat was stationed at Springdale, Montana, then was transferred to Columbus, Montana. When he met and fell in love with Bob Tatham's daughter Blanche in 1910 in Springdale, Pat kept the relationship going by traveling N. P. passenger and freight trains back and forth to Springdale.

Pat Huntley and Blanche Tatham were married December 21, 1910, in Billings. The newlyweds attended a performance of *The Chocolate Soldier* that night.[10] Blanche called Pat "Perce." Blanche was a person with smiling blue eyes, and an easygoing and slow-to-anger personality. In later years, she enjoyed ceramics and decoupage.[11]

To Pat and Blanche, Chet and three sisters were born. Celia Wadine Huntley, born February 12, 1914, married Tristram Cummins and they had two children. Marian Huntley, born September 23, 1916, married Dean Turner and they had three children. Margaret Huntley, born July 29, 1920, married Howard Shutes and they had three children.[12] Huntley's parents and a sister, Marian, are buried in the Huntley plot in Bozeman, Montana.

The Farm Near Saco

The Huntley family tried homestead farming 15 miles north of Saco, (pronounced "Sayco"), Montana, in the Milk River country, for about eleven years beginning in 1912. Each family claimed 320 acres for a total of 960. Saco, then a small town of 425, was about 160 miles west of the North Dakota border, and 40 miles south of the Canadian border. When James Hill was building his Great Northern Railroad across Montana in 1887, towns were named, according to legend, by a group of Great Northern executives. A group of station agents from towns along the railroad went to St. Paul, Minnesota, Great Northern's headquarters. They decided to have a blindfolded clerk spin a globe and wherever the man's finger landed, a town was named for that place.[13] Founded in 1892, Saco was named after Saco, Maine. When Blaine and Valley counties were split in 1915, Saco became part of the new Phillips County, named for sheep and mine operator Ben Phillips of Chouteau, Montana.

Chet Huntley, ca. 1913. By permission of Chet Huntley Collection, Museum of the Rockies archives, Bozeman, Mont.

On this 960-acre ranch, the Tathams and the Huntleys raised some sheep, a dozen cows and alfalfa.[14] This part of Montana is gently rolling hills and prairie, few trees except along rivers and creeks. It can be warm in the summer, to put it mildly, and cold as the arctic in winter, except when the Chinook winds blow in from the west. Farming was year around. Chet mentioned one spring:

I sat in the warm sunshine on tops of the hills overlooking the ranch house, the barns, the fields and the lake bed. I [lay] down and put my head on the grass. I could hear it! I could hear spring! The ground was a moving, writhing, stirring mass of movement and growth. Millions of tiny shoots were probing at the warm earth, drinking in its moisture, absorbing its goodness and sending their growth to the sunlight. The earth, the sky, the air, the universe were throbbing with life ... and it was good![15]

Harvests were classified by Mother Nature. For example, northern Montana weather was not kind in 1916. The harvest was poor, but Pat's and Blanche's spirits remained high. The 1917 rains brought green and generosity to the land. Hail ruined their 75 acres of flax that summer. In 1917, the Huntleys had a good harvest, so they went to Missouri to visit the Tatham relatives for the winter. The locusts ate the 1918 crop. Huntley said, "Grandma's turkeys profited from the locusts.... In exaltation, [the turkeys stuffed] their craws to the bursting point with the inexplicable harvest of live feed."[16]

Drought finally took many immigrants of that part of Montana to other parts of the state or to other parts of the United States.[17] The Huntleys were part of the 53,000 who migrated from the farm.

Two other plagues would hit Montana's grain-growing plains. One was the Japanese barberry bush used as landscaping, the other was Russian thistle. The bush hosted a winter spore that killed the wheat. The thistle came with Russian wheat seed imported into the United States. It choked out the grain and thrived on drought. It reseeded itself when the wind broke the shallow roots "in early fall [and it] bounce[d] and tumble[d] across the land." The thistle would pile up "against the fences, stretching the wire and breaking fence posts."[18] The Huntley family tried using it as cattle feed during the winter, but it had no food value; the cattle appreciated the Chinook wind when it melted the snow and exposed the grass underneath.

Blanche said there existed a Montana friendliness then. "...We visited and would have all sorts of dances from daylight 'til dark; and of course on Sunday, the minister would come, and everyone would go some place in the afternoon, or have company. And the neighbors would always help neighbors; they'd bring their horses over when it was a time to do the haying or bring in the grain, and we'd do the same."[19]

The Methodist Episcopal Church of the North Montana Conference established a church in Saco in 1904, and began a

Sister Celia "Wadine" and Chet, ca. 1916, on Huntley-Tatham ranch north of Saco, Mont. By permission of Chet Huntley Collection, Museum of the Rockies archives, Bozeman, Mont.

preaching service at Huntley school in 1916 that had ended by 1922. Several ministers served this appointment during those years, so none could be singled out for the next story. Huntley's grandfather, Bob Tatham, did not like the Methodist minister who came to preach in the Huntley school house. Mrs. Tatham finally had to call her husband "on the carpet" over his cussing when he called the minister "that trombone-playing pious, hypocrite son-of-a-bitch." Huntley said the minister's trombone playing was so "excruciating" that, if his grandfather did attend, his hands would soon cover his ears. Chet thought the minister was "awkwardly slick," had "too much talcum powder on his freshly shaved face," suits that did not fit, and "told unfunny jokes."[20] Concerning other facets of religion, Chet said he read the Bible and found the Psalms to be the best part.

Within a mile of the Huntley farm, the Huntley school was built. Chet started his education there. The student body, all in one room —first to eighth grade, numbered a dozen. He did not "remember learning to read." His teacher, Ada Sommers, "employed the phonic system of instruction. She flashed the cards on which the letters of the alphabet were printed, and in unison we sounded them."[21]

Huntley's "prejudice in behalf of the phonic system has been strong, but the method has all but disappeared. Here and there it is given a

Huntley School, Saco, Montana. Photograph by Gary Svee. Print courtesy of *Saco Independent* and permission of *Billings Gazette.*

Interior of Huntley School, Saco, Montana. Moved to Saco and restored in 1968 by the Saco Garden Club. Photograph by Gary Svee. Print courtesy of *Saco Independent* and permission of *Billings Gazette.*

revival—frequently as a kind of curiosity. [His] generation of Montana youngsters learned to 'sound out' the words, and [he could not] recall a youngster in the later grades or in high school who had any difficulty with reading. Spelling, furthermore, seemed to be an effortless and automatic byproduct of learning to read."[22] Blanche Huntley said "school through the eighth grade, was very important." All the Huntley children went on to college because of their interest in education.[23]

In 1920, when the family moved into Saco, and he was enrolled in school there, the school's population was up to 200 children. He said during those early weeks every boy in his class and "then some" beat him up, and his grandfather encouraged him to fight back. He did and soon gained their respect.[24]

His Whitehall English and speech teacher, Callie Allison, paid tribute to him in a column in the Whitehall, Montana, newspaper, the *Jefferson Valley News*, in 1974. She said, in part,

> ...The students of Whitehall High School can justly be proud of Chet as one of their student body, for he has been a credit to his alma mater.

Rarely does a man of Chet's diversities of talent and abilities, of his enthusiasm and energy, and of his intelligence, pass through the four years of a small high school in a small Montana town that is marked by a small dot on the map....

As his former teacher, I watched the growth of Chet throughout the years and was convinced that some day he would become a man who would be respected for his thoughts and honesty....

To him America was a land of many opportunities; no one knew better than he because he had found those opportunities and they led him to his success. He loved America; he loved his native state Montana; ... the casual living, the down-to-earth people.[25]

Pat Huntley brought home the first radio receiver in late 1920. The family could hear KDKA, Pittsburgh, or Bill Hays from Hastings,

Huntley School children, Saco, Mont., ca. 1919. Back row (l-r): Steve Osier; Carrie Franklin; Mrs. Cord, teacher; Bertha Osier; Rudy Waal. Second row (l-r): Bisgard Kappel; Margaret Bushe; Ruth Kappel; Florence Franklin; Dan Pinkerman. Seated, front row: Elna Waal; Chester Huntley; Gertrude Kappel; and Vic Palm. Photograph courtesy of *Saco Independent.*

Nebraska. Hays was a 26-year-old Scottish immigrant. A music store employee and Methodist church choir director, he was recruited to be KFKX radio's first personality. Hays made it a "good show" at station breaks by announcing, "KFKX, Haastings, Neebrrawska."[26] Neighbors and townspeople dropped in to hear this machine in the Huntley's living room. Montana's first continuous radio station still on the air today is KFBB-AM, 1290 then, now KEIN, 1310, started in Havre in 1922, then moved to Great Falls in 1929.[27]

On occasion, Pat worked for the Great Northern Railroad as a fill-in telegrapher. Pat, deciding the farm was not going to be a fruitful venture anymore, moved his family into Saco and returned to Northern Pacific Railway employment. He began at Silesia, southwest of Billings, in September 1922. Blanche said that "hailstorms, fire, drought, locusts" finally caused the Huntleys to leave the farm.[28] He decided that returning to the Northern Pacific would be "more comfortable and rewarding" than the Great Northern. Chet believed his father's love of fishing the "streams of the mountainous southern [Montana] counties" had something to do with it.[29] Chet had on his NBC office wall a framed memo Pat wrote in August 1923 ordering all Northern Pacific trains "to pause for five minutes in memory of President [Warren] Harding's death."[30]

Leaving the Farm

Chet wrote a few words about the family moving from the farm to Saco for a while. Some included his grandmother's (Frances Tatham's) death from pneumonia in October 1921. She is buried in the Saco Cemetery. Bob Tatham died in 1959 in Casper, Wyoming, and is buried there.

The Huntleys and the Tathams sold the Saco farm in 1924. They were part of the 53,000 who left Montana farming during the 1920s. In the years ahead the Huntley family would live in various southern Montana towns: Big Timber, Norris (1925), Pony, Whitehall (January–August 1926) and Bozeman, to name a few, along the Northern Pacific. In several cases, Percy worked in Alder (August 1926-April 1927) and Twin Bridges (1927) while the family stayed in Whitehall. Blanche said, "We were just a roaming family. [Montana is] a big state, and we saw it all of it."[31] Pat retired in 1960, and he and Blanche spent their final years living in Reedpoint and Billings, Montana.

The depots the Huntley family lived in were two-story buildings along the railroad tracks in each town. Usually in these small towns the railroad employees and families lived in such quarters because of housing shortages.

The railroads also believed that their employees with families could be more responsible and stable and could be good representatives within the community. Because money was kept at the depot, agents who lived there helped "discourage burglars." If the railroad carried fire insurance, having someone living there meant lower rates for the railroad.

The accommodations were no more than two bedrooms, kitchen, living room and one or two closets. Most railroad employees and families did not stop with two children. The Huntleys had four. Two-story depots/living quarters posed problems. For example, indoor stairs so the family had to carry groceries, coal for heating, or even water to the second floor. The winters in Montana are cold, so the living quarters could be drafty. With the depot standing next to the tracks, trains could be both noisy and, at times, earth shaking, if they did not have a reason to stop in that town.

Since this building was also home, it was dangerous for small children. Playing around the building could be injurious because of open-sided freight wagons filled with baggage or freight that might fall if tampered with by inquisitive children. Playing on or near the tracks could be dangerous, too.[32]

Living in Big Timber in the middle 1920s, Chet reminisced about selling the *Minneapolis Tribune* newspaper. "That was the only newspaper I sold as a boy. The country was full of Scandinavians and they would come in off the farm and buy the papers like they were going out of business."[33]

A telegram Chet sent to a friend named Ronald survives that gives us a moment of Chet's life at age 12. The Huntleys were living in Big Timber in 1924. He had joined the Boy Scouts and told Ronald that the troop was going to camp north of Livingston, Montana, the next week. It was an eight-day camp and cost $6.[34] He eventually became an assistant scoutmaster in Whitehall where he helped them with volleyball games in 1927 and 1928.

Pat's telegraphy occupation would play a role in starting Chet toward a career in broadcasting. "During the World Series, Pat Huntley would write down play-by-play reports as they came over the wire, and Chet would announce the action out the depot window to assembled fans."[35]

Whitehall

Whitehall, Montana, became the family's home in 1926. The town was founded in 1890 when the railroad built into that region. Its population in

1920 was 629; in 1930, 553. Named for a large white house of a local settler, Whitehall was originally a stage stop between Helena and Virginia City.

In 1928 Chet worked for the Whitehall State Bank as a teller. When it was robbed, he earned a $50 reward and banked it so it would help with his college expenses. According to Whitehall historian Roy Millegan, there was "some dispute" that Chet, in his book, made a little too much of the bank robbery.[36]

More on his book can be found in Chapter VIII below, called "Other Events."

In a Dec. 28, 2001, letter from Mr. Millegan, he stated, "Chet used to go into the local [Penslar's] drug store, where there was always a fountain in those days, and ordered a cherry Coke, twice a day."

An "A" student in school, Chet was a "popular" and busy student during his high school days, according to Whitehall's present-day high school librarian, Jeff Vial. Fellow student Edward Alexander and Huntley were the first debate team in 1927. They "deserve a great deal of credit and praise for the work they have done in debate" that year, said the 1927 Trail editor. Chet was the secretary-treasurer of the nine-member Parliamentary Club during 1926-1927. Huntley won the 1928 state declamation

Whitehall Mont. High School—1929. Photograph from 1929 *Trail* yearbook. By permission of Jefferson Valley Museum. Whitehall, Mont., and Montana Historical Society, Helena.

contest that was held in Missoula. In Missoula, his school entered for the first time the Little Theater Tournament in 1928. Chet played the part of "Robert Crawshaw" in the comedy *Wurzel-Flummery*. Their group won third place.

A popularity contest was published in the 1927 Trail and in the list of "seconds" Chet was voted "most conceited." In the 1928–1929 calendar of the 1929 Trail Chet was "kicked out of library 8th period" on December 11, 1928. On March 1, 1929, Ed Alexander and Chet "lost their 4-leaf clover." The Whitehall Debate Team lost to Butte (Montana) in debate.

In the 1929 tournament, he played the part of "A Southern Sergeant" in the play *The Clod*. As a member of the high school dramatic club, "The Teasers," he helped present a one-act comedy, *The Love of Pete*, in the Little Theater mentioned above. As a member of the Boys' Glee Club in a

Whitehall High School debate team — 1927. Edward Alexander, left; Chet Huntley, right. By permission of Jefferson Valley Museum, in *Trails*, 1927 Whitehall High School yearbook.

comic opera titled *The Lass of Limerick Town,* he played "Captain Pomeroy Worthington." A member of "The Forum" club that was organized to sponsor debates, Huntley and fellow student Edward Alexander were the school's debate team in 1927, 1928 and 1929. In 1928, they won the championship for Montana's southern district. They were runners-up in 1929 against Butte. "Chester was named the second best debater in the state" that year.

Other interesting items found during his second and fourth years of high school included: 1) he wrote next to his picture in one fellow student's 1927 "Trail" yearbook: "Yes, this is me. Mustn't let you forget that fact. Hope your Soph. year is as happily spent as mine." 2) On the "Just Jokes" page of the 1929 "Trail," Chet and his sports coach/history teacher, Lawrence Walker, are involved in this story:

> MR. WALKER: "What are the national sports of Mexico?"
> CHET HUNTLEY: "Bull fighting and golf."
> MR. W: "Golf isn't played in Mexico."
> CHET: "Sure it is. Didn't you ever hear of the golf of Mexico."

As a four-year member of the basketball team, Chet was on squad

The Forum—1929. Back row (l-r): Edward Alexander; Chester Huntley; Alice Hay, James Woodward. Center row (l-r): Carol Speck; A. Harbison; Clifford McCall. Front row (l-r): Callie Allison (sponsor); Clifford Crane; Jack Pace. Photograph from 1929 *Trail* yearbook. By permission of Jefferson Valley Museum, Whitehall, Mont., and Montana Historical Society, Helena.

Boys' Glee Club, Whitehall High School—1929. Back row (l-r): L. Pinter; Ray Hixon; Chester Huntley; James Dzur (director). Center row (l-r): Clifford Crane; Robert Manlove; Jean Thompson (pianist); William Nichols; Clyde McCall. Front row (l-r): Jack Pace; I. Halverson; M. Westmoreland; Carol Speck. Photograph from 1929 *Trail* yearbook. By permission of Jefferson Valley Museum, Whitehall, Mont., and Montana Historical Society, Helena.

"A" of two squads. The team won the subdistrict tournament, came in second in the southern district, but only won one game of three in the state tournament in 1929. He was a four-year football team member. For example, in 1929 the team won four of six games and were the "undisputed champions of the western section of the southern district." The school could not finance a trip to Billings, Montana, to play for the southern district championship that year, a first for the school! He was "Boys' Athletics" editor for the 1929 *Trail*. Involvement in other areas of school included: scientific treasurer, (1927–1929), Student Council (1927–1929), basketball (1926–1929), Forum (1928–1929), Teasers (1926–1929), Junior Play (1928), Senior Play (1929), Glee Club (1927–1929), *Whitehallite* school paper staff (1928), *Trail* yearbook staff (1929) and declamation (1926–1929).[37]

In a class of 24, Huntley graduated from the Whitehall [Montana] High School in 1929. The graduates were proclaimed the "Wonder Class." This group of teenagers were to become teachers, administrators, attorneys and one future nationally known newsman.

During the summer of 1929 the Northern Pacific Railway hired Chet to fill in temporarily for depot agent-cashier-clerk Bill Hastie.

Following high school graduation, the Huntleys moved to Bozeman so Chet could start college. Pat continued to work in Whitehall and commuted to Bozeman. Bozeman was then a community of 6,900.

It must have been an eye-opener to go from a high school graduating class of 24, to a student body of about 1,200 Montana State College (now university) students. Chet enrolled as a pre-med student (etymology) at MSC in Bozeman. This was his first goal but the Huntley family's financial status during this period in America's history made the "required schooling impossible."[38] In a 1960 interview he spoke of his pre-med years. "It became very apparent to me that my life work was not in science. I was getting my worst grades in science while English, speech and the like were a snap."[39]

Huntley was a tall

Chet Huntley's graduation picture from 1929 *Trail* yearbook. By permission of Jefferson Valley Museum, Whitehall, Mont., and Montana Historical Society, Helena.

young man with swept-back hair. Fellow students recalled that Chet was "a student who acted like any student on campus" and was interested in girls; that he liked trying new words on fellow students (Chet "always learned a new word a day"); that Chet dressed well and always wore a tie ("He was a real fashion plate"); that once, when he needed money, a friend bailed him out by "buying his riding pants and boots"; and that he always had an interest in the theater arts.[40] His involvement in debate and dramatics while at Montana State, and a rise in national oratory contests, won him a scholarship in that field.

By October, he was pledged with the Sigma Alpha Epsilon fraternity. In 1931, he was elected president of the Alpha Psi Omega, a new dramatic fraternity at Montana State. A member of the Montana State College Players, he played Jimmy Ludgrove in the drama "*The Perfect Alibi*, on November 20, 1932. Other plays during his years at MSC were *Mary Rose*, as leading man, and *Granite*. He directed *The Monkey's Paw*.

Huntley was a member of the 1932, nine-member Pi Kappa Delta, "a national honorary debating fraternity organized for the purpose of fostering debate, oratory and extemporaneous speaking." In addition, he was a member of the Sigma Alpha Epsilon fraternity.[41]

In the 1932 MSC yearbook, the *Montanan,* where he was athletics and associate editor, it was written about Huntley, "unfortunately his dramatic style of speech was not regarded as favorably as the conversational types employed by the other speakers and in the finals he received seventh." However, at the end of the article, it was written, "This is the highest rating any MSC speaker has ever been awarded in national contests and indicates distinct superiority."[42]

Huntley wrote for a 1966 book by *Seventeen* magazine some thoughts on speaking:

> Beautiful speech is not difficult to acquire. A single school year of instruction is sufficient to master the sounds and the rules which govern them. From then on it is merely a matter of reading aloud. Correct speech is actually just as entertaining and satisfying as playing a stack of favorite phonograph records. Voice quality, too, can be altered or changed with no great effort. The human larynx is an incredible instrument. It will do just about anything the brain tells it or demands of it. Upon request, and with a bit of practice, the human sound system will overhaul itself and become a thing of rare beauty.[43]

Huntley's father was working only two days a week during the Depression, so Chet worked as a waiter, a telegram delivery person, washed windows and sold pints of his blood.[44] During his summers and weekends out of high school and college he worked on farms and ranches.[45] He mentioned, in a 1959 speech, his 1931 summer.

> I was working a hay crop on a ranch over in Ross's Hole and a horse nipped me on the arm, with the consequence that I wound up [in Missoula] in the Northern Pacific Hospital with a thriving infection. I recall that a friend came by and I rode with him from Missoula to my home in Bozeman in his old Model T Ford. Just this side of Butte, a connecting rod burned out and we put the tongue of my shoe in between the connecting rod and the crankshaft. To my knowledge that Ford went the rest of its life with my shoe-tongue. I suppose the only moral of that story is that the Model T invited,

commanded, and permitted a good deal more ingenuity than the contemporary models.[46]

Huntley's interests in farming and ranching would eventually get him into trouble with the federal government. In his later years, he could say with deep pride that he had more "manure on his boots than any Eastern dude."

Seattle's Cornish School of Arts professor E. R. Lovejoy, in the summer of 1932, interviewed Huntley "for dramatic material for moving pictures."[47] From this interview and his oratory style, he received a scholarship. That fall, he transferred to and was enrolled for a year and a half at Cornish. One play he starred in March 20-25, 1933, was *As You Like It* by William Shakespeare. His character was Dennis. This school was created by Nellie Cornish in 1914 in Seattle. Its prime focus was on dance. However, as the school grew, the curriculum became more diversified. The school established, in about 1932, the nation's first radio school. While at Cornish, Chet was stage manager in the drama department.

In the winter of 1934, Huntley transferred to the University of Washington, Seattle. In the winter of 1935, he completed his Bachelor of Arts degree in drama with minors in zoology, history, literature and journalism from the University of Washington, Seattle. He did not apply for graduation until 1942, graduating that June.[48] The university was established in 1861 and later was housed in the former buildings of the Alaska-Yukon-Pacific Exposition which was held in 1909. Huntley was one student among 9,600 in 1933. Seattle, founded in 1853, was the largest city in the Pacific Northwest with a 365,500 (1930) population. Its largest employer was Boeing Aircraft, established in 1916.

According to the *Jefferson Valley News*, May 31, 1934, Chet was fined $25 on May 8 for speeding in Seattle. He was hoping his friends would bail him out as he did not have the money. Chet ended up serving eight days in jail. The judge would not let him have a school book to read during his incarceration. On May 17–18, he had the leading role in the university play, *The Little Clay Cart*.

On March 21, 1935, Huntley played "Tom Collier" in *Animal Kingdom*, a play by Phillip Barry, at the Studio Theater in Seattle. These parts were a prelude to his future involvement in radio programs and movies mentioned below in Chapter III.

III. The Radio
(and Early Television)
Years: 1934–1955

Huntley's 1930s radio news reporting covered such national historical events as President Franklin Roosevelt's New Deal programs, the pre-
World War II news of Germany's invasion of various countries in Europe;
and Japan's expansion in the western Pacific Ocean region.

Of all Washington state's historical events, the biggest was the Depression of the 1930s, the beginning of the Columbia River Basin Project, and
the Bonneville Power Administration's building dams and providing
hydroelectric power to the Pacific Northwest and other western states.

Huntley told an interviewer at the time of his retirement in 1970,
"back in '37 or '38, I felt the [U. S.] government was the answer to all our
problems. But the federal government, I've concluded, is now [1970] an
insufferable jungle of self-serving bureaucracies."[1]

A short history of radio news gathering is required in this section.
Radio newscasts during the 1930s were taken from several sources: rewrites
of newspaper stories, police records, courthouse sources, press releases,
people calling in and the wire services such as Associated Press, United
Press International or International News Service. The AP began offering
its service to member newspapers in 1922 with a notice that its news

bulletins were not to be used for radio broadcasts. UPI and INS were willing to supply radio with their bulletins. By the mid-1920s newspaper journalists expressed worry that radio news would threaten their business. By 1933 newspapers had brought enough pressure to stop UPI and INS service to radio. By 1940, publisher and broadcaster problems were resolved. Major networks such as the National Broadcasting Company — NBC — (1926) and the Columbia Broadcasting System — CBS — (1927), by the summer of 1933, and later ABC and Mutual Broadcasting System (MBS), began offering world, national and even regional coverage. CBS established full news bureaus in London, New York, Washington, Chicago and Los Angeles. NBC assigned a few people to gather and report the news but not to the extent that CBS did. With competition, radio stations began giving thought to hiring a news director or assigning the local news to a staff member.[2]

Chet Becomes a Newsman

Chet said, "the Depression years taught me the value of a dollar, how to study, and how to talk myself into my first job as a radio announcer."[3] He was also "one of the few men of any seniority in the [newscasting] business who [had] no newspaper experience to speak of."[4] CBS' Edward Murrow was another.

Beginning his broadcast career in 1934, at seven-year-old KPCB radio, 710-AM frequency (now 50,000-watt KIRO), one of eight radio stations in Seattle, Huntley earned $10 a month. He said, "his first job was the first one he could find. 'I got off a streetcar, walked into a radio station and got a job.'"[5] He received the job because KPCB's program director had just been fired. It was reported he "overheard the station manager firing the program director and, as the dispirited fellow came out, [Chet] confidently walked in. A few minutes later the 24-year-old Huntley was the new program director."[6] His job description also included announcer, salesman, janitor, writer and disc jockey. He supplemented his salary by the station's laundry service and could use sponsorship accounts to trade for food. There was no wire service for radio news, so he bought a *Seattle Star* (newspaper) each day and rewrote the news for a 15-minute newscast each night, he admitted.[7] His first commercial was for a local funeral home.

"I remember the old days— you sat down [at a microphone], the red light came on [meaning 'on the air'], and there you were — you pretty much had to feel your way,"[8] Chet declared in 1968. He remembered that first radio position in another interview. "I was convinced that radio was a good medium for news. A lot of things were happening, so I got on the newspaper's radio station [KPCB]. I ran sort of an underground news broadcast. I bought the newspaper from the corner and rewrote it. I also ran the transmitter, spun records, wrote ad copy and swept out" the station.[9] In addition, Chet hosted KPCB's one-man grand opera broadcast, providing commentary and sound effects every Sunday afternoon from 2 to 5 P.M.,[10] in the fall of 1934. According to the *Jefferson Valley News*,

> With seven sound effect records (some he recorded himself) and complete operas recorded in Europe — it takes 15–20 discs to record a complete opera — Huntley has been giving sustaining programs over KPCB several weeks. First, speaking into the microphone himself, Huntley announces the opera — 'it will be Rigoletto as recorded in La Scalla this afternoon' — gives a historical background to the subject and its composer and describes the ensuing act. Then Huntley starts one of his sound effect records playing. You hear the instruments being tuned and the leader's baton rap for attention. Then (Huntley has to be quick fingered to present his opera) he sets the first record of the opera playing. He changes records as each one ends and intersperses natural-sounding effects at the proper places, doing some ... of his comments between acts.[11]

The program was the first of its kind on radio, according to the music industry's *Billboard* magazine. There were 26 operas, with nine of the most popular re-broadcast for a total of 35 weeks.

Several historical events were happening in the state of Washington while Huntley was going to school and just after graduation. President Roosevelt's Great Depression programs, one of them the National Recovery Administration (NRA), provided the Washington state labor movement with tools to organize among the workers. In Seattle, strikes included those by the waterfront/maritime employees in 1934 and 1936. Also striking were lumbermen, affecting 40,000 people, that closed mills and camps for a while in 1935. A newspaper strike shut down the *Seattle Post-Intelligencer* and the *Seattle Star* for several months in 1936. These were news items and Chet reported them.[12]

In 1936, Chet applied for a position on KHQ-AM, 590, Spokane, Washington, where he was hired as a newscaster and a writer. KHQ, now KAQQ, began broadcasting in 1922, one of three radio stations in the community. Spokane, then 115,500 in population, was in a farming area of Washington state's eastern center. The area was first settled by the North West [fur] Trading Company in 1810. A larger settlement by 1871, Spokane had become a community in 1878, and incorporated as a city in 1881.[13]

Later, at KGW-AM, 620, one of seven radio stations in Portland, Oregon, in 1936–37, Chet became a writer, newscaster and announcer. KGW,

on the air since 1922 and an NBC Blue Network affiliate, was one of two
stations then owned by the *Oregonian* newspaper. The Blue Network, of
"slightly less quality," was one of two NBC networks established in 1926.
According to legend, the red and blue were what the radio engineers used
to color code their network maps. Portland, first settled in 1829, had begun
its steady growth by 1845. It was and still is the largest city in Oregon. In
the mid-1930s, the city's population was 302,000. Portland is located on
the Willamette River south of its confluence with the Columbia River,
and a majority of its factories were powered by electricity from the river.
This made Portland soot- and smoke-free. Products produced during the
1930s ran from flour and cereal to foundry wares. Portland's major
employer was the Kaiser shipyards. The city was and still is a docking site
for several shipping companies. For the first three decades of the 20th century, Portland was also known as the music center of the Pacific Northwest.

Events reported by KGW News were the construction of the Portland
airport, struggles by the labor unions to unionize, and the Portland Public Forum. This forum, an eight-month program, involved adult education jointly sponsored by the federal government, the Oregon Works
Project Administration and the Oregon education commissioner. The
Portland Public Forum was one of ten national demonstration projects.[14]

Chet's next move was to Los Angeles and KFI-AM, 640, 1938-39.
Here he was part-time newscaster, part-time vacation relief announcer.
KFI was on the air in 1922 and one of 14 stations in the Los Angeles area
when Huntley arrived. In 1939 he was hired by the Columbia Broadcasting System (CBS).

Huntley supplemented his income by doing voice-overs for "scores
of movie trailers [and] introducing dance bands on late-night broadcasts"[15] and acting/announcer parts in movies mentioned below. The late
night dance band announcing, for $15 a week, was done at Earl Carroll's
restaurant in Los Angeles. He mentioned he "wasn't proud of having to
moonlight, but he liked the music and he enjoyed listening to grandiose
schemes of the band's young piano player, Stan Kenton."[16]

While living in Seattle and attending the University of Washington,
Chet met Ingrid Rolin. On February 23, 1936, they married in Seattle. In
1939, he commented on her as, "the prettiest, housekeepingest, best cook
and finest Swedish wife you ever saw." She could make a dollar stretch
into two. On occasion her cooking helped him win a sponsor for his radio
programs.[17] They had two daughters, Sharon (born in 1940) and Leanne
(born in 1943). Sharon would marry Dan Arensmeier; Leanne would
marry Eskandar Khajavi. While he was working in California, they lived

in "a beautiful home in Van Nuys."[18] Ingrid and Chet were divorced in early 1959. In the Huntley collection can be found a picture of Chet and a pretty blonde woman. Unfortunately, the back of the photo did not have names. Because of this, a photo of Ingrid and Chet is not included in this biography.

When the Huntleys moved to the Los Angeles area in 1939, the city's population was just under 1.5 million. The city was founded in 1781. By 1869 Los Angeles was southern California's social and political center. San Diego was the economic center because of its harbor. After the first World War, Los Angeles' Chamber of Commerce started attracting industrial plants, by publicity to eastern corporations. Several

Chet broadcasting on KFI radio, Los Angeles, Cal., ca. 1939. Photograph in Chet Huntley Collection. By permission of K. Ross Toole Archives, Maureen and Mike Mansfield Library, University of Montana, Missoula.

industries picked Los Angeles: first, the movie industry, and Chet would get into it in a minor way. Second, rubber companies decided to build their plants there because of its location to Asian rubber plantations, Imperial Valley's cotton fields, and southern California's tire market. The auto industry decided to build in Los Angeles, too. High technology also found a home: aerospace built plants in Long Beach (Boeing), in Santa Monica (Douglas), and in Burbank (Lockheed). The city and its suburbs experienced substantial growth in population. Neighborhood homogeneity encouraged by developers caused blacks and Orientals to be excluded from new communities. Property was priced so that similar income families were grouped together. The Los Angeles area was "strongly influenced by urban crises back East and by a whole national ideology where the city is feared and hated." Rating itself as a "good community," "it tried to define itself as a sort of counter-city, free from most urban diseases, from social conflicts and modern sins." During the second World War, Los Angeles suffered from a housing shortage. Housing was made available to immigrants who came to work in the war industries. Local authorities hoped these immigrants would return to their respective states after the war, but that did not happen.[19] The first freeway, the Santa Monica, was completed in 1940. Smog began developing over the city in 1943.

While working in California from 1939 to 1955, Huntley reported on the continued migration of Midwest farmers to California which was helping to produce a high unemployment rate. As World War II became part of American history, Huntley also reported on the economic upsurge as California became a center for aircraft and ship building. A sad side effect of the war was the detention of Americans of Japanese descent to both instate and out-of-state camps, and the confiscation of their property.

In his autobiography, Huntley mentioned his non-involvement in the military:

> I have been startled with the realization that I was born at about that precise time in the early twentieth century to have seen this nation of ours engaged in four foreign wars [World War I, World War II, Korea, Vietnam], to have remembered all of them, and yet to have been either too young or too old to participate in any of them as a combatant. We Americans born in that brief span of years around the turn of the century and shortly thereafter are unique in having experienced more wars than any other generation of our country, which is perhaps only a sad commentary on this violent century.[20]

He registered for military service on October 16, 1940, and was classified 2-A-L. At that time, the Huntleys were living in Burbank, California.

CBS Years

The CBS years included reporting on: the events of World War II; President Franklin Roosevelt's death in 1945; most of Harry Truman's years (1945–1951) as President; the beginning of the Cold War (1946): Soviet and American relations deteriorating as a result of each's interpretation of the others actions, with Soviet influence branching out to other European countries and America reaching out to form the North Atlantic Treaty Organization (NATO) (1949) with various European countries; the Berlin airlift in 1948–9; the McCarthy Communist scare of the early 1950s; and the beginning of the Korean War in 1950.

For twelve years, 1939–51, he was associated with CBS' KNX, 1070, and CBS News as a newscaster, correspondent and analyst. The position paid $65 a week in his first year. KNX went on the air in 1922. Chet completed his Los Angeles newscasting with ABC, 1951–55.[21] He mentioned KNX being part of a "genuine news network. I was correspondent for 11 western states," he stated of his radio years in a 1960 interview. For CBS, he was a "correspondent"; after World War II, he was elevated to "commentator." "They don't give you a title until you are a pro," he stated.[22]

In January 1941, CBS transferred Chet into their news and special features bureau. His assignment was to be editor of war information, writer and director of their special events, and to help with public affairs programs, public relations, news and analysis. During World War II, he was a regional director for two war bond campaigns. The United States Department of the Treasury, in gratitude, awarded him a medal.

After Japan attacked the United States at Pearl Harbor, Territory of Hawaii, in late 1941, the U. S., in 1942, evacuated Americans of Japanese descent from the west coast to various locations across western America. Chet reported about one group from Poston, Arizona, on a national CBS radio hookup on May 26, 1942.

As a correspondent in the Pacific region on "two or three brief assignments" during the war, he was "shot at quite a few times; and [that was] pretty exciting."[23] Chet remembered World War II radio news reporting in a 1959 speech. "It kept a nation reasonably well informed ... quickly, accurately, and without editorial axes to grind. A tremendous public confidence in radio news was established. As for the radio commentators or news analysts, while the public tended to split the question of their accuracy or degree of responsibility, still the public found them interesting."[24]

Concerning the 11-state area he covered as a CBS correspondent, the World War II era and beyond saw the U. S. government become involved, through its Atomic Energy Commission, in atomic bomb testing in New Mexico where the first bomb was exploded on July 16, 1945. A testing center was built northwest of Las Vegas, Nevada, and nuclear bombs were first tested there in 1951. Uranium was discovered in northwest New Mexico in 1950. A nuclear research facility was built at Las Alamos, New Mexico.

Defense plants were created in Oregon. The shipyards in Portland built war and cargo ships. Military supplies were made in that state's factories. In Utah, the U. S. government created military bases, then expanded them after the war. In Arizona, cloudless days were an asset that caused the U. S. government to construct a number of military bases to train pilots.

The mining of precious metals in Nevada and Colorado kept their economies going. In Montana, the need for grain and meat helped its economy boom. However, when the war ended, grain prices fell and agriculture income dropped causing the people to leave Montana's farming areas. Camp Minidoka, near Idaho Falls, Idaho, became a relocation camp for Japanese-American citizens from Washington and Oregon. These Japanese-Americans, because of a farm worker shortage, worked the sugar beet and potato fields around Idaho Falls. A nuclear reactor testing station was constructed near Idaho Falls. The station produced the first electricity made from nuclear energy, in December 1951. Food processing and manufacting brought Idaho a post-war economic boom.

As already mentioned World War II began in the Territory of Hawaii in 1941. The National Memorial of the Pacific Cemetery was developed and dedicated near Honolulu in 1949. A year later (1950) the territory wrote a constitution that was used for its 1959 statehood bill. In Alaska in 1942, the Japanese bombed the Aleutian Islands at Dutch Harbor — two islands, Kiska and Attu, were occupied. U. S. troops drove the Japanese out in 1943. The Alcan Highway into Alaska from Canada was completed in 1942.

Chet covered the creation of the United Nations when delegates met in San Francisco in the spring of 1945.

In 1943 Huntley was assigned to the special events staff at KNX radio. For the Pacific Coast CBS stations, he produced and voiced a ten-minute news and commentary program. While in California, Huntley made known his concern over the lack of black Americans in broadcasting, especially drama. "When Pillsbury Flour balked at sponsoring a program featuring blacks cast in roles that were outside the normal stereotypes that were common in radio at that time, Chet [researched and] offered an opinion that sponsor sensitivity to blacks in normal roles also accounted for the lack of news coverage of events in the black community." The author added, "I presume that the reason for less Negro news was due to sales resistance. Sponsors would probably fear boycott of their products."[25]

Huntley produced an award-winning 30-minute series, "These Are Americans," for KNX that was broadcast in 1942 (see below). He did a second series titled "These Are Americans, Too" that was broadcast in 1944.

In 1942 and 1954, Huntley won the George Peabody Award for excellence in news analysis. The 1942 award was for the series "These are Americans." This series "attempted to show Angelenos, [natives of Los Angeles] at that time angered by recent Mexican zoot-suit riots in [Los Angeles], that most Mexican-Americans [were] good citizens."[26] Also, a part of this program was about blacks in the military and in broadcasting. For this commentary, the New York University (New York City) presented to him an award.

The zoot-suit was clothing cut loosely at the top, but with pants tapering at the ankle worn by some Mexican-Americans. Mexicans and Californians had close ties. Military personnel stationed in the Los Angeles area did not understand this. A gang attacked a group of sailors walking around town but the attackers were never found. However, "the sailors described them as Mexican and a feud began." Bands of soldiers, marines and sailors roamed the town looking for zoot-suited Mexicans to attack.

The police sided with the servicemen and a week-long riot started. Public indignation toward the police and servicemen brought an end to the problem. Parts of the city were closed to the military men, organizations were created to help protect the minorities, and the police department was reorganized and reeducated in minority culture.[27]

The zoot-suit riots provided "the cautionary incentive" to produce six fifteen-minute programs titled "These Are Americans, Too." Involved were the Hollywood Writers' Mobilization (HWM), an entertainment-based liberal group of writers, and local civic groups. Sponsored by HWM and the CBS Department of Education — Western Division, the program ran for six weeks from late January to early March 1944. Huntley, a member of the Writers' Mobilization, wrote and narrated the program. Introducing the first program, Huntley said the series was "about the American Negro: about his problem, about his education, about his place in industry, business, the arts, the armed forces and his position in our society." The programs "worked from the assumption that a change in race relations and the extension of greater opportunities to African Americans were not only inevitable but also imminent. Its primary goal was to coax white Americans into accepting the idea of equal opportunity and fair play for African Americans while calming their fears about the practical implications of such a political and social shift."

"These Are Americans, Too" was a regional broadcast. It did not receive a "southern white reaction." Huntley repeatedly reassured the radio listeners, especially Caucasians, "who were fearful of the impact of great black freedom on the racial status quo." The program, overall, did not spend much time "justifying the extension of full rights" to blacks. It focused its attention on managing the "transition in race relations." In a later interview, Huntley said he received a letter from a man who asked him the definitive racial inquiry, "[W]ould you want your daughter to marry a Negro?"[28]

The Ohio State University Institute for Education by Radio presented him with a special news citation.

In October 1945, he covered the United Nations' formation in San Francisco for CBS Radio News, and its tenth anniversary for NBC News in 1955.

He narrated episode 16 of "The Trial," part of the Nuremberg, Germany, war crimes trial. The episode was broadcast May 19, 1946, on the CBS Radio network.

In 1949, CBS sent him to Europe for several weeks. Huntley reported on the progress of the Berlin airlift. The Soviets had blockaded Berlin beginning in June 1948 because the Western Allies decided the Western German zones, including Berlin, needed to be unified. The airlift ended in September 1949. The North Atlantic Treaty Organization (NATO) that initially included Belgium, Canada, Denmark, France, Iceland, Italy, Luxembourg, the Netherlands, Norway, Portugal, the United Kingdom and the United States was formed from a military agreement designed to hold the Soviet military forces in Eastern Europe. The Geneva Convention met to decide on further rules for prisoners of war. Russia developed the atomic bomb. Konrad Adenauer began his term as West Germany's Chancellor; Walter Ulbricht began his term as East Germany's Communist dictator.

Television, especially in the large cities, was making inroads into radio listener- and viewership by the late 1940s. Chet Huntley moved toward that medium, too. During the 1950s the television set became a furniture piece in the American home. This leisure-time activity brought national and world scenes into the American living room. Television soon became a ratings game between networks and between network television news organizations.

In 1946, Huntley was a founding member of the Radio News Club of Southern California. He later became its president. Chet recognized that broadcast news journalism should not be "a plaything, an instrument of a broadcast owner's own political biases or business objectives." He "spearheaded the battle against a powerful radio station owner [George "Dick" Richards and his group of radio stations, one of them, Los Angeles' KMPC-AM] who commanded, on pain of dismissal, that his news employees slant the news to fit the owner's political, economic, and social biases." For example, the news was against Franklin Roosevelt's New Deal and against Roosevelt personally. "Pigboy" or "Tumbleweed" was what former Vice President Henry Wallace was to be called. President Harry Truman was to be called "Pigsqueak." When Eleanor Roosevelt was involved in an auto accident, Richards "ordered KMPC to make it seem as if she had been drinking."[29]

The final item that caused Richards' downfall came in January 1948. Richards had invited General Douglas MacArthur for his birthday, along with Richards' stations' personnel, to a Los Angeles restaurant. Richards was hoping to start the campaign to get MacArthur elected U. S. president. KMPC's news director Clete Roberts had been sent to Tokyo to film and record material for the party. Richards had reviewed the material and gave instructions about it. A radio was brought into the restaurant so everyone could hear the program as it was broadcast over KMPC.

Richards had instructed Roberts not to mention MacArthur's age. However, Roberts noticed and mentioned MacArthur's hand tremor. Richards became angry. Radio commentator Walter Winchell picked up the comment, quoted it on his program and Richards' anger grew. Roberts lost his job. At the next Radio Club of Southern California meeting Roberts told his story. Huntley and the Club reacted.[30]

Huntley sent affidavits to the Federal Communications Commission (the federal licensing authority for, at that time, all radio stations and announcers, etc.) "documenting Richards' policies." As a witness before the FCC on October 18, 1950, Chet provided key testimony against the owner. "Hearings were being held when Richards died." Assured by his heirs and stockholders that this practice "would be discontinued, the commission closed the case" and the Richards group was allowed to keep its licenses.[31]

Radio and Movie Parts

During the 1940s, Huntley was a narrator or small part actor in several radio programs and movies. In 1942 he was the radio announcer in the 92-minute RKO pictures *The Big Street.* Starring Henry Fonda and Lucille Ball, the melodrama, about a "timid busboy who devoted himself to a self-centered nightclub singer,"[32] was based on the short story "Little Pinks" by Damon Runyon. Runyon was producer and Irving Reis was director.

Between 1942 and 1944, Chet narrated a first-person true human adventure radio drama on the CBS West Network titled "I Was There." CBS broadcast "dramatic accounts of leading events told by persons who were there." The 30-minute program broadcast three separate incidents. During the two years of its existence during World War II, the themes were wartime adventures. The network believed the programs would be made more believable by including its regular news commentators such as Knox Manning and Chet Huntley. The music was provided by Lud Gluskin and was produced by Robert Hafter.[33]

He was listed on a radio program called "Mail Call — A Letter from

Home" for the Armed Forces Radio Network. The January 20, 1943, program listed actress Alice Faye, actor Cesar Romero, band leader Tommy
Dorsey and Chet Huntley as participants.

Gung Ho!, an 88-minute, World War II movie about U. S. Marines
recapturing a crucial Pacific island, was narrated by Huntley. The Universal Pictures Co., Inc., release starred Randolph Scott, Noah Beery, Jr.,
Peter Coe, and J. Carroll Naish. Released in 1943 the movie was based on
the story "Gung Ho!" by W. S. LeFrancois. It was produced by Walter
Wanger and directed by Ray Enright.[34]

In a 1943 release, he was the announcer for the 1942-filmed, 101-
minute, RKO pictures, Flight for Freedom. It starred Rosalind Russell and
Fred MacMurray. The aviation drama story was written by Horace McCoy.
I Cheated the Law! was a 1949 film by Belsam Productions and a 20th Century–Fox release. Chet played himself in this legal crime drama. The 71-
minute, black and white movie starred Tom Conway, Steve Brodie and
Barbara Billingsley.[35] Chet played "Landers" in the 1949 Universal International Pictures release Arctic Manhunt. The movie, starring Mike Conrad and Carol Thurston, was about an ex-convict's attempt to find
sanctuary in the Arctic "as a missionary among the Eskimos." The story
was based on Ewing Scott's "Narana of the North." It was produced by
Leonard Goldstein.[36]

Chet narrated another crime drama about drug smuggling in New
York City, Port of New York. The 79-minute, black and white Contemporary Productions movie starred Scott Brady, Yul Brunner, and Richard
Rober. Produced by Aubrey Schenck and directed by Laslo Benedek, the
movie was scripted from a story by Arthur Ross and Bert Murray.[37] In
1950, a movie drama about God on the radio and the "profound effect on
Anytown U. S.A.," The Next Voice You Hear, was made. The 82-minute,
black and white MGM movie starred James Whitmore and Nancy Davis.
Chet was the radio personality.[38]

Anti-Communism

The late 1940s and early 1950s "were bad times for liberals" in radio
and television.[39] Huntley's years with CBS ended in early 1951 because
"his bosses were unhappy with his liberal commentary, and because he
refused to sign a loyalty oath."[40] The loyalty oath was a statement that he
was not a Communist and his allegiance was to America. Ten years later,
he added, "It's still a moot point whether I was fired or resigned."[41] At CBS,
he was earning $750 a week. Huntley always insisted on giving background

information on "both sides" of any issue. One of those issues, Communism, would arouse West Coast pressure groups that tried to drive him off the air as early as 1950.[42]

Concerning Communism in the United States, Huntley said it "has been a despicable and miserable little dust devil inflated by its enemies." Around the world, it had had a "miserable performance and track record everywhere[.] We are compelled to acknowledge that Marxism is still a force to be reckoned with."[43]

U. S. Senator Joseph McCarthy (R-Wisconsin) began holding hearings on Communism in America in February 1950 that lasted for four years. In a Wheeling, West Virginia, speech, February 9, 1950, McCarthy pulled from his pocket a sheet of paper with people's names; they were, he claimed, "members of the Communist Party" who worked for the U.S. State Department.[44] On investigating the State Department, for example, no Communists or Communist sympathizers were found by the Senate Foreign Relations Committee. Making additional accusations, McCarthy gained quite a following. Sadly, thousands of Americans came under suspicion and were affected by McCarthyism: ministers, journalists, college professors, actors and actresses, film directors, librarians, to name a few. Those accused of Communist affiliation were blacklisted (refused consideration for employment). Loyalty oaths to the U. S. government were required by many employers. McCarthyism declined by 1954 because of the end of the Korean War, and the Senate accused McCarthy of conduct unbecoming a senator. By 1958, several U. S. Supreme Court decisions had helped secure the rights of citizens accused of being Communist sympathizers. Newsmen who spoke against McCarthy were Elmer Davis, Edward Murrow and Chet Huntley. Huntley commented in 1961, "Maybe it was a mistake [to attack McCarthy], and to this day I'm not sure, but I felt I should define my attitudes."[45]

Huntley supported UNESCO and criticized McCarthy and "various other right-wing causes." (UNESCO was and is the United Nations Educational, Scientific and Cultural Organization. UNESCO's mission was and is to further peace among all nations by way of education and science. A boycott was called against Huntley's sponsor, a coffee company. The company and various liberal groups stood with him. As the controversy intensified, the company's sales increased as Huntley's supporters "urged their friends to buy the product. The opposing group could not rally the support to boycott."[46]

In 1950, Huntley's criticism of McCarthy brought an accusation of his being a Communist, which he denied. He sued for $200,000. In January 1954, he won his lawsuit against one of his leading accusers, Mrs.

Rae Suchman, over this slander. She had to publish a retraction which was printed in the Hearst-owned Los Angeles *Evening Herald and Express.* The newspaper had given Suchman and her group "unprincipled and enthusiastic support," so it had to be painful to print the following: "I wish to state publicly that I have found no evidence which would indicate that Mr. Huntley is other than a patriotic, loyal American. I have no evidence which in any way links him with any subversive organization or undertaking. This statement is a public apology by me for any contribution I may have made to organized efforts to silence him or to induce advertisers to withdraw sponsorship of his broadcasts." The court ordered her to pay Huntley $10,000 "which he never collected."[47] The group's campaign had cost Huntley at least one sponsor. The *New Republic* magazine added: "Now that they have been given a lesson in the fundamentals of Americanism, lack of evidence may cause them to stop their running attacks on [syndicated columnist] Drew Pearson and Mrs. [Eleanor] Roosevelt as well."[48] Huntley said, he "didn't want [the money], but the judgment still stands to keep the party from opening her mouth again."[49] Because of his courage on this subject, Chet won CBS' Edward Murrow's admiration and friendship.[50] Chet also won the admiration of many in the entertainment business. In one of his biographies, Edward Murrow said, "Two of the best known news broadcasters on the [Pacific] Coast" are Chet Huntley and Nelson Pringle. They are "old friends of mine."[51]

A Few Movies and a Travelogue

Before we say something about the ABC years, Huntley was involved in several more movies and specials during the 1950s. He had a small acting part as a baseball broadcaster in the 1952 20th Century–Fox, black and white, 93-minute movie *The Pride of St. Louis,* starring Dan Dailey and Joanne Dru. It was a biopic of baseball personality Jay H. "Dizzy" Dean. Dailey played the part of Dean.

Chet offered commentary in the 1954, 104-minute, black and white MGM movie *Executive Suite.* It was produced by John Houseman and directed by Robert Wise and starred William Holden, Barbara Stanwyck, June Allyson, and others. Based on a novel by Cameron Hawley, the movie told the story of a furniture company president's death that prompted the company's executives to orchestrate power plays to fill the vacated position.[52] The movie was nominated for four Academy Awards: best supporting actress (Nina Foch), best cinematography (black and white), best interior decoration (black and white) and best custom design (black and white).

A 60-minute travelogue he narrated in 1954 on the Mau Mau uprising in Africa was titled "Mau, Mau." An anti-European guerrilla movement called the Mau Mau existed among the Kikuyu tribe in British-ruled Kenya. The Kikuyu were disrupted socially by European settlement and missionary work. In 1952, Kenya's colonial government declared a state of emergency that existed for 11 years. This rebellion helped force Great Britain to grant independence to Kenya in 1963. The travelogue was broadcast in the early summer of 1955 and received a bad review by the *New York Times Film Review*. The reviewer, however, gave that Huntley's was a "worthy narration."[53]

The last movie Chet, as himself as a news correspondent, acted in was a 1958, MGM-Virginia and Andrew Stone Productions, 96-minute suspense thriller titled *Cry Terror!* It starred James Mason, Rod Steiger, Inger Stevens, Neville Brand and Angie Dickinson. The movie was directed by Andrew Stone and produced by Virginia and Andrew Stone.[54]

ABC Years

Huntley's ABC years included the end of Harry Truman's years as president (1951–1953); the Korean War (1950–1953); President Dwight Eisenhower's campaign, election and first years as president (1952–1955); and the beginning of a liberal U. S. Supreme Court under former California governor Earl Warren as chief justice (1953–1969) that swept away the legal basis for racial discrimination in such cases as *Brown vs. Board of Education of Topeka, Kansas* (1954).

He was offered a position with the ABC Radio Network (later local television, too) at KABC-AM and TV in California and began there on February 28, 1951. A commentary from this era is found in the Appendix below.

His ABC supervisor, Sam Zelman, remembered Huntley as a conscientious, hard worker, an avid "reader but not really an original thinker. He was known to read, at that time, the *Economist* and *Foreign Affairs Quarterly*. He may have started out as a radio announcer, but he grew into a journalist because he cared about news."[55]

ABC assigned him to the 1952 national political conventions as a reporter. More can be found in the Chapter V below.

One news story Huntley reported for ABC News was "Operation Doorstep," the atomic bomb testing at Yucca Flats, Nevada, in the late 1940s and early 1950s. Huntley was there for the thirty-third testing, and the second nationally televised blast on March 17, 1953. The network telecast the early morning detonation and returned eight hours later for another live report, both thirty minutes long, for the aftermath. The Atomic Energy Commission wanted to see what effect the blast would have on two mock houses and, within 3,500 yards of the blast, a group of U. S. Army troops. What the coverage presented was the "necessity for civil defense preparation."[56]

In 1954 he won the Peabody Award, which was given for "Skill in analyzing the news" and "talent for mature commentary." He feared "he might become famous." Concerning going to New York to accept the above award, he said, "I'm a little afraid of going to New York because I have a feeling a job offer will be made."[57]

Signing with NBC

A reported salary dispute was one reason for Chet's departure from ABC in 1955. Furthermore, because his news analysis and anchoring had made for the highest-rated program on ABC, and because of his awards, NBC scouts took a serious look at him. In truth, the scouts "were seeking talent to compete" with Edward R. Murrow.[58] According to one source, NBC president Sylvester "Pat" Weaver saw Chet, then ABC's affiliate local anchor in Los Angeles, at an industry luncheon present a speech that impressed him.[59] In June 1955 NBC hired Huntley. Reuven Frank said that when the news spread across Los Angeles that Huntley had been hired by NBC, NBC News president Bill McAndrew and Huntley were having lunch at the Brown Derby restaurant. Comedian/actor/television show host Groucho Marx noticed the men, walked to their table and said to McAndrew, "Now, you treat him right or your name will be mud out here."[60] Chet did radio network news and television local news at NBC's Los Angeles bureau. Later, McAndrew and J. Davidson Taylor brought Huntley to New York.

The Huntleys moved to New York six months later in the fall of 1955. His office and broadcast microphone were on the fifth floor at NBC in 30 Rockefeller Center, New York. "There was no specific assignment. I was just a staff correspondent," he explained in 1970.[61] Reuven Frank, his producer, and Huntley began a news commentary program titled "Outlook" in early 1956. The two men, up through the years, would film numerous NBC News specials such as "Outlook," "Chet Huntley Reporting," and "Time Present." All three were the same program with different names. The reader can read about one of these and other specials in the Appendix.

Future co-anchor David Brinkley, wrote in his autobiography, that Huntley "was handsome. If the Marlboro man had been invented by this time, they could have photographed Huntley on horseback smoking a Marlboro. He had a serviceable baritone, looked good on the tube and was experienced in doing news on television." NBC hired him "where for a time he sat around and did occasional odd jobs, such as filling in on the "Camel News Caravan" when [John] Swayze was on vacation." Once in a while, Huntley or Brinkley were assigned to Swayze's anchor position where Brinkley "found it about as uninteresting [at 30 Rockefeller Center] as it had been at the Washington end — simply writing and speaking little captions to introduce little pieces of film about as exciting as writing labels for the drawers of file cabinets."[62] Brinkley once put Huntley's style in two words: "relentlessly serious."[63]

IV. "The Huntley-Brinkley Report": 1956–1970

Huntley's NBC years included events in American history such as: Part or all of the terms of Presidents Eisenhower (1955–1961), John Kennedy (1961–1963), Lyndon Johnson (1963–1969) and Richard Nixon (1969–1970); the Central High School, Little Rock, Arkansas, desegregation event (1957); the U.S.S.R. putting the Sputnik satellite into space in 1957; Dictator Fidel Castro taking over the island of Cuba in 1959; the 1960, 1964 and 1968 political party conventions; the Vietnam War where nearly 550,000 troops would be placed by 1969 with a $100 billion cost; the University of Mississippi desegregation in 1962; Black Americans' civil rights and voting rights becoming law (1965); Medicare (1965)—providing millions of elderly Americans with some health insurance; War on Poverty (1965) that focused on children and young adults, providing them with better education and remedial training; the assassinations of the Kennedy brothers, John (1963) and Robert (1968), and of Martin Luther King (also 1968); the rioting in Watts in Los Angeles and other cities (1965); the space program to put an American on the moon by 1969; and attacks on the news media by the Nixon Administration (1969–1970).

Not all these events will be highlighted in the following two chapters. This chapter highlights the beginning of the Huntley-Brinkley duo, their highs and lows, a typical day for Chet and how their program was broadcast.

As we begin, mention needs to be made of President Eisenhower. (More can be found in Chapter V below.) In a nutshell, "detached" and "coolly rigid" is what media author William Porter called Eisenhower's relations with the media. The media viewed Eisenhower as that era's "American hero," and "treated him gently." Eisenhower gave his press secretary, James Hagerty, the "freedom and authority to speak in his behalf." And Hagerty did.[1] Between the media and the President, this was the situation during Eisenhower's terms. It would not be the case with Johnson and Nixon!

David Brinkley

Future co-anchor David Brinkley, a native of Wilmington, North Carolina, was born on July 10, 1920, to William and Mary Brinkley. David was the youngest member of a family of two sisters, Mary and Margaret, and two brothers, William and Jesse.

During his high school years, he reported for his hometown newspaper, the Wilmington *Morning Star*, and worked for, at that time, Wilmington's only radio station, WRBT.

He graduated from high school in Wilmington, then went on to the University of North Carolina and Vanderbilt University.

Brinkley served in the U. S. Army, 120th Infantry, Company I, in 1940.

Returning to journalism, he went back to the renamed Wilmington *Star-News*. Later, United Press International hired him. He worked in the Atlanta, Georgia, Montgomery, Alabama, and Nashville, Tennessee, bureaus. In Washington, D. C., in 1943, NBC, in ten minutes, hired Brinkley after CBS said they did not know who he was. He was stationed in Washington, D. C. In 1956, he was teamed with Chet Huntley at the political conventions. Their news program, "the Huntley-Brinkley Report," was on the air for nearly 14 years. It won nearly every news award. In 1970, when Huntley retired, Brinkley co-anchored, with John Chancellor and Frank McGee, the "NBC Nightly News," and later, provided commentary only on the program. In 1981, he left NBC and moved to ABC News, Washington. Between 1981 and 1996, on Sunday mornings, he anchored his own ABC News commentary and interviews program, "This Week with David Brinkley." Additional journalists were George Will, Sam Donaldson and Cokie Roberts who provided their opinions in a round table format. In 1996, at the age of 76, he retired from news broadcasting.

Mr. Brinkley has been married twice. His first marriage was to Ann

Fisher in 1946. They divorced in 1968. Three sons were born to this union: Alan, Joel and John. He admits his career cost him his first marriage, keeping him away from home too much. His second marriage, in June 1972, was to Susan Benfer; a daughter, Alexis, was born to this union. Mr. and Mrs. Brinkley live in the Houston, Texas, area.

Mr. Brinkley is six feet, two inches tall, and weighs 170 pounds. Often presenting a humorous angle to a story, touched with irony, he is a reserved person, and displayed an on-air ease. More on his character is found in the following chapter.

He is the author of three books: *Washington at War* (about Washington, D. C., during World War II), *David Brinkley* (his autobiography), and *Everyone Is Entitled to My Opinion* (his commentaries from his fifteen-year ABC news program).[2]

Chet pondering a news story in his NBC News office, date unknown. Photograph in Chet Huntley Collection. By permission of Museum of the Rockies archives, Bozeman, Mont.

Beginning

In 1956, Huntley signed his first seven-year contract with NBC News. A news department writer, Pat Trese, recalled, "The day he [came into 30 Rockefeller Center] we sat in the control booth and watched him in the studio. He didn't have many skills. He could lean on one arm and then the other [while speaking], and he had a pipe." The director, for no particular reason, asked Chet to stand up. "That was it. Standing up *made* him, and he did it for the next few years. It broke all the clichés that he was stuck in about how an anchor was supposed to look—it freed him to be himself. When he stood up, he was really a presence. He filled the screen."[3]

Huntley was aware that NBC hired him to be "the new [Edward] Murrow" (CBS' senior newsman). Chet Huntley sounded like Edward Murrow when you listened closely! Huntley wondered if he should include the smoking on camera. Reuven Frank, then NBC News' producer and, in later years, its president, told him, "You got a choice. You can either be the second Edward R. Murrow or the first Chester R. Huntley. Do it straight, and whatever personality you have will come out."[4] Chet did smoke but never on the air.

"The Huntley-Brinkley Report" came about because of two events. The first was that NBC executives "had tired of" John Cameron Swayze. Reuven Frank said there were "two factions" fighting over who would replace Swayze. David Brinkley could do the best "because he had grown up in Washington and knew not to take some things seriously," Frank believed.

Second, others wanted Huntley, "a newcomer" from the west coast, "who, it was said somewhat mockingly, 'liked to read *The Economist* and interview Conrad Adenauer.'" Putting Huntley and Brinkley together was "accidental." Frank said, "we couldn't agree on one man, so some said, 'Let's use both.'"[5] He also thought it was "one of the dumber ideas [he] had ever heard."[6]

Brinkley wrote Frank and Julian Goodman, NBC's Washington bureau manager and Brinkley's longtime friend, "wanted Huntley and me. Everyone agreed on Huntley. He was new, he was experienced, and he was good." NBC vice president J. Davidson Taylor wanted White House correspondent Ray Scherer and Huntley, not Brinkley. News executive William McAndrew wanted Huntley and somebody else.[7] (Another contender was novelist John Hersey but he did not want the job, either.[8]) McAndrew's thought was "why did everyone agree we needed two people while CBS did very well with [Douglas] Edwards alone?" In the end, the decision was sent upstairs to NBC's top man, David Sarnoff. However, somewhere in the climb, the decision was made for Huntley and Brinkley. "NBC hung back for two months before it was willing to announce our names in public," Brinkley stated.[9]

Taylor was not willing to give up thinking Huntley and Brinkley "would be too boring and fill the air reciting dull facts nobody cared about." Hiring "a song-and-dance man," Barry Wood, Taylor thought he could instruct Huntley and Brinkley to liven up the 1956 conventions in "an entertaining manner." However, the duo did their own interpretation. Taylor also tried to push the pair to "wear two bright red blazers with the NBC chimes embroidered on the breast pockets."

Brinkley asked Taylor, "You get this out of Guy Lombardo's saxophone section? I won't wear it." (Readers may remember Lombardo's band was famous for their red blazers.)

"Huntley agreed and the blazers" disappeared. Brinkley added, "I do think we saved a whole generation of local news broadcasters from having to come on the air looking like animal trainers."[10]

Because so much attention was lavished on coverage of political conventions, this author has elected to cover most of the 1952 and 1956 conventions in the next chapter. However, some aspects of the 1956 conventions are highlighted below.

With the 1956 election year, NBC was not willing to lose the Democratic and Republican conventions to CBS and its news department. "The Camel News Caravan" was leading in the news ratings but the NBC News executives: "did not think [John Swayze] knew enough political history or knew enough of the political system's featured players and strutting prima donnas to carry the load of discussing and explaining them and the convention procedures for four days and four nights"; and they thought Swayze's program was "carefully scripted" even to the point that Swayze could "rehearse and memorize his stories." On the other hand, political conventions were ad-lib and unrehearsed.[11]

In a 1966 *McCall's* magazine interview, Chet said, "NBC wasn't willing to believe that either of us could do it. So in effect they were hedging their bet by putting us both on, figuring if one of us blew it, the other could help him out. They wouldn't want to admit that now, but it's true. And as it turned out, it worked."[12]

Brinkley suggested to Frank, NBC's production genius, and Frank agreed, that one simple rule was needed to cover the conventions: "In talking over a television picture, never tell the viewers what they can easily see for themselves. If you cannot add anything useful to what is in the picture, keep quiet. It worked then" and it continues to work to this day.[13]

Chet explained during the *McCall's* interview, "Well, for the first time I had the feeling that if I were to run out of gas, I'd just say, 'David,' and look at him and nod, and there'd be someone there to pick it up. It was very comfortable. There was never a feeling of 'Oh, my gosh, I'm on this subject, but what do we do next?'"[14]

Brinkley met Huntley in person for the first time when both were NBC News reporters when Brinkley flew from Washington to New York to do a segment for Huntley's "Outlook" program before the conventions started. Huntley and Brinkley worked together for the first time on August 8, 1956, as they co-anchored the Democratic Convention. Their coverage of the conventions earned top reviews. Chet said, "I had seen David Brinkley exactly once before in my whole life. We sat down together, the red lights blinked, and there we were."[15]

To give the reader some idea of Huntley's convention reporting, this piece is his opening the third day of NBC's convention coverage.

> This session today is, more or less, ladies' day at the National Democratic Convention. It featured Mrs. Katie Lockheim, the director of women's activities of the Democratic National Committee. And the delegates here also heard from a number of the Democratic representatives in Congress, all of them ladies. It would seem that the women of the Democratic Party do have something of a justifiable complaint and some references have been made to it already. Namely, these women are, by no means, low in numbers inside the Democratic ranks and their strength is certainly being felt more and more all the time. And yet when they say they come to a National Democratic Convention and make their speeches and make their appearances on the rostrum that the men stay away in droves. So something is going to have to be resolved or else there will be another feud in this convention.[16]

He did make a pronunciation mistake while at the Republican Convention. He called former President Herbert Hoover "Hoobert Heever."

New York Times television critic Jay Gould, then the most respected and the most feared of all critics, told his audience with intense flattery:

> A quiet southerner with a dry wit and a heaven-sent appreciation of brevity, has stolen the television limelight this week at the Democratic National Convention. He is David Brinkley, who together with Chet Huntley has been providing the National Broadcasting Company's running commentary from Chicago....
>
> The National Broadcasting Company's team of Chet Huntley and David Brinkley swept away the stuffy, old fashioned concept of ponderous reportage on the home screen. They talked as recognizable humans, sprinkled their observations with delightful wit and were easily the TV hit of the week.[17]

As then CBS News vice president Sig Mickelson wrote, Huntley was "the straight reporter, Brinkley the sardonic commentator, fast with the irreverent quip. It was a radical departure from the conventional pattern but well adapted to a political convention with a plethora of party pageantry but very little news."[18]

CBS News executive Richard Salant, who became an NBC News employee in the late 1970s, stated Huntley and Brinkley were "very good together. Their contrasting styles—Chet deep voiced and serious, David light and wry—were just right for the 1956 conventions, and the evening news."[19]

One television news author (Maury Green) suggested news anchors, "in particular," are one or the other: "sex symbols or father images." Green suggested Huntley was a "father image"; Brinkley, the "sex symbol." He believed the "public subconsciously forms" these images of these two men to which the public then "reacts." Huntley and Brinkley, Green suggested, had "a brilliant combination of both images."[20]

CBS lost in the ratings. For both conventions, the ratings went to Huntley and Brinkley. Theodore White said, "the rivalry between CBS and NBC ... produced the great changes in both the commerce of television news and the impact on politics."[21] The competition between the two networks during future conventions became intense. According to Zachary Karabell in 1998, CBS covered them not in "its most thoughtful and original way as the story developed ... [but] ... to beat NBC to get the bigger audience and critical acclaim."[22] CBS did not succeed during the Huntley-Brinkley years.

On October 26, 1956, John Swayze and NBC's "Camel News Caravan," on the air since 1948 as NBC's original TV news program, ended. Frank said two rehearsals were held for the new "Huntley-Brinkley Report"—one on Saturday and one on Sunday. On Monday, October 29, Huntley and Brinkley began their almost 14-year news marriage.

NBC's creating a two-person anchor team with Chet in New York and David in Washington was innovative. The double anchor operation was one of Frank's broadcast journalism contributions. New York and Washington were linked by cable. To describe how the duo worked, Frank switched "between the two cities as if the men were seated side by side in the same studio." Their carrier was AT&T. In the beginning, NBC and AT&T worked out a word code where a word in the script was used to make the switch between New York and Washington. "When Huntley finished a segment," he said, "David"— switch, and Brinkley began his segment; when David was finished, David would say "Chet"— switch. This was why the duo ended a news story by each speaking his partner's name. It gave the AT&T technician the "cue" switch to either city. The audience always thought that each was talking to the other when he was not.[23]

Brinkley's specialty was national news from Washington; Huntley, in New York, reported on America and the world. "The two frequently divided aspects of the same story, giving the broadcast a sparkling space. The secondary details of stories, which might have been lost if only one anchor were reporting, were now highlighted by the very act of having the other anchor tell it. The scripts were tightly written, the coordination between the two anchors was well orchestrated, and the broadcast seemed to be in more places where news was being made."[24] Frank said unless either was on vacation, or on assignment, the two men did not "step" on the other's time. Brinkley's segment was about one third of the program; Huntley's took up the rest. Understandably, the audience "thought they shared the time equally."[25]

In 1956, TV news was simple. Brinkley stated, "You just use pictures when you have them and words when you don't, and stop once in a while for a commercial, there's no other way to do it."[26]

That Monday night, October 29, 1956, at 7:45 P.M., Eastern time, "the Huntley-Brinkley Report" went on the air. Brinkley said the "new and much anticipated program" was "terrible." Frank called it "the worst evening news program in the history of American network television." No kinescope recording exists of that first night, and he "remembered sitting at [his] desk when it ended, filled with abject despair."[27] Brinkley did not think that first program was that bad. However, Frank was upset because so much news was happening that week and NBC "lacked the facilities to cover it": France, Great Britain and Israel seized the Suez Canal (see below); Democratic presidential candidate Adlai Stevenson attacked President Dwight Eisenhower; Hungary had an uprising and Russia rolled its tanks in to put it down.

Linking the Red and Mediterranean seas in Egypt, the Suez Canal had been seized by Egypt from their French and British owners during the previous summer. Britain, France and Israel carried out a joint land and air attack against Egypt. President Eisenhower had the United States, through the United Nations, propose a cease fire. The President also suspended some loans to Great Britain. France and Great Britain were not happy! They withdrew their armies and let the United Nations troops take over. The handling of this crisis helped Eisenhower win his second term a few days later.

At that time, NBC did not have reporters and cameramen in the field. They relied on film from such companies as Movietone. *New York Times* television critic Jay Gould commented, "The program was not too smooth technically and was plagued by needless gadgetry, but presumably will improve as the bugs are ironed out." Then Gould kicked Huntley and

Brinkley, "For depth and clarity of editorial organization, however it wasn't in the same league" with CBS's "Douglas Edwards with the News."[28]

Variety magazine described Huntley as an "authoritative N[ew] Y[ork] anchor man, much improved from his initial efforts as a sometime replacement for [John] Swayze. The magazine said of him and David Brinkley, "both are extremely affable and presentable gents who also happen to know their business. They are relaxed, friendly, not ... solemn ... which is refreshing."[29]

Variety called the pairing "problematical." The magazine suggested that NBC's theory of a two-man anchor needed to happen because television was moving toward 30-minute programming. The TV news programs in the 1950s were fifteen minutes. Also, NBC's news was broadcast a half-hour later than CBS' news.[30]

During their nearly 14-year partnership, both men maintained their relationship was happy, "despite NBC insiders' reports that the men often bridled at each other. Chet said, 'We're both adults. We've never pretended that we have to travel in tandem,'" but he maintained, "we've never had a harsh word."[31] Huntley said he "had to bite his inside cheek to keep from breaking up at Brinkley" and his delivery style during their first year.[32]

Frank claimed he made all the decisions on "the Huntley-Brinkley Report" and in his nine years with Chet and David he had "one serious disagreement" but it was not highlighted.[33]

As previously mentioned, Huntley anchored the world and national news (his gift was foreign news stories) and Brinkley handled what was happening in Washington, D. C. An "exceptionally gifted and an attractive" newscaster, Huntley "carried about two-thirds" of the "Report." His "greatest strength was on the air." His presence, with a "magnificent, resonant voice," made him "admired and believed." Huntley was a great reader. Pat Trese, a "Huntley-Brinkley Report" writer, said Huntley "was just beautiful, absolutely unflappable. He was one of those guys who made everything you wrote sound better."[34]

Frank commented on NBC News' news gathering of that period:

NBC News was beginning to accommodate itself to our way of seeing pictures, to our proposition that television news was, above all, seeing things happen. Cameramen were enthusiastic, reporters and bureau chiefs less so. Our system was to have cameramen film news events, to edit their film into a narrative, then, as the last step, to write a script that included the description of the event and its news relevance. We did not use reporters on the scene, who would speak a script to which pictures were matched — risking the danger of throwing away the best pictures because they had not been scripted for. So although we had some good reporters, we used them very little, far less than CBS did and perhaps more than we should have.[35]

Barbara Matusow wrote "many viewers were irate [that John Swayze had been taken off the air], including his biggest fan, President Eisenhower. Ike's press secretary, James Hagerty, called in NBC White House correspondent Ray Scherer to pass the word that the President was unhappy about the switch."[36]

For several months, "the Huntley-Brinkley Report" did not do well. Advertisers were few, the program had a small audience.[37] The duo went months without a sponsored minute.

When the ratings were still in the cellar that summer, NBC News president McAndrew was thinking about dropping Huntley because Brinkley had seniority. McAndrew told Reuven Frank, "You'd better prepare Huntley. David has seniority, and we'll keep him. But Chet may have to go."

Frank said, "The saddest lunch I ever had in my life was that one with Huntley. They were both good men. But not enough people were watching. I told Chet to expect the worst."

McAndrew kept top management at bay, "then, as Huntley phrased it, 'the country vote came in.'"[38] By the end of 1957, Huntley-Brinkley was number one.

During part of the summer of 1957, the program was broadcast without commercial interruption. In the spring of 1958, Texaco Oil picked up the tab and was their sole sponsor for three years. Then, "Camel cigarettes became a half-sponsor."[39]

CBS News executive Av Westin suggests some of the poor rating was due to the fact that "many NBC affiliates had dropped the program when it had switched times [7:45 to 7:15] so 'the Huntley-Brinkley Report' was not available in many cities."[40] Frank said that "Outlook," Huntley's news analysis program, had ventured into the South and reported on the segregation issue too often.[41] NBC's southern affiliates would not carry "the Huntley-Brinkley Report" because these affiliates saw New York-based networks as favoring racial integration.[42] Reuven Frank explained that civil rights were NBC News' "top story, weekdays and Sunday." This kept Southern opinion leaders annoyed. One leader said Huntley's eyebrows undermined NBC's "objectivity and fairness."[43]

In December 1957, the Nielsen ratings service gave "Douglas Edwards with the [CBS] News" an 18.6 share (seven million homes) to Huntley and

Brinkley at 11.4 (four million homes). By 1958, Huntley and Brinkley had pulled even with CBS News. Then they had stepped up to number one by 1960, and they stayed there until 1967.[44]

What were the reasons for their success? First, both men offered commentary now and then, not only news reports. Second, both presented "the facts, put them in context, and suggested likely consequences." And third, Huntley felt he had an "immense responsibility ... to report the news fairly, accurately, and professionally."[45] In addition, Huntley "insisted that TV news should be more than a dry recitation of bulletins."[46]

One story that highlighted Brinkley's style, or as one author suggested, "an almost revolutionary new tone to broadcast journalism," was reporting a "rather silly debate" by the Republicans on renaming Nevada and Arizona's Boulder Dam, Hoover Dam. Brinkley suggested the squabble could end with the former President changing "*his* name to Herbert Boulder."[47]

In April 1962, CBS took Douglas Edwards, their original TV news anchor for the last 14 years, off television and put Walter Cronkite in his place. Cronkite did not knock Huntley-Brinkley out of their number one position until 1967. Part of that may have happened because Huntley crossed the picket lines during the 1967 AFTRA strike (see below). During the summers of 1965 and 1966, Cronkite edged passt Huntley-Brinkley. By the fall of each year, Huntley-Brinkley were back on top.

Several NBC officials, not named, suggested the following smug explanation for the seasonal up and down: NBC's "nightly news audience, being brighter and more affluent, spent the summer sailing off Martha's Vineyard or attending music festivals in Europe, while Cronkite's viewers, presumably the dull and the indigent, estivated in front of their television sets because they had nothing better to do."[48] In 1969, the ratings for the three network news programs were CBS: 31 share, NBC: 30 share and ABC: 12 share. The 1970 ratings put CBS News at 15 percent of the American households, and Huntley-Brinkley at 14.6 percent.[49]

During the 1960s and early 1970s, American TV watchers "made network news-watching a nightly ritual." Reportedly, watching the news were 93 percent of television owners; Huntley and Brinkley had more than one third of the owners' viewership.[50] By 1961, the duo was seen on 182 NBC affiliate and five NBC-owned and operated stations. Frank claimed the 1960s were NBC years, with it being so far ahead in the ratings, it was a "one-horse race."[51]

One person who was a steady watcher was President John Kennedy. "When Huntley-Brinkley or the Cronkite show was on, no one disturbed" Kennedy.[52] Another was Kennedy's father, Joseph. Chet was quoted as saying Joseph Kennedy would call after most "Huntley-Brinkley Reports" to either say the program was "beautiful," or "just give us hell about something."[53]

Who created the well-known sign off: "Good night, Chet; good night, David"? It was Reuven Frank. Neither Huntley nor Brinkley thought much of it.[54] Brinkley commented, "We both hated it. Huntley thought it was sissified. I argued we should say good night to the audience, not to each other, and I thought it sounded contrived, artificial and slightly silly. We lost. We used it. It worked."[55]

Their sign-off, "Good night, Chet; good night, David," was found on billboards and buses all over the United States.[56] They became more well-known than many movie stars. In 1965, a consumer-research company released its survey that Chet and David were "recognized by more adult Americans than Cary Grant, James Stewart, the Beatles and John Wayne."[57] Even 30 years after their famous duo ended, and if Brinkley is recognized on the street, people still call out, "Good night, David."

A woman viewer wrote in 1959 that when she and her husband "went to sleep at night, they always used the Huntley-Brinkley sign-off, one of them saying, 'Good night, Chet,' and the other replying, 'Good night, David.'"[58]

The team inspired a "couplet to the tune of the popular song 'Love and Marriage'":

> Huntley-Brinkley, Huntley-Brinkley,
> One is solemn, the other's twinkly.[59]

During one of President Kennedy's inauguration balls, January 20–21, 1961, comic Milton Berle and singer Frank Sinatra sang the above couplet.

Odds and Ends

In checking Walter Cronkite's autobiography, *Walter Cronkite, A Reporter's Life*, this author found it surprising that Cronkite said nearly nothing of his competitors! Cronkite only mentioned NBC when it went to 30 minutes a day after CBS did in 1963. In a short interview, he told this author that during the years they were anchors and on occasion were in the same room, they probably exchanged no more than "ten words." Mr. Cronkite considered Huntley a "good journalist," "well respected" and the serious, "dour" anchor.[60] The biographers of Edward Murrow mentioned "the Huntley-Brinkley Report" as "stiff competitors."

Another man who brought NBC alive was Robert Kintner. He was a "driving, difficult man with a great instinct for excellence and a great feel for what television was."[61] When he was involved in the political conventions, he could be very abrupt.

One ridiculous event blown into "massive proportions" was when President Johnson had a bad cold in 1964. Frank had NBC broadcast news bulletins throughout the day interrupting the NBC programming schedule![62]

Huntley's typical workday included waking up by 8 A.M. (Later on in his career, he would wake up at 6:30 A.M. to read several newspapers.) Taking the subway, or a 10-minute taxi or a 30-minute walk, he arrived by 9:30 A.M.[63] at the NBC studios at 30 Rock. He wrote

> his radio "think pieces" as he called them — two a day and four for the weekend — and taped them at noon. After lunch he answer[ed] letters "most of the fan letters are kind" or work[ed] on a news "special" show.
>
> At 4 o'clock he [huddled] with the producer, editors and newsmen who [made] the show what Huntley [called] "group journalism." All day they had been collecting film and reportage from NBC correspondents around the world, and all hands [decided] what stories [went] on the air. Huntley [gathered] their reports, research and wire service and [wrote] his part of the show.
>
> "The guy who voices the news has to write it as much as he can," was his philosophy.[64]

Over 300 persons helped put together the daily "Huntley-Brinkley Report." Seven were directly responsible for its 6:30 and 7 P.M. broadcasts. In later years, between 2:30 and 4:30, over closed circuit TV link, Huntley, Brinkley and a half-dozen co-workers would discuss and decide that evening's program.

At 6:10 P.M., Chet would head for his anchor desk where "technicians darted around him, maps and severed heads of famous people flashed in rehearsal on screens fore and aft and promptly at 6:30, the voice rolled out, 'Chet Huntley, NBC News, New York.'"[65] At 6:30 P.M. (later in 1970, 7 P.M.), "the Huntley-Brinkley Report" was on the air.

Huntley usually arrived home about 7:45 P.M., and after a couple of drinks, dinner was served at 10 P.M. Tippy Huntley, in a 1961 interview, mentioned their entertainment. "We [had] two or three couples in for dinner and an evening of good conversation. We [liked] to mix our guests. Ideally we [had] two couples who knew each other or [had] common interests, and a couple with a dissimilar background." Because he was "so close to the day's news, guests" started by asking him what he thought "about the latest world crisis and [ended] up telling" Chet what *they* (his emphasis) thought. He "liked to listen." There was enjoyment in a "good stimulating discussion with your guests at your own table."[66]

When the Huntleys sold the New Jersey farm (see Chapter X), Chet turned to "cooking, reading, sorting out his thoughts about the state of the world, and dodging phone calls. Tippy said, 'He learned to hate [the phone]. Interruptions [drove] him crazy.' This was not to say he was anti-social." He would rather spend an evening playing cards or just be in conversation with friends. A friend and a lawyer, S. Hazard Gillespie, said, "He can sit through an evening of perfectly miserable cards [bridge] and be as cheerful as can be."[67]

As "celebrities," the news anchors, up through the years, were invited to speak at various functions. At the Waldolf Hotel in New York, in the sixties, Huntley, Brinkley, Cronkite and Peter Jennings were guests. With hundreds of people in the audience, one man asked them, "You guys in TV are just in show business." Huntley charged back, "Now hold it! My only concession to show business is that I stop in the makeup room every day and have these bags under my eyes painted out." And Cronkite said, "Yeah, Jennings stops in and has them painted *in*...."[68]

Broadcasting the News

It needs to be noted here that the network news departments "did not systematically preserve tapes of their evening news broadcasts." This writer found that the University of Wisconsin, Madison, the Vanderbilt University Television News Archive, Nashville, and the United States Defense Department "all filmed evening news coverage." This preservation started because of the "great controversy over the reporting of Vietnam." So, since August 1965, America has preserved, in some form, evening news programs in all three of the above archives.[69]

To present one problem of newscasting, especially transmitting the story from one part of America to New York, the following story provides a clue. Segregation of white and black students in separate public schools was declared unconstitutional in 1954 by the U. S. Supreme Court in *Brown vs. Board of Education of Topeka, Kansas.* (In summary, a black man and father, Oliver Brown, filed a lawsuit against the Board of Education in Topeka. His daughter, who had to attend a black school further away and across dangerous railroad tracks, could not attend an all-white public school close by.) President Eisenhower was trying to integrate gradually but when the Little Rock crisis developed, the event ruined that gradual integration. The State of Arkansas and Governor Orval Faubus refused to implement the court's ruling. In September 1957, segregation hit crisis proportions at Central High School in Little Rock, Arkansas. It became a national event when President Eisenhower sent Federal troops to enforce the ruling. NBC's senior correspondent, John Chancellor, was assigned there and filmed the events each day, then flew the film to Oklahoma City where a cable connection existed with New York. Little Rock did not have a link. This reporting brought Chancellor his first national audience. It helped fuel further dislike of NBC by Southern broadcasters.

Huntley was present as the first newscaster to introduce and host Telstar, the first satellite-television linkup between Europe and the United States, when it came on line in 1962. The satellite link helped improve television news instantaneously. Chet began his portion by stating, "We had intended to begin by taking you to Washington where the President's news conference was under way … but because of early acquisition at Andover we got the Telstar circuit early and the President doesn't begin for several minutes. So, we now take you to a baseball game in Chicago— and perhaps its fitting that the sporting event — one of civilization's earliest ceremonials— be the first special event televised across the sea."[70]

Going to 30 Minutes

In September 1963, CBS News was the first to go from a 15-minute to a 30-minute broadcast. NBC followed a week later. Rueven Frank told Edward Bliss in 1985 how NBC went from 15 minutes to 30 minutes in one week:

> The change was not made on short notice, at least in terms of those days. It had been suggested for some time, but affiliates balked. When the CBS announcement was made, Bob Kintner [president of NBC] used that to force the change through…. I had spent the summer planning, doing a little hiring, and writing a long memo about what kind of program we expected to have…. Every weekend in August we prepared a half-hour program … and I commuted between Washington and New York on Friday, Saturday, and Sunday as we tried it out. We established the program's offices in London and Tokyo, redesigned the look, and physically moved within 30 Rock to larger quarters, never a small matter. This was in sharp contrast to the very beginning of Huntley-Brinkley, where Swayze did his [last] report on Friday [October 27, 1956] and we [Huntley-Brinkley] began ours [Monday, October 29] with only one dry run on Sunday afternoon [October 28].[71]

Affiliate stations, at first, objected. They were not willing to lose advertising money with NBC taking an extra 15 minutes. NBC came up with a plan that would pay part of the national advertising dollars back to the affiliate and NBC-owned stations. Presidential historian Theodore

White said with the networks going to 30 minutes "the reluctant affiliates found their audiences were not 'depressed' by news, but hungry for it."[72] Huntley and Brinkley used their first 30-minute broadcast to interview President John Kennedy. Part of that interview can be found below in Chapter VI.

Cronkite wished the duo "reasonable" success on going to 30 minutes. This suggested a "growing sensitivity and disturbing awareness" in the television news ratings game.[73]

NBC bought a three-column page-length newspaper ad in the *New York Times* to announce "the Huntley-Brinkley Report" increase to 30 minutes as well as the local station's 30-minute news program. With the picture was this prose: "Tonight, Chet Huntley and David Brinkley, backed up by the worldwide 800-man staff of NBC News, begin the new 'Huntley-Brinkley Report.' Expanded to a full 30 minutes, the series now covers world and national events in deeper detail, and illustrates its reports with nightly, exclusive on-the-scene films."[74] *New York Times* television columnist Jay Gould critiqued the new 30-minute news program, saying, in part, "The [Huntley-Brinkley-Cronkite] rivalry had its lighter moments. Mr. Brinkley confided that he and his colleagues had received an opening night telegram wishing their venture 'a reasonable amount of good luck'; and it came from Mr. Cronkite." Later, Gould wrote, "In other respects, however, it cannot be said that either the C. B. S. or N. B. C. half hour constituted a particular innovation in TV journalism." He thought both programs were not much different from their 15-minute formats, but the main difference was more "headline bulletins, not any appreciable increase in true depth or diversity of coverage."[75] *Variety* magazine reviewed this increase in time by mentioning "twinkly Brinkley and his Gotham-berthed Chetmate are still a hot team." Frank and others at NBC News "have come through admirably, if hardly venturesome in probing for something new." The magazine gave confirmation to the 30-minute format and could see "the Huntley-Brinkley Report" and "the CBS News with Walter Cronkite" rivalry "being a lulu."[76]

With NBC doing so well after the 1960 conventions, the CBS executives brought in new news executives. In 1963, CBS' new news president Richard Salant truly believed Huntley and Brinkley would not survive the increase to 30 minutes from 15 minutes. Salant crowed, "NBC is a fine organization but all they've got going for them in a pitcher and a catcher. We've got Walter [Cronkite], an infield, an outfield, and a strong bench." Brinkley came back with an irritated response, "If Huntley and I are only a pitcher and catcher, then by that standard, CBS has only a pitcher *or* a catcher.... Mr. Salant is going into an area he knows nothing about."[77] It

Chet Huntley and David Brinkley at the 1965 Presidential inauguration. Photograph in Chet Huntley Collection. By permission of K. Ross Toole Archives, Maureen and Mike Mansfield Library, University of Montana, Missoula.

would take CBS four years to catch up in the ratings (see "AFTRA strike," in Chapter VI below) but Salant would not be CBS News president.

Too Famous

Huntley and Brinkley would become too famous. When Minnesota U. S. Senator Hubert Humphrey was campaigning for President in 1960, Brinkley went on the trail with him. However, Brinkley had to quit the media team because Brinkley "was drawing more attention" than Humphrey. Brinkley's anonymity was lost and his days of being a working journalist in the field were over.[78]

Chet stated, in a 1966 interview, a couple of humorous stories about the duo's identity.

> ...[H]alf the time I'm called Brinkley or Chet Brinkley, or David Huntley. He gets the same thing. I am frequently bemused by the fellow who does a bit of trading on our good nature by bringing his wife or girl friend or business associate over to the restaurant table, slapping me between the shoulders,

and saying, "David, old boy, I want you to meet Doris (or Charlie or Stan or Florence). She (or he) watches you every night."

There was the lady in the lobby of the Kempinsky Hotel in Berlin one night who walked up a bit uncertain on her feet, impaled me with a fixed stare, and asked, "Now which one are *you*?"

And there was Miss Murphy, a stewardess on the "Red Eye" special, the overnight from San Francisco to New York. Slowly, I became aware that Miss Murphy was studying me rather intently, so I assumed a pleasant counte-nance as she knelt in the empty seat next to me and asked, "Aren't you ... well ... don't you ... do you have something to do with television?"

"Yes," I said.

"Well," she went on, "do you know those two fellows who do the news every night ... David and what's his name ... the other one?"

"Yes," I said, "I know them very well."

Miss Murphy was impressed. "Well ... that other one ... the long-faced guy who is always frowning ... the serious one ... I can't stand him, but oh that David! Well, I tell you, I've got a stir for him that's just awful! Is he married?"[79]

Chet did not answer.

In 1965, "The Huntley-Brinkley Report" was on 187 affiliates across the United States. By 1974 "the NBC Nightly News" (successor to "the Huntley-Brinkley Report") was on 210 stations.[80] Their viewership was 24 million; their advertising bill exceeded $28 million for 1965–1966.[81] In 1965, there were 800 NBC News employees. In Vietnam, in 1965, Saigon had the largest news bureau outside Washington and New York. NBC cor-respondents were Garrick Utley, Jack Perkins, Dean Brelis and Ron Nessen. NBC had about 30 employees working there.[82] When Huntley retired, there were 1,000 NBC News employees, worldwide.

On November 15, 1965, NBC became the first network to have its news stories recorded in color.[83] *Variety* mentioned "the color in some segments prove so dazzling to the eye, that the content of the news deliv-ered becomes secondary." The November 15th Peacock-colored edition of "The Huntley-Brinkley Report" opened with footage of Chet and David in their studios, of the Yarmouth Castle burning, field reports from Viet-nam and Salisbury, Rhodesia (now Zimbabwe), and a Washington, D. C., press conference. The magazine mentioned the "danger of color prettify-ing what is in reality a grim event" such as in Vietnam and a U. S. Marine's reaction to a comrade's death.[84]

News analyst and former NBC news correspondent Robert MacNeil, in 1990, looked at a 1960s Huntley-Brinkley tape and commented "how thoughtful and slow it seemed. No gimmicks, no graphics, no captions to speak of, and the commercials lasted a minute for Salem cigarettes."[85]

News anchors during the 1950s and 1960s had to read film narration live. This was an operation that was delicate and dangerous. The anchors rarely saw the film until it went on the air. "The script would contain instructions, such as 'Pause for five seconds to let sound of locomotive come up,' and a writer would stand behind Chet and tap him on the shoulder, cu[e]ing him to begin reading again." Huntley read two words per foot of film, or three words per second. If someone had died, he would slow down to two words per second.[86]

His news reporting philosophy was defined in an interview with TV critic Marie Torre: "I don't mean simply reading a bulletin which says 'Senator So-and-So declares that farmers do not want a Congressional bill that will arbitrarily jack up farm prices.' Given alone, that statement can mislead. It doesn't give any insight into the whole issue. After I tell what the Senator said, I'll relate what the opposition had to say, and to the best of my ability, give the latest developments in the matter."[87] In another interview, he said, "Sometimes we wonder if we have overdone the tightness [of their news program], but time is limited. You have to say what you mean the first time."[88]

Time magazine classified him as stubbornly independent, and "that trait communicated itself to his millions of viewers."[89] Huntley enjoyed going against the "prevailing ideological tide."[90] He said, in another interview, that he "once considered himself as a 'classic liberal.'"[91] Defined, Huntley explained, "I mean an open-mindedness, a feeling that ideas are not dangerous and let's consider them all."[92]

The editorial policy was set by Rueven Frank; the "Report's" tone was set by Huntley and Brinkley. In their early years, editorializing was a part of the program, more from Huntley than Brinkley. A couple of times a week, Huntley would have an "opinion piece."

Huntley never lost his interest in foreign events. This writer found few stories on his foreign news trips, so if this biography is shy on this reporting, little was found. One that is available concerns President Eisenhower's Doctrine. It stated that U. S. military aid and financial help would go to any Middle East country that needed it to fight Communist aggression. Crises in the Middle East and Asia would include that in Lebanon where American troops were sent to fight rebel forces, keep the pro-Western government in power and protect U. S. oil interests. Huntley went to Beirut to interview the U. S. Marines stationed there. He remained to interview Lebanon's Premier, Sami Es-solh, who had endured an attempted assassination by terrorists. In Asia, China decided to shell the Quemoy and Matsu Islands. Eisenhower sent the U. S. Navy to help move supplies to the islands from Taiwan, ending a threat to the latter country.

KBMN Radio station owner/manager Bill Merrick stated that Huntley's love and affection for Montana was shown when the NBC affiliates, radio and television, held their annual convention. "Chet would always make his way to the Montana delegation to visit with us."[93]

Brinkley commented on the duo's compatibility in 1966. "If Huntley and I were entirely dependent on our own resources, we would not last a week. We have somehow hung on for 10 years because the resources of a news program are the world and the human race and their folly, wisdom, comedy, tragedy, gaiety, and nonsense. It is all a gaudy performance with a huge cast, people tune in to see that, not to see us. So, in effect, Huntley and I are pointers."[94] Reuven Frank said, "Huntley made Brinkley possible. Brinkley alone could never make it, because he doesn't have the authority that the audience wants. Huntley did. He had that great leonine head and that Murrow-like voice."[95]

Huntley mentioned that his eyebrows raised a "minor ruckus" in 1963 when a "southern editor complained that they were editorializing." Chet said he "couldn't be responsible for what his eye-brows did on the air. And he went on reporting the news."[96] Vice President Spiro Agnew always thought when Chet's eyebrows were arched, he was editorializing too much and "when he was reading a news item critical of the Nixon Administration."[97] He humorously commented on his delivery in 1965: "I have a faculty for ruining every good story I tell. I have a deadly serious face."[98] In another interview with *McCall's* magazine he was asked why he never smiled on camera and during that interview he did. Huntley replied, "I guess I look like the stock villain who comes to foreclose the mortgage and throw the widow out. The real reason, I guess, is that in most of the news there isn't much that will provoke a laugh."[99]

The Huntley retirement will be highlighted at the end of Chapter VI.

Throughout the 1960s Huntley and Brinkley were the nightly news staple in homes across America, including this author's. Chet and David vividly brought the world to the Johnston family in the wonder of a black and white (later color) television set. As I researched this segment, I was surprised to find that Brinkley only carried one third of the newscast. Watching the program during the 1960s my perception was Brinkley carried half the news reporting. I remember Brinkley's wit as he offered commentary at the end of the program. Huntley remained the serious one. Like many viewers, I thought they were in the same studio with different cameras. Little did we know that the mention of each other's names at the end of a news story was not just a friendly jest but a cue to switch to the other city and NBC studio. Clever!

V. Political Conventions

Political conventions have been held since September 1831 when the Anti-Masonic Party first met. Such meetings, held ever four years since 1832 by the now Democratic and Republican parties as well as other parties, nominate and select their leaders, debate, decide and approve their programs and organize their campaigns. Television began covering political conventions in 1940.

For this biography, we begin with 1952. U. S. Army General Dwight Eisenhower was courted by both the Republicans and the Democrats for the 1952 presidential nomination. Initially, he had refused to try for the nomination because he did not think military personnel should seek political office. He also did not want to run against President Harry Truman. However, Truman decided not to run for reelection. Eisenhower then decided to accept the Republicans' invitation as there had not been a Republican president in twenty years. He took a leave of absence from the Army, and when it looked like he was going to be nominated, he resigned from the military.

The 1952 Republican Convention nominated Eisenhower and elected him on the first ballot. California U. S. Senator Richard Nixon was selected as his vice presidential candidate. Illinois Governor Adlai Stevenson and Alabama U. S. Senator John Sparkman were nominated and elected by the Democrats.

Both conventions were held in Chicago.

Huntley's and Brinkley's first known televised involvement with political conventions occurred in 1952. Both were assigned to the conventions as reporters. Huntley represented ABC News; Brinkley, NBC News. Brinkley said he could not do much as a reporter-anchor. The NBC floor director, Bob Doyle, had a camera traveling all over the floor with Brinkley offering commentary. Sometimes, though, Brinkley could not get past the second sentence in his descriptions when the camera would switch to another area. Delegates were seen eating hot dogs, reading newspapers or even sleeping in their chairs during the proceedings. The descriptions were a hit with the NBC audience. The Republicans did not think much of this coverage and issued a notice to its delegates to be careful of what they were doing. The Democrats did not care.[1]

Doyle said he "was the pool director for the '52 conventions.... The cameras were better. The audience was now between fifty and eight million.... The Democrats tried to make it more interesting for television, but you can't shut up a politician, except when Bess Truman kicked Harry. He objected to something and she gave him a boot in the ankle. I had that on the air. Bess was a tough cookie."[2]

However, in the ratings, NBC was second behind CBS and their anchor, Walter Cronkite. ABC was third. The *New York Times* reporter Herbert Mitgang believed the networks became obsessed with ratings.[3]

Later, during the 1960s' conventions, Mr. Brinkley, concerning live events such as the space program or the political conventions, said, "Delivering the news isn't all that difficult. It's the ad lib situation that counts. You cannot get rattled. If I don't know something, I'll throw it to Chet. If he doesn't know, he'll toss it back to me." Huntley added, "Our egos are not acute."[4]

Those who have watched political conventions may have noticed that Huntley and Brinkley did not use "many notes for Election Night coverage because it was easier to depend on their memory than to riffle desperately through mountains of printed matter. 'The two-man operation,' says Huntley, 'is what makes this possible. By the time David runs out of gas (and each of us can recognize the signs pretty well at this stage), I'm ready to get the ball rolling again.'"[5]

The 1956 conventions have been covered in the last chapter. The highlight of the 1956 Democratic Convention was the last time the vice presidential nomination was an open contest. Massachusetts U. S. Senator John Kennedy lost the nomination to Tennessee U. S. Senator Estes Kefauver. Kefauver ran with Illinois Senator Adlai Stevenson but lost a second time to President Eisenhower.

Newspaper radio/television columnist Jack Gould told his newspaper audience about the 1956 convention coverage: "... [T]he new television luminary of the convention was easily David Brinkley of the National Broadcasting Company. His succinct and wry observations were most welcome during periods of inactivity. Together with Chet Huntley Mr. Brinkley gave the N. B. C. News department what it has needed for nearly a quarter of a century, a sense of humor." Later, Gould would suggest, "TV would be better off sometimes if it worried less about making history and more about reporting it. N. B. C. in particular is prone to re-invent television; some of its electronic gadgetry was more distracting than helpful."[6]

"The Huntley-Brinkley Report" also covered mid-year elections. During the 1958 national elections, Gould had to point out a problem NBC encountered in telecasting. Huntley and Brinkley "seemed noticeably ill at ease primarily because they were the victims of a cumbersome method of switching cues." Later he added, "N. B. C. News covered the election adequately, to be sure, but not with any great style."[7]

Huntley, in a full page ad in the *New York Times* concerning watching the 1960 conventions, explained:

> Remember in watching the conventions that wild and exuberant demonstrations on the floor have little real political significance. Enjoy them as the shows they are — but don't make the mistake of judging a candidate's strength by the size of the demonstration organized for him. For more meaningful signs, keep an eye on any fight that may develop over the seating of delegations, and watch the rostrum to see who is trying to get the ear of the chairman in order to be recognized and address the convention. Contrary to the smoke-filled-room school of thought, a national political convention is not a private, closed affair today. It's an open, public and quite transparent event. It's a many-headed, many sided spectacle that's made for television and the television viewer. The issues, the drama, the excitement, the humor, and sometimes even the foolishness are carried into your living room precisely as they occur.[8]

According to Gould, "the dry wit of David Brinkley of N. B. C. just about stole the show" in 1956 and NBC executives were looking to repeat the performance in 1960.[9]

When the 1960 Democratic and Republican conventions were broadcast, Huntley and Brinkley were in NBC's booth. CBS stayed with Walter Cronkite. It did not work. On the third day of the Democratic convention, CBS tried teaming Murrow with Cronkite,[10] but everyone was tuning to NBC. "The two [Murrow and Cronkite] were courteous to each other. There was no conflict but they did not mesh as a team. They were no Huntley and Brinkley."[11] With "brisk political repartee," Huntley and Brinkley broadcast with humor and substance. When the conventions were over, the audience stayed with NBC. *Newsweek* magazine said NBC made the conventions "a fresh, light wind ... by applying the light wit and dry satire of David Brinkley in easy converse with the world's most informed straight man, Chet Huntley." The duo were obviously complementary to each other — "Brinkley the *apéritif*, Huntley the cordial — that neither could have done so well alone. They relaxed and let history write itself." In addition to Huntley and Brinkley, the convention floor "creepee-peeping reporters" were Frank McGee, Merrill Mueller, Herb Kaplow, Sander Vanocur and Martin Agronsky.[12]

During that convention and on camera, Huntley said to Brinkley, "There has been talk about whether Nixon and [New York Governor Nelson] Rockefeller like each other. Now I find similar speculation applies to us. This may be something like taking a loyalty oath, David, but for the record, I like you." Brinkley replied: "I like you, too, Chet, ... if I didn't I could not stand all of this togetherness in this tiny booth all these hours."[13] Living in that ten by twelve foot broadcast booth, the duo aroused sympathy with viewers. One sent them pastrami sandwiches. The Governor of Maine sent them a precooked lobster dinner.[14]

For a long time, NBC ended their broadcast each night with "This program has the largest daily news circulation in the world."[15] Their NBC coverage earned a 51 percent share of the audience; CBS, 36 percent; ABC, 13 percent.[16]

Huntley and Brinkley became so well known that they were feature stories. For example, the duo landed on the cover of the March 13, 1961, *Newsweek* magazine and were featured in a story within. Inside the magazine was a cartoon by Robert Day that presented a church worship service. One minister had his arms crossed behind one corner of the pulpit; another smiling minister stood on the right side of the pulpit speaking. A man in the audience was shown turning to his wife, and stating, "Ah, the Huntley-Brinkley approach."[17]

Surprisingly, Theodore White, the author of the three *The Making of the President* (1960, 1964, 1968) books, mentions almost nothing of television news coverage, except the following: (During the 1964 campaign, after the California primary, NBC, CBS and ABC decided to "pool their resources" and did America a service? (author's question mark) by creating a cooperative called the Network Election Service. The networks were later joined by United Press International and the Associated Press.) White called it the "happiest and most valuable" creation to the rivalry of the national networks that were becoming "cannibalistic," "desperate" and "dangerous." This service set up a tabulating center where, at that time, a "staff of 100,000 people was deployed to give Americans the quickest, most honest and most complete vote count in their history."[18]

In the 1964 election, from all indications, the Republican Party never wanted much television coverage. For example, Republican vice presidential nominee William Miller was not happy with the media in the summer of 1964. He complained that "the Huntley-Brinkley Report" had interviewed a member of the "Minuteman" group who endorsed the Republican presidential nominee Barry Goldwater. Miller stated this was "deliberately designed as an illustration of the kooks that support Goldwater. They don't bother to put [Communist party spokesman] Gus Hall on and ask him if he supports [Lyndon] Johnson."[19]

David Brinkley offered this story concerning the 1964 Republican Convention in San Francisco. NBC News personnel were roomed in the Mark Hopkins Hotel. The Republican delegates "detested" the news media. Huntley and Brinkley heard how bad the media were every time they traveled up or down the hotel elevator:

"Chet and I agreed never to say anything, since a fistfight in an elevator would resemble a scene from the Marx Brothers.... After a few more of these elevator scenes, I worked out a little exchange with Huntley when we were riding up and down together, saying to him, 'The security squad waiting down stairs?'

'Yes, all of them,'" [Chet said].

Brinkley said it shut the insulters up for awhile.[20]

In another article in 1966, Huntley mentioned this convention, too:

I suppose the Republican Convention in San Francisco in 1964 was the most trying assignment we've ever had. Politicians are, for the most part, rather generous about their reputations. They are accustomed to criticism, analysis, or comment. They realize they are part of the political process.

But the majority of the delegates to the 1964 Republican Convention were newcomers. At one point, Henry Cabot Lodge, in utter exasperation, said, "Who are these people? I've never seen any of them before!"

Some of them were rough. Brinkley was getting it in the lobby of his hotel, the Mark Hopkins; and my wife was shocked one evening when a lady assaulted me in the lobby of the Clift, shaking her fist under my nose and warning that Barry [Goldwater] would soon fix me.

I think it was the second day of the convention, when I checked in at the Cow Palace and went up to the [NBC] booth about a half-hour before air time. David beckoned me aside, "Look," he said, "you probably haven't heard about it, because you would be the last to know; but there is a movement around here to get rid of one of us, and I think it is you. In any case, if that's right, I just want you to know that if you go, I go, too!"

Sure enough! There was a movement — a strong one. Bill McAndrew, Julian Goodman and Bob Kintner put out the fire, and I never did learn all the details.[21]

Reuven Frank said anti-press sentiment was evident even with souvenirs. Young Republicans selling souvenirs outside the Cow Palace had a best seller with the button urging "STAMP OUT HUNTLEY-BRINKLEY!" When they ran out, more were ordered from their New York supplier.[22]

Later, former President Dwight Eisenhower spoke to endorse Arizona U. S. Senator Barry Goldwater for president. To defend Goldwater, Eisenhower stated, "Let us particularly scorn the divisive efforts of those outside the family including sensation-seeking columnists and commentators...." The delegates exploded. Eisenhower was startled. Many left their chairs, rushed to the edge of the hall below where Huntley and Brinkley and other news personnel were stationed in their glass studios above the floor. The delegates shouted at and waved their fists at the media. With Eisenhower's "official support and sanction," Huntley and Brinkley were "quite happy to be in our booths high up and out of reach." Brinkley did not know what the delegates "might have accomplished had they been able to get to us, but [the delegates] were furious enough to do anything."[23]

To cover San Francisco's Republican Convention, NBC took care of their two stars by engaging nurses, doctors, and a dentist "in case one of them gets a toothache." To satisfy Chet's and David's complaint that "they almost starved during the 1960 conventions," Julian Goodman said, "we are going to have one man in charge of feeding just Huntley and Brinkley."[24]

In a 1965 book and a 1968 New York Times advertisement, several other stories were told concerning the 1964 conventions. Correspondent John Chancellor supposedly did "not have a good time." From the Cow Palace's floor he covered the convention and when he "refused to move when an assistant sergeant at arms ordered the aisles cleared" Chancellor was escorted off the floor by San Francisco police. NBC cameras followed Chancellor toward an exit. "It's awfully hard to remain dignified at a time like this," he commented. When he disappeared into a tunnel, he announced, from the television screen, "This is John Chancellor — somewhere in custody." A few moments later he reappeared on the convention floor and began again. "As I was saying ..." Turning to the sergeant at arms, Chancellor asked, "How do I get to Alaska?"[25] Chet quipped, "I think this is a first, a man broadcasting his own arrest on television."[26]

At the 1964 political conventions "NBC's success was awesome.... At one point in San Francisco," at the Republican Convention, NBC "seemed to have submerged the entire opposition.... NBC routed CBS even more dramatically at Atlantic City," at the Democratic Convention.[27] Cronkite anchored the San Francisco convention but that changed. Cronkite was replaced with CBS radio's Robert Trout and a Washington reporter, Roger Mudd,[28] but Huntley and Brinkley still beat them. Cronkite viewed Huntley's and Brinkley's success on "entertainment value."[29]

NBC President Robert Kintner enjoyed the audience share NBC received. When he called Robert "Shad" Northshield, an NBC News producer, Kintner said, "NBC has eighty-six per cent of the audience." In trying to reply Northshield found Kintner, true to his character, had hung up. A few moments later, Kintner called again. When Northshield identified himself, Kintner said, "I don't think you were excited enough. Do you understand what I said?" Northshield, again trying to reply, found Kintner had slammed the phone down. Shortly Kintner called again, and said, "I still don't think you understand." Northshield, exasperated, caught him before he could hang up, saying, "Look, we're very busy here. What do you want, one hundred per cent?" Kintner replied, "At least you've got that right" and hung up.[30]

Yes, the convention had celebrities. However, the news personnel found themselves to be celebrities, too. At the convention on its second day, Chet noticed from the broadcasting booth a possible disturbance in a corner of the auditorium. Through the intercom, Huntley asked correspondent Frank McGee to investigate. "Chet picked the wrong man." The person of the disturbance was McGee himself. He was "frantically trying to fight his way through a crowd of over-eager autograph seekers."[31]

Another highlight that kept viewers on NBC was when correspondent Sander Vanocur caught President Lyndon Johnson after he had finished his acceptance speech and was leaving the hall at 12:30 A.M., and interviewed him for 16 minutes. Vanocur was in the right place at the right time. Johnson was in an ancedotal mood and Vanocur got an "exclusive" long, spontaneous interview. CBS "was no where in sight!" NBC ran the "exclusive" the rest of the night.[32] *Newsweek* magazine reported Vanocur hoisted himself up to President Johnson's box and engaged the President in a long exclusive interview.[33]

It was enjoyable to notice CBS "keep attributing [NBC's] edge entirely to Brinkley's humor." CBS "could not accept that NBC did the basic work better than [CBS]. Brinkley ... was not some fellow telling jokes. He was an experienced Washington journalist who was also gifted with wit and style. Huntley's solidity and Brinkley's wit put a stamp on our work," Frank said.[34]

In an ad in *Broadcasting* magazine, NBC printed two pages of quotes concerning how well Huntley and Brinkley did during the 1964 conventions. A few include: "'NBC's Chet Huntley and David Brinkley were again in a class by themselves'.... Bob Williams, *New York Post*"; "'Huntley and

Brinkley haven't had a single bad moment'.... Lawrence Laurent, *Washington Post*"; 'NBC was best by a wide margin in the coverage of the night's proceedings' ... it got more perceptive and brighter comment from its two men at the top, Chet Huntley and David Brinkley'.... Percy Shain, *The Boston Globe*."[35]

Huntley reviewed the 1964 election year with these words: "The American election year was marred by too-recent tragedy [President Kennedy's assassination]; too much vulgarity and meanness; too little nobility and inspiration. But the continuity of the system by which we govern ourselves remains intact."[36]

President Johnson won the 1964 election. Senator Goldwater truly believed the media caused his defeat. Nine years later, in a letter to Huntley, January 10, 1973, Goldwater wrote: "I am convinced that there was a determined effort on the part of a majority of the major press representatives and the press to misrepresent me."[37]

NBC broadcast the 1968 conventions in color. Their cameramen also had lightweight wireless mini-cams. It gave NBC more mobility. Brinkley, after a demonstration, quipped, "It's going to make a convention floor as intimate as a cocktail lounge ... but with better visibility."[38] At one point, NBC had 80 percent of the audience during the Democratic convention. Robert Kintner asked Brinkley to stop in his office. Kintner offered Brinkley "a warm glass of whiskey — no ice — a damp handshake, and a gruff word of thanks," Brinkley recalled.[39]

One happy notation, or sad one, depending on how the reader gauges it, concerns Chet and food. After an eleven-hour session he went to eat one night in a nearby NBC food booth and found his lobster dinner had been eaten by a Tennessee politician invited in by an NBC friend. "Chet looked sadly at the waitress and sighed, 'Well, the way this convention is going, it may be the last full meal the poor man will have for a while. No use complaining.'"[40]

Miami, Florida, hosted the 1968 Republican Convention. Barry Goldwater was not on the schedule to speak. Nevertheless, Republican officials believed Goldwater should even though it made Nixon supporters nervous. The 1964 candidate spoke on the "need for party unity[. T]he response was overwhelming. [He didn't] recall anything like it in [his] entire political career." Brinkley called it "the most spontaneous, emotional, enthusiastic Republican response of the entire convention."[41]

The 1968 Republican Convention was quiet compared to the Democratic Convention in Chicago. With President Johnson not running again and Robert Kennedy having been assassinated in Los Angeles the previous June, the violence and dissent inside and outside the meeting caught news coverage and was heavily criticized. John Chancellor mentioned, "When the 1968 Democratic National Convention delivered its presidential nomination to Hubert H. Humphrey, there was discord in the convention hall, and rioting in downtown Chicago, where anti-war demonstrators battled police. It was a night of ironies—a gentle man reaching his life's goal in circumstances that belied everything he had preached in a long political career."[42]

The media was put on the carpet for what they broadcast during that event, especially the coverage of the violence. Scenes included police with tear gas charging demonstrators past the Hilton Hotel to the convention center; police clubbing marchers; a New York delegate who refused to show his pass and police dragging him out of the center; and guardsmen with bayonets chasing demonstrators into Grant Park. Frank said, "Most of the horrors testified to later at the commission of inquiry were in fact not seen on television — police shouting 'Kill 'em! Kill 'em!,' or clubbing kneeling young women and well-dressed, middle-aged bystanders."[43]

Huntley's voice "cracked with anger" over this violence. "I tried to cast myself as the voice of restraint. That night in Chicago I was mad, but when we had an on-camera bull session after the convention shut down, I pointed out that there was a definite brat element out there in the streets, that it was not a total slaughter of the innocents."[44]

"Outrageous and unfair ... the zenith of irresponsibility in American journalism," recalled Roman Pucinski, a Chicago congressman. "Network media personnel such as [NBC]... have done violence to the truth by their unfair coverage at Chicago and the public deserves better at the hands of this great industry," said Oklahoma congressman Ed Edmondson.[45] Frank stated, "But what we did show sickened those who watched, and they hated us for it."[46] Chet declared in his Wednesday "Chet Huntley Reporting" radio commentary,

> We in the calling of journalism have hesitated to talk about our problems here in Chicago, with the conviction that you and others have problems of your own. But the hostility toward newsmen, the hostility toward others not part of the city establishment, the hostility toward any sort of criticism, and the fear of telling it how it is have become too much and it became our duty to speak out.
>
> [Citing the number of injuries and beatings or harassments, Mr. Huntley said] the significant part of all this is the undeniable manner in which Chicago police are now going out of their way to injure newsmen and prevent them filming or gathering information on what is going on. The news profession in this city is now under assault by the Chicago police.
>
> [The NBC correspondent charged that] "a variety of impediments against free flow of news had been installed here in Mayor Richard Daley's city. His

control has even extended to the Democratic convention where all sorts of annoying and petty restrictions have been applied. In view of all this it is little wonder that young insurrectionists of our society have come here by the thousands to taunt and harass the city administration. It is such 'fair game.'"[47]

For many viewers, the networks "had devoted far too much time" to the convention's violence. "This general feeling was a product perhaps, of the frustration felt by the American majority." Frustration included the year long anti-Vietnam war protests, the disenchantment of the young, and the rebellion of black citizens across America. The networks were asked how much reporting was devoted to the violence? In 35 hours of coverage, NBC reported the violence for about 36 minutes "during the convention sessions, 28 minutes [was] devoted to the demonstrations outside of convention sessions."[48] The news chiefs of the TV network organizations, when looking back at their coverage of the convention, "appeared content to leave well enough alone." Frank said, "everything that was done may not have been exactly as it should have been done, but everything was done as well as it could have been done under the circumstances." He had "high praise for his people."[49]

The public thought it was more. Frank declared "Chicago 1968 was where network television had lost its innocence. After years of telling pollsters they trusted television above all other media of news, the American audience, history's most middle-class majority, was writing [NBC, for example] that the era of trust was over!"[50] TV Guide's Neil Hickey suggested an answer: "The Chicago convention is being called the great Rorschach event in recent American history: observers of every bias are interpreting it according to their own needs and fantasies. Similarly, an impressive body of psychological literature attests to the existence of a remarkable phenomenon called perceptual selection, which means that witnesses to an event perceive it — and quite sincerely so — the way they *want* to perceive it, and reject coldly what their prejudices and presumptions find uncongenial."[51]

The networks would not give Chicago's Mayor Richard Daley free time to respond to the violent broadcasting, so Daley and many others filed a complaint with the Federal Communications Commission over the FCC's "right to question the accuracy or alleged bias of coverage of controversial issues and public events."[52] NBC Network's Washington attorney, Howard Monderer, filed a ten-page letter October 22, 1968, with the FCC, in part saying:

... that the Communications Act and the First Amendment bar the F.C.C. from any form of regulation that might constitute censorship.... [T]he mere transmission of a broadcaster of a formal inquiry by the commission implies that the commission may take action of some kind if it deems the response unsatisfactory. Nothing could be more deleterious to the journalistic function of the broadcaster than to compel him to be guided, not by the professional, experienced judgment of reporters, editors and news executives, but by an attempt to anticipate what would please the commission or those who might complain to the commission.[53]

At the end of the 1968 Democratic Convention, NBC bought a *New York Times* full page ad with the title "NBC News Election Year '68" with the subtitle: "Six Straight." Six pictures of the Democratic and Republican conventions since 1960 were printed and the following:

This week, NBC Democratic convention coverage attracted a larger audience than the competing network's coverage or the third network's combination of entertainment and abbreviated coverage.

It marks the sixth consecutive time more viewers watched a national political convention on NBC than on any other network.

This preference for NBC News — typical when the networks cover a major event — is strong confirmation that people regard it as the leader in broadcast journalism.

We're proud of the work done at this year's Republican and Democratic conventions by Chet Huntley, David Brinkley, John Chancellor, Frank McGee, Edwin Newman, Sander Vanocur and all their able colleagues. Each contributed to a superlative job.

But not to be overlooked as a factor in NBC News' leadership is its excellent reporting and analysis during the days, months and years *preceding* these particular conventions.

It all adds up.[54]

Huntley said, "the political conventions, elections, [and] election campaigns [were] exciting."[55] He would comment on the 1972 elections as an independent commentator on KBMN radio in Bozeman, Montana, and on his part-owned Horizon Communications radio network.

During the November 1968 election day, exit polling was an experiment by the networks. The procedure did not become a basic reporting feature until 1980.[56]

VI. The 1960s:
The Space Program, Vietnam, Assassinations, and Media Problems

Through the 1960s, "the Huntley-Brinkley Report" would anchor or co-anchor events such as

- President John Kennedy's death and funeral in November 1963;
- The arrival of the English rock music group called the Beatles (1964);
- The death of Martin Luther King, Jr. (1968);
- The assassination and funeral of Senator Robert Kennedy (1968);
- The funeral of President Dwight Eisenhower (1969);
- President Richard Nixon's eight-day fact-finding tour of western Europe, and traveling to Paris, France, to cover the Vietnam peace talks; and,
- The launch of the Apollo space program.

The Late 1950s and the 1960s

In its early days, "The Huntley-Brinkley Report" covered a number of events that would leave a permanent mark on U.S. history, including President Eisenhower's second administration (1957–1961), school integration and the space program.

In 1959 Eisenhower and Soviet Premier Nikita Khrushchev agreed to visit each other and hold a summit meeting in Paris, France. Khrushchev's visit to the United States, the first by a Soviet leader, took place in September.

Eisenhower, a dedicated viewer of "The Huntley-Brinkley Report," "told Huntley that his telecasts in advance of the Khrushchev visit [were] a major factor in determining the official U. S. approach."[1] When Eisenhower and Khrushchev met in Paris, the Soviets had downed an American U-2 spy plane over the Soviet Union. A United States apology was demanded by Khrushchev when he met Eisenhower in Paris. Eisenhower refused, Khrushchev walked, and the invitation to the Soviet Union was withdrawn.

In 1959, revolutionary leader Fidel Castro fought his way to the dictatorship of Cuba and made it a Communist state. The next year, he seized all U. S. company-owned property. Eisenhower broke off diplomatic relations with Cuba on January 3, 1961. Huntley said Castro "demonstrated an improved technique of hiding within a popular revolution and captured it at its frenzied moment of success."[2]

Eisenhower was the first president who could not run for a third term because Congress had approved and Americans ratified the 22nd Amendment limiting presidents to two full elected terms. This legislation was developed so that another president could not follow in four-term President Roosevelt's steps between 1933 and 1945.

A decade of diverse events was the 1960s. The U. S. Supreme Court decision on *Brown vs. Board of Education of Topeka, Kansas* (1954) had been a civil rights factor in the middle 20th century. By the 1960s civil rights leaders were unhappy with the movement's slow progress. On this movement, NBC News filmed several documentaries both in America and in Africa (see Appendix below).

Violence and crime increased after 1960. This was attributed to poverty, drug addition, weakening of the family and mental illness. Government aid and a healthy economy did not help the poverty problems in America's central cities, either. Black Americans living in decaying, poor neighborhoods vented their dissatisfaction in riots in such places as Los Angeles, Chicago, Detroit, Cleveland, Newark and New York ghettos, especially after Martin Luther King's assassination in 1968. Violence would touch Huntley's life, too, as we shall read below.

Americans were making steady movement from cities to their suburbs. By 1970, 70 percent of Americans lived in urban areas. Changes in lifestyle such as new sexual attitudes and practices, style of living, dress codes and behavior of teens and young adults caught the media's attention. Huntley stated in a 1964 column, "There are some who consider [hemlines] not major news. Well, to these untutored male eyes, hemlines are like yo-yos, moving up and down in a path which repeats over the circle of years. As they rise, apparently, old dresses can be altered. When they fall, new ones must be bought. If this is true, as it was in the post war 'new look,' an arbitrary, faraway decision on hemlines could be as big a domestic economic event as a national strike."[3] Chet said on the "Today" show on NBC on July 31, 1970, that he hoped the miniskirt would not fade away.

The early post-World War II baby boomers (born between 1946 and 1964) were beginning to graduate from high school in 1963 and 1964 and head toward college, military service or the job market. Americans were seeing news reports and documentaries of a small portion of these persons known as radicals and hippies rebelling against cultural and political authority. This would touch Huntley, too.

Major literary writers during the late 1950s and the 1960s included, for example, Herbert Gold, J. D. Salinger, Mary McCarthy, Susan Sontag and Frances Fitzgerald. Others include Edward Albee — *The Zoo Story* (1958) and *Who's Afraid of Virginia Woolf* (1962); Betty Friedan — *The Feminine Mystique* (1963); Truman Capote — *In Cold Blood* (1965); and Norman Mailer — *Armies of the Night* (1968). Chet had two books of his own published.

Major movies include *Dr. Strangelove* (1963), *The Graduate* (1967), *Bonnie and Clyde* (1967), *2001: A Space Odyessey* (1968), and *The Wild Bunch* (1969). On television such westerns as "Gunsmoke" and "Bonanza" dominated the ratings during the late 1950s and into the 1960s.

The Bay of Pigs invasion to take down Fidel Castro in Cuba in 1961 was a complete failure. The ill-fated coup was initially planned by the Eisenhower Administration and the Central Intelligence Agency. President Kennedy decided to continue with the invasion and took full responsibility for its failure. Reuven Frank explained that the invasion was more of "a footnote to a past event than a news story."[4]

Created in 1961 by the U. S. Government, the Peace Corps helped developing nations meet their own needs in various occupational categories. Volunteers over the age of 18, on two-year tours of duty, with their living expenses paid, included teachers, health care specialists, and rural development and agriculture experts. About 10,000 mostly young adults were deployed to work in 46 countries by the end of the Kennedy Administration in 1963.

In early 1963 NBC News presented a series of four, 60-minute films around the main title of "Profiles of Communism." Chet narrated three of the four segments: "The Death of Stalin" (January 27), "The Rise of Khrushchev" (February 3), and "An Encyclopedia of the Divided World of Communism" (April 3). In the first segment, Huntley saw Josef Stalin presiding over a terroristic police state and believing that a "war with the imperialists is inevitable." The second segment presented Nikita Khrushchev's rise from a bureaucrat to a world leader in the Communist Soviet Union following Stalin's death in 1953. The fourth segment put in perspective the split between the Soviet Union and China Communist. The Soviets expelled NBC News from Moscow and the Soviet Union because of the first two segments. This put NBC at a real disadvantage. CBS News offered space to NBC but NBC declined because it might get CBS expelled, too. It finally took Secretary of State Dean Rusk's intervention to get NBC back into the Soviet Union by the end of 1963.

President John Kennedy was on a two-day campaign (November 21-22, 1963) through Texas, first in San Antonio, Houston and Fort Worth; then Dallas. It would become "the most extraordinary weekend in the history of television." In meeting the challenge, "television news would never be regarded in quite the same way again."[5] When President Kennedy was assassinated that day, NBC and the other networks went on the air (commercial-free) through the funeral on November 25. They broadcast everything: the available footage on the shooting, Lee Harvey Oswald's arrest and murder by Jack Ruby, Air Force One bringing the slain president, Mrs. Kennedy and President and Mrs. Lyndon Johnson to Washington, D. C., the viewing, the famous farewell salute by John Kennedy, Jr. and the funeral. NBC broadcast the event for 71 hours and 36 minutes.

Unfortunately NBC was the last network to get on the air to broadcast the assassination. According to Brinkley, just after the shots fired at Kennedy, correspondent Robert MacNeil telephoned the New York headquarters news desk, and yelled, "This is MacNeil in Dallas!" An employee answered and said, "just a minute," then went to look for someone to take the call. The employee never came back, so the reporter was sitting on the most important news story of his career and could do nothing. What turned out, as Brinkley said, to be a quiet Friday newsday would become several days of continuous coverage.[6]

NBC finally got on the air at 1:45 P.M., Eastern time (15 minutes after Kennedy was shot) because NBC local affiliates were running their regular afternoon programming and had no one to turn them off! The Washington NBC affiliate's manager was out to lunch. "No one knew where he was, nor [*sic*] would take responsibility for bouncing" a fashion show. In New York Huntley somehow interrupted WNBC-TV's "marshmellow" program "Bachelor Father." When Brinkley finally got on the air, he was described by a fellow newscaster as being in a "controlled panic." According to presidential historian William Manchester, the Associated Press, which NBC relied on too much, committed some errors in reporting. NBC repeated those errors. For example, When the President's plane, Air Force One, had been in the air over an hour headed back to Washington, NBC reported that "LBJ was remaining in Dallas."[7] Johnson was on the plane.

NBC was the only network covering Lee Harvey Oswald when he was shot on live television on November 24 in Dallas while being transferred from city jail to the county jail. Correspondent Tom Pettit was standing two yards away. Usually mild-mannered, Pettit gasped, "He's been shot — Lee Oswald has been shot! There is panic and pandemonium! We see little in the utter confusion!" Oswald died later that day. His killer, Jack Ruby, did not get away. He was arrested, jailed, later tried, convicted and died of cancer in a Texas prison in 1967.

Continuous coverage of Kennedy's funeral was from 6:59 A.M., Sunday morning November 24, until 1:18 A.M., Tuesday, November 27. NBC's programs "outnumbered those of the other two networks combined."[8] When Kennedy's closed casket was viewed in the Capitol's rotunda, NBC was given the main camera angles, with "pooled" shots with ABC and CBS. Brinkley received "letters and wires demanding" an explanation of why Kennedy's casket was closed during the national viewing. He "refused [any explanation] though [he] said it was at the request of the family, or for reasons which seemed obvious. To [Brinkley] it *was* obvious. I feel strongly that the coffin should be closed at funerals."[9]

Wisconsin Senator William Proxmire offered a tribute for the television coverage: "Not only was the coverage dignified and immaculate in taste, it was remarkably competent and frequently it soared with imaginative, if tragic beauty. The intelligence and sensitivity of commentary and continually expressed dedication to this country's strength and solidity in its hour of terrible grief was superb."[10] Huntley mentioned sometime during the four days that "I didn't always agree with JFK, but I liked his style." Later, he wrote, "In seven seconds, he [Kennedy] wrote his piece in history and terminated a hopeful era."[11]

Brinkley, at 9 P.M. and 11 P.M., November 22, summed up his thinking of the sad event:

If we have come to the point where a President cannot appear in public without fear of being shot, then we are less civilized than we think we are…. It is one of the ugliest days in American history. There is seldom any time to think anymore, and today there was none. In about four hours we have gone from President Kennedy in Dallas, alive, to back in Washington, dead, and a new President in his place. There is really no more to say except that what happened has been just too much, too ugly, and too fast.[12]

Chet also offered commentary titled "Hatred":

It is a logical assumption that hatred … far left, far right, political, religious, economic, or paranoiac … moved the person or persons who, today, committed this combined act of murder and national sabotage.

There is in this country, and there has been for too long, an ominous and sickening popularity of hatred. The body of a President, lying at this moment in Washington, is the thundering testimonial of what hatred comes to and the revolting excess in perpetrates.

Hatred is self-generating, contagious, it feeds upon itself, and explodes into violence. It is no inexplicable phenomenon that there are pockets of hatred in our country, areas and communities where the disease is permitted, or encouraged, or given status by those who can and do influence others.

You and I have heard, in recent months, someone say, "Those Kennedys ought to be shot." A well-known magazine recently carried an article saying Chief Justice [Earl] Warren should be hanged. In his defense, it said it was only joking. The left has been equally bad.

Tonight, it might be the hope and the resolve of all of us that we have heard the last of this kind of talk, jocular *or* serious; for the result is tragically the same.

This is Chet Huntley.[13]

The space age began on October 4, 1957, when the first artificial satellite, *Sputnik 1*, was launched by the Soviet Union. Nearly a month later, November 3, they sent up *Sputnik 2* that carried a dog as a passenger. This shocked Americans that the Soviets had beat them in this knowledge. There were Americans who thought the Soviets could develop or already had developed long-range missiles that could be fired at the North American continent. From this Eisenhower ended up supporting an acceleration of the space program. *Explorer 1*, the United States' first satellite, was launched into orbit on January 31, 1958. America was in the space program. Astronaut Alan Shepard, Jr., became the first American in space on May 5, 1961, soaring from Cape Canaveral, Florida's NASA launching pad.

Sometimes the anchors betrayed their selectivity in news reporting. Chet reported on the "Navy's enthusiasm" about their atomic submarine *Nautilus'* Arctic cruise that year. According to Navy scientists, that military branch "gained 100 times more information from this trip than all previous air or surface explorations." Huntley commented, "The Russians may be ahead in space exploration, but apparently we know more about the bottom of the Arctic Ocean than anyone else in the world."[14]

Later NBC, just as the other networks did, covered live the launch of space vehicles such as *Gemini* beginning June 3-7, 1965. According to Reuven Frank, Bob Kintner wanted reporter Frank McGee out as anchor of the space coverage. Kintner wanted Huntley and Brinkley. Frank said both Chet and David "had, at best, only casual interest in the topic, and it showed." McGee remained the "expert commentator" second to Huntley and Brinkley.[15]

Gemini, or GT-4, was propelled into space with James McDivitt and Edward White II as astronauts. White was the first astronaut to walk in space. It was the first space launch and recovery telecast with Huntley and Brinkley as anchors. This was NBC's first launch in color and 200 NBC employees staffed the launch. *Newsweek* stated Huntley and Brinkley were "not in control of their subject matter and served up little more than casual conversation." The magazine suggested NBC's "knowledgeable, articulate [correspondent] Frank McGee would have been better left alone for the whole flight instead of being shipped off to New York after launch."[16]

When three astronauts, Virgil Grissom, Edward White II and Roger Chaffee died in an *Apollo* space capsule fire on the launch pad at then Cape Canaveral, on January 27, 1967, Huntley offered the following commentary:

> The nation has laid to rest three of its soldiers who volunteered in the struggle against the confining frontiers of human knowledge. It may be of some comfort to the nation to realize that these men had known success and achievement in their own brief time. They were spared the loneliness of martyrdom. For a whole generation of sometimes doubting youth, and adults as well, they brought new respect to old virtues of self discipline, physical excellence, and determined application of mind and body.
>
> Relatively few are permitted somehow to taste the exhilarating draught brewed of a whole nation's pride; but these men did. Hopefully it had occurred to them on the final days or hours of their lives that they had made us so very proud.
>
> Even in the final seconds of their lives, Virgil Grissom, Edward White II, and Roger Chaffee made their entries in this nation's new science. As the space exploration goes on, other young men will soar and travel in the profit derived of this loss.
>
> Chet Huntley, NBC News.[17]

Apollo VIII went to the moon in late December 1968 with Col. Frank Borman, Capt. James Lovell, Jr., and Major William Anders. These men became the first to orbit the moon. When they returned on December 27, and while waiting for them to splash down in the Pacific Ocean, Huntley filled the time reading letters NBC had received concerning *Apollo VIII's* trip. As Frank stated, "some letters pointed out that Borman was in a government vehicle when he read from the Bible [Genesis chapter one], which violated the separation of church and state. Huntley welcomed Borman to television, where no matter what you say someone will write to object."[18]

NBC's highlight was the July 20, 1969, *Apollo XI* landing on the moon. *Apollo XI*'s crew, Michael Collins, Neil Armstrong and Edwin Aldrin, Jr., took their spacecraft to the moon. Collins, in the main capsule, released the module, *Eagle*, carrying Aldrin and Armstrong, to drop gently down on the moon's surface at 4:17 P.M., Eastern time. It is estimated that one billion people, worldwide, saw the landing and heard Armstrong say, "One small step for [a] man; one giant step for mankind." (The word "a" was lost in transmission, according to NASA.) It is reported that ninety-four percent of Americans with television sets tuned in to see the event. The network covered the event for 31 consecutive hours. Huntley shared the anchor duties with Brinkley and Frank McGee. Two astronauts, Tom Stafford and Eugene Cernan, helped with commentary. In recorded history ABC, CBS and NBC television "had provided the single most striking sequence of images of the century."[19]

Apollo XIII was launched to the moon on April 11, 1970. On the way the mission encountered a catastrophic event but still the space capsule was able to go around the moon and back to earth. A 1995 movie was made of the events titled *Apollo 13*. It starred Tom Hanks, Kevin Bacon, Ed Harris, Bill Paxton, Gary Sinise and Kathleen Quinlan. Director Ron Howard included segments of the original telecasts of Chet (NBC), Walter Cronkite and Jules Bergman (CBS), and Frank Reynolds (ABC).

Huntley said in the 1970 *Life* article, covering the Apollo astronauts was "an exercise in boredom. The networks all got trapped. Most astronauts are dull as hell, nice guys, mechanics. The only ones who had a mind of their own didn't last long."[20]

The English Rock music group the Beatles—John Lennon, George Harrison, Paul McCartney and Ringo Starr—came to the United States on February 7, 1964, for their first American tour. NBC covered the arrival in New York. Later that evening, Chet informed the television audience that "like a good little news organization, we sent three cameramen out to Kennedy airport today to cover the arrival of a group from England known as the Beatles. I feel there is absolutely no need to show any of the film."[21]

Vietnam

America's foreign policy directed its attention to containing Communism following the Second World War. It became more evident during the 1960s with the Cuban Missile Crisis in 1962 and the Vietnam War. These foreign policy decisions, especially in Vietnam, brought challenges from protestors of all kinds to try to bring changes. A majority of the demonstrations were peaceful. However, some were violent. Several will be highlighted as we advance in this chapter.

Vietnam, in Southeast Asia, had been controlled and governed by France between the 19th century until World War II when the Japanese occupied it in 1940. France regained control after the war. Ho Chi Minh and his Vietminh gained control of northern Vietnam in 1946 and fought the French to defeat at the Battle of Dien Bien Phu in 1954. A peace settlement by an international conference in Geneva, Switzerland, divided Vietnam at the 17th parallel temporarily. The Geneva Accords, as they became known, called for reunifying the country through general elections in 1956. North Vietnam became Communist; South Vietnam became non-Communist. A rebellion in South Vietnam began in 1957 by the Vietminh. North Vietnam began publicly supporting the Vietminh in 1959. President Harry Truman believed the United States must help any nation threatened by Communism. Presidents Eisenhower, Kennedy and Johnson also adopted the Truman Doctrine. They feared a domino effect that if one nation in Southeast Asia fell to the Communists, others would fall, too.

Between 1957 and 1965, the Vietnam War was a fight between the Viet Cong (Communist-trained South Vietnamese rebels) and the South Vietnamese Army. Civilian and military advisors had been assigned by President Eisenhower to assist the South Vietnamese president Ngo Dinh Diem and that country's army. This continued under Presidents Kennedy and Johnson.

Hong Kong-based NBC News correspondent James Robinson made the first television report of the Vietnam War on January 5, 1962, during the special "Projection '62," anchored by Frank McGee.

Robinson bluntly announced, "Well, Frank, like it or not — admit it or not — we are involved in a shooting war in Southeast Asia."[22] By 1963, 16,000 military advisors had been deployed to South Vietnam. In 1965, the United States became fully involved with ground troops: Army, Marines, Air Force and Navy. There were 184,000 military personnel there by the end of 1965; 385,000 by 1966; 486,000 by 1967. Sadly, 15,000 had been killed, 60 percent of them in 1967 alone. Between 125,000 and

400,000 people in New York heard Martin Luther King on April 15 denounce the war. No congressman or senator was willing to speak.[23] In 1968, there were 510,000 troops in Vietnam; this author was one of them.

The Vietnam "conflict" (author's interpretation) (1961-1975) kept "The Huntley-Brinkley Report" busy reporting it. NBC broadcast an average of 12 Vietnam War-related stories per week between 1965 and 1970.[24] It was reported by Dr. Charles Bailey, who studied five years of all three networks' broadcasts, that Huntley and Brinkley "never offered formal commentary" or editorials during or at the end of their broadcasts. William Whitworth stated they did deliver commentary/editorials.[25]

Television news would see a historical turning point in their reports beginning in September 1963, with the Vietnam "conflict." Coming into America's living rooms every night, the "conflict," because of new television technology, "became the first evening news war in history."[26]

On their first 30-minute radio-television "Huntley-Brinkley Report" interview with President John Kennedy, Chet in part, asked the President,

> "Mr. President, in respect to our difficulties in South Vietnam, could it be that our Government tends occasionally to get locked into a policy or an attitude and then finds it difficult to alter or shift that policy?"
>
> The President: "Yes, that is true. I think in the case of South Vietnam we have been dealing with a government which is in control, has been in control for ten years. In addition, we have felt in the last two years that the struggle against the Communists was going better. Since June [1963], however, the difficulties with the Buddhists, we have been concerned about the deterioration, particularly in the Saigon area, which hasn't been felt greatly in the outlying areas but may spread. So we are faced with the problem of wanting to protect the area against the Communists. On the other hand, we have to deal with the government there. That produces a kind of ambivalence in our efforts which exposes us to some criticism. We are using our influence to persuade the government there to take those steps which will win back support. That takes some time and we must be patient, we must persist."[27]

During Kennedy's term, Porter wrote, Kennedy wanted the media to "ignore" Vietnam and "concentrate on those matters which made his administration look good."[28] It did not happen!

However, for example, in the early part of 1962, the Pentagon's public-affairs office director assured Kennedy that NBC had been convinced that United States interests would be negatively reflected if NBC presented coverage of "rough treatment by South Vietnamese soldiers to Viet-Cong prisoners, with a United States Army captain appearing in the sequence." The film did not appear on "The Huntley-Brinkley Report" and was shelved.[29]

President Johnson, at the beginning of his term, had a good relationship with the press. However, as the media refused to handle Vietnam as a "1940s crusade for universal freedom,"[30] a rift developed between the Johnson Administration and the media as will be highlighted ahead.

A June 14, 1965, speech given by Chet to Rotarians in Billings, Montana, was paraphrased by the *Billings Gazette*: "it is impossible to assume [the] Communists would allow a free and open election" if they ever took South Vietnam. Chet stated, "Critics also say that the Viet Cong constitute a native, home-grown force — in other words, a civil war." The newspaper reported him saying, "Broadcasts from Hanoi do not make this true."[31]

Huntley reported from South Vietnam three times (1965, 1966 and 1968) during the seven years "The Huntley-Brinkley Report" covered the war. He said it was "pretty sickening." He thought President Johnson made "some horrible mistakes," but he did not elaborate.[32] NBC broadcast Huntley hosting "Vietnam — December 1965" at Christmas time that year. During his second tour in the summer of 1966, Huntley and his camera crew visited the U. S. Navy LSD 26 the *Tortuga*. They recorded a story on its river patrol base activities.

In a September 11, 1966, NBC "White Paper" documentary, "Vietnam — War of the Ballot," he expressed doubts about America's involvement in South Vietnam. "If the South Vietnamese fail politically, at what point would we, could we, recognize it and in front of the world, acknowledge it. It's a puzzlement. In the military phase of the struggle, where it cannot be won, we do well. We have not lost a battle. In the political area, where the decision lies, we have yet to win one."

Huntley's additional thoughts were stated in 1967: "I was there in 1955 and I saw the stupidity and selfishness of the French. We inherited this problem from them, and God, it's irritating to hear [French President Charles] DeGaulle acting holier than thou about it. I'm for escalation, but I'm not for pulling out. The big cliché has become, 'Stop the bombing.' Well, we've stopped the bombing five times now; why the hell isn't the [blame] on the other side?"[33]

In a radio commentary in 1968, Chet said:

> Historians might one day, when this Vietnam War has ended, discover that it broke all known records in throwing off platitudes. They have floated out of the Vietnam confusion like clouds of little bubbles. For example, the Vietcong are frequently defined as patriotic nationalists. The war is frequently called a civil war. Ho Chi Minh's purposes are sometimes described as only a desire to unite his country.
>
> We have had "seek and destroy,"the "redoubt or garrison tactic," "stop the

bombing," and finally, there is the one which reads, "There can be no military decision in Vietnam." If [captured documents] can be given any credence whatsoever, it becomes clear that military results are going to determine when and under what circumstances the enemy will come to the negotiating table....

This is why the Committee on Political Settlement in Vietnam, with Dr. Clark Kerr acting as its frequent spokesman, makes such sense. It asks for some reciprocal assurances from the enemy."[34]

As he prepared to retire from NBC in 1970, he provided more:

I do not subscribe to the argument that we were wicked to go there in the first place, that Ho Chi Minh was a benign and tolerant old patriot, that the Hanoi regime is really made of a corps of democrats, or that the Thieu government is comprised of a gang of villains. We went to Vietnam in the first place because a people was being cut to pieces by guerrilla terrorism directed largely from Hanoi, and because we mistakenly thought it was basically a thrust southward by monolithic Chinese Communism. We responded, in large part, to a cry for help.

We are in the process of discovering, most painfully, that, given the characteristics of the Vietnamese people, given the terrain and the geographical location of Vietnam, and given the enemy's type of warfare, Vietnam may be beyond the outer reaches of our power. That this realization should contain some shock quality and that it is painful should not surprise us.[35]

In an interview with David Frost in 1970, Huntley was asked again about the war. Chet believed the war needed to be debated as a "public issue" as far back as 1956. However, since it was not debated, the college students of the 1960s rose up and made their voices known. The war "accumulated like a small hurricane, way over the horizon, and grew.... Finally when the American troops reached approximately five hundred and fifty thousand [in 1969], then for the first time some attention was paid to it and the debates broke out." Those debates began on the college campuses. "It was far too late to hold a debate then," he said. Chet stated that America responded "to a genuine appeal for help." America had no interest in their territory, trade, treasure, "no advantage of any kind." The war went downhill when President Johnson was convinced early on that more troops could win it and the war would be over and everyone would "live happily ever after."[36]

One news item that Huntley reported each week was battle deaths. A phrase he included with the number of soldiers killed was "most of them were young men."[37] An example was an August 14, 1969, "Huntley-Brinkley Report" story: "Last week, before the resumption of the fighting, the number of American men killed in Vietnam fell to the lowest level in two years. Ninety-six Americans ... most of them young men ... were killed...."

In the Appendix below will be found an overview of two Department of Defense films Huntley narrated. One author suggested Huntley and Cronkite were "questionable" in hiring them-selves out to the government. J. Fred MacDonald further stated about Huntley, "At a time when his profession needed the utmost objectivity to report accurately to the American citizenry," Huntley "lavished praise" on the military.[38]

In 1965, stories on the sophistication or superiority of American aircraft over Vietnam were telecast. Chet narrated a Department of Defense film on the A-4 Skyhawk. The Navy plane made more bombing raids than any other navy plane. Huntley said the A-4 produced "spectacular" results, and "should have even better shooting in the days ahead" because of improving weather.[39] A few months later, the various network news broadcasts were trying to help America define various Vietnamese terms and phrases. One was "National Liberation Front." Huntley defined those three words as "Hanoi's name for its own forces."[40]

Chet became "worried that too many TV reporters in Vietnam concentrate[d] on" trying to get their filmed village burnings by the U. S. Marines, such as Cam Ne in 1965 (reported by CBS' Morley Safer), to "ensure an appearance on the air at home." He stated, "the military [thought] too many correspondents [were in Vietnam] for their own personal aggrandizement."[41]

When a field report was filmed and sent in, it gave only a small picture of the wider significance of the war. The bigger picture was summarized by the anchor. Such "battlefield roundups" would precede and set the context for the network's film reports. Into such reports were inserted other sound/film bits about the war. Let us remember that these reports and introductions were written by staff and were read by Huntley. For example, on January 10, 1966, Chet reported:

> American and allied forces were on the offensive on three fronts today in Vietnam. An assault by units of the First Air Cavalry Division, kept secret for six days, wound up on the east bank of a river separating South Vietnam and Cambodia. The enemy was clearly visible on the other bank, but refused to fire. The sweep has netted virtually no enemy personnel, but three large camps and tons of equipment and supplies have been destroyed. In the Iron Triangle 25 miles north of Saigon the story is about the same.... The South Koreans 10 miles north of Qui Nhon have turned in one of the big victories of the war, catching an enemy regiment and killing 185 and capturing 609 suspects. In air operations over South Vietnam four American airplanes were lost yesterday and today.[42]

A few months later, he said, "Last week when Hanoi and Haiphong were bombed for the first time the Communists claimed they had shot down seven American airplanes and claimed it was a significant victory. In fact only one airplane was lost in the raid. The same night, Wednesday, they tried hard to shore up morale in Hanoi by parading a captured American pilot through the streets of the capital."[43] Chet reported on and "gave a reassuring view of the [Vietnam] fighting and, perhaps without knowing it, of the strategy of attrition."[44]

On May 3, he told the NBC audience: "From Hill 881 to the Mekong Delta ... the enemy has chosen to stand and fight conventionally in relatively large numbers. And it has been his undoing. The U. S. has immeasurably greater firepower and mobility.... The principal campaigns so far bear this out. In the Mekong Delta South Vietnamese operating west of Hué killed 150 ... the 4th Infantry Division killed 136."[45]

The latest Johnson biographer said, "Johnson refused to let war opponents dominate the media with 'Communist' inspired accounts of the war. At the end of February [1967], he told the president of NBC News that the networks were slanted against him.... During dinner [at Washington State] U. S. Senator Henry Jackson's house, [Johnson] told NBC's Ray Scherer that 'nothing good was ever written about his Vietnam policy.'"[46] Continuing this theme, the Johnson administration "saw every negative Vietnam story as a blow to America's war morale." NBC aired a "highly critical report" showing troops fighting with M-16 rifles that "jammed often, which was bad for morale." It showed Marines arriving at Camp Carroll where, "if the present rate of fighting continues, more than half of them will be wounded or killed." In addition, the program cited "complaints that some Marines are being returned to Vietnam after less than a year away."[47] "'A report from Vietnam on [the] Huntley-Brinkley [news hour] tonight [July 18, 1967] was devastating,' [Johnson aide] Harry McPherson told [Johnson press secretary] George Christian."[48] On September 20, 1967, Johnson said to a group of Australian broadcasters, "Press coverage of Vietnam is a reflection of broader and deeper public attitudes, a refusal by many Americans 'to see the enemy as the enemy.' ... NBC ... [is] committed to an editorial policy of making us surrender."[49]

As opposition to the war increased, the "centerpiece of movement mythology" was the testimony in America's capital. On October 21, 1967, 100,000 demonstrators descended on Washington and the Pentagon. This building was besieged by some 50,000 persons.[50] Another report said only a "few thousand occupied the plaza and steps of the Pentagon."[51] Brinkley called the march "a coarse, vulgar episode by people who seemed more interested in exhibitionistic displays than [in] any redress of grievances."[52] The next day President Johnson and his family took a ride around the fringe of the city's demonstration just to see "what a hippie looked like."

Lady Bird Johnson complained about the garbage the militants left behind.[53]

Huntley stated in a speech at the Rochester Institute of Technology on June 2, 1967, "The right to dissent is a blood relative [to peace]. Respect it, use it, too." Later he thought protesting the war, burning draft cards, profanity and flag burning were "carried to excess." Finally, he emphasized, "I don't think you are as effective as you might be in enlisting our aid [oldsters, as he put it], if you resort to overstatement of your protest or dissent."[54]

On March 5, 1969, he was invited to give a speech at a national peace luncheon at the New York Hilton Hotel. After his short speech (see Appendix below), he introduced Senator William Fulbright. When Senator Fulbright came to the podium to speak, he did not get the opportunity. The group of half-dozen war protestors calling themselves the Veterans and Reservists to End the War in Vietnam shut the forum down.[55] The reader is invited to turn to the speeches in the Appendix of this book and read Chet's commentary on the event.

The antiwar demonstrations would continue into the Nixon and Ford administrations and past Huntley's death. At his retirement from NBC in 1970, he mentioned, "We've listened to the extremists long enough — and rather politely: they are arrogant, ill-mannered boors [who] have no program — only a tantrum."[56]

NBC blew its accuracy with reporting the aftermath of the Tet offensive, January 31, 1968. Four hours after the Viet Cong fired their first shot at the U. S. embassy in Saigon, "The Huntley-Brinkley Report" stated,

> The Vietcong seized part of the U.S. embassy in Saigon early Wednesday, Vietnam time. Snipers are in the buildings and on the rooftops near the embassy and are firing on American personnel inside the compound. Twenty suicide commandos are reported to be holding the first floor of the embassy. The attack on the embassy and other key installations in Saigon, at Tan Son Nhut Air base, and Bien Hoa, north of Saigon, came as the climax of the enemy's biggest and most highly coordinated offensive of the war. There was no report on allied casualties in Saigon, but they're believed to be high. The attacks came as thousands of civilians were celebrating the Lunar New Year, and at times it was impossible to distinguish the explosion of mortar shells and small arms fire from those of the firecrackers the celebrants were setting off....[57]

The networks guessed at what happened and used bird's-eye interpretations on what followed the battle. They said the six-and-a-half-hour Vietcong occupation appeared to be the United States' most embarrassing defeat in Vietnam. The Vietcong never got into the embassy building.

The snipers were U.S. personnel firing at 19 VC commandos inside the embassy grounds. The most embarrassing U. S. defeat in Vietnam was not a small group of commandos fighting on or near the U.S. embassy!

A few days later in Saigon, South Vietnamese brigadier general Nguyen Ngoc Loan had an alleged Viet Cong officer brought to him. The captured officer had not been cooperative in providing information. Loan walked over to him in the middle of a Saigon street, put his pistol to the officer's head and shot him. NBC was the first to broadcast the killing. NBC News' Bob Kintner defended the broadcast not so much for the killing but because it was "newsworthy."[58] It was estimated that 20,000,000 viewers saw the murder.

During February 1968, the Battle for Hue, South Vietnam, was telecast 18 times by the networks between February 1 and 15. NBC reported from Hue five times. On occasion, the news employees rewrote the wire copy that provided scripts for the 6:30 anchors. Sometimes the geography was confusing. Huntley reported this example:

> After two weeks of stalemate caused, at least partly, by the United States reluctance to join in an attack on artistic and architectural treasures, the Marines today entered the walled Citadel in Hue on the left bank of the Perfume River. Five hundred men crossed the river in assault boats and executed a wide flanking movement, entering the Citadel from the northwest to join up with South Vietnamese troops fighting their way toward the Imperial Palace and the southeast corner of the Citadel, which the enemy still holds.[59]

Peter Braestrup in his book corrected several geography statements. Braestrup said the Marines simply boated across the Perfume. They did not execute a "wide flanking movement." The Marines went to the east corner where the South Vietnamese First ARVN Division headquarters were located. The Citadel walls did not run north-south east-west. "They linked corners which pointed in the four principal compass directions. Thus the 'southeast corner' was in reality the south corner; but the map of Hue was usually tilted, for easier reading, and confusion resulted."[60]

On February 15, Chet reported, "The situation in Hue has become so critical that today the city's mayor, Col. Pham Van Khoa, said he plans to execute a number of Vietnam prisoners in public. An unidentified American advisor reportedly is encouraging the mayor. He was quoted by UPI as saying, 'There will be summary executions of VC and hopefully some of the infrastructure.' By infrastructure he meant enemy leaders. The Defense Department late today told NBC it has no information at this time on the report."[61]

Braestrup said the "planned executions" were irrelevant to the battle situation then happening in Hue. They were later "knocked down,"[62] and Khoa was dismissed for "incompetence and panic." The wire services were "keen on execution stories."[63]

Some of NBC News' insights into what was happening during February 1968 also came from captured VC propaganda film. Chet led a report on February 16:

> ...The sniper firing has subsided now in Saigon. Those Vietcong not killed or captured have presumably gone back to their villages where they can take refuge. One such village, according to the Vietcong, is Cu Chi, 20 miles northwest of Saigon.
>
> We have obtained film made by the Vietcong more than a year ago of their activities near this village. A North Vietnamese English narration of the film seems to indicate that the villagers spend much of their time working in opposition to the South Vietnam government.[64]

Huntley then introduced correspondent Douglas Kiker who interpreted the background of the film and scenes. Many more reports could be included but space does not allow.

With all the coverage during February 1968, one writer said the news broadcasts of two-three minute sound/film bites showed viewers "more infantry action over a longer span of days than most American troops [saw] who were in Vietnam during the Tet Offensive."[65] One writer said, that following Tet, "the pillars of establishment opinion," CBS News, *Newsweek*, the *Wall Street Journal* and NBC News, "gave way and called for de-escalation."[66] For two months after Tet, the administration said nothing. With the President taking no action, his job rating went down. Three topics contributed to this:

1) Johnson did not take any action to the "rally round the flag" effect that would have boosted his popularity in "the aftermath of a foreign policy crisis";

2) the North Koreans seized the intelligence ship the U. S. S. *Pueblo*; and

3) Johnson did not "maintain the initiative on a major public issue."[67]

Administration press aide Jack Valenti suggested to Johnson that he talk to Huntley, who "... turns out to be a very vigorous supporter of the President. In private conversation he is committed to the President's course of action in Vietnam and approves of both his objectives and his tactics. Senator [Birch] Bayh [of Indiana] told me that Huntley was overjoyed at the unexpected meeting he had with the President at the White

House — after the meeting he talked continually of how impressive the President was and how strong and wise he appeared to be."[68]

Valenti "suggested to Bayh that Huntley" should go public with his Vietnam support. Brinkley had made known his opposition to the war. Johnson never did meet with Huntley and make that support public.[69] Another source believed Huntley was "considered an Administration supporter."[70] However, correspondent Liz Trotta said Huntley and Brinkley "never declared themselves for or against the war on the air."[71] Dr. Charles Bailey, in analyzing the 1965-1970 "Huntley-Brinkley Reports," stated Huntley "seemed to interpret stories in a way to emphasize his judgment that the war, although ugly, was just." Later, Bailey said that Huntley "was more and more saddened by the human costs of the war and more pessimistic about the chances of peace. It seemed that the balance tipped so that, to Huntley, by his tone and style, the war was still just, but not worth the price."[72]

Brinkley once asked President Johnson why he did not "give up on Vietnam and save American lives that Brinkley thought were being needlessly lost. Johnson replied, 'I'm not going to be the first American President to lose a war.'"[73]

When Johnson made his famous announcement on live television on March 31, 1968, "I shall not seek, and I will not accept, the nomination for another term as your President," Huntley, in an oral interview, said he was "surprised."[74] Johnson, in his autobiography, made no mention of any media coverage![75]

As Richard Nixon took over the Presidency in 1969, he decided there would be a controlled effort to shift the news from Vietnam to other events. When press conferences were held, only "paraphrasing or official statements" were offered. Nixon also used more prime-time speeches. He wanted to make sure he had direct communication to all Americans. Nixon was going to have media coverage "without the journalists."[76]

President-elect Nixon wrote Chet a letter concerning future press coverage. Nixon was "deeply grateful ... for the coverage I received from NBC." Later in the letter, Nixon stated,

> In the years ahead, I realize there will occasions when you may not agree with the policies of the new administration. I want you to know that I will appreciate receiving the benefit of your criticism as well as your praise. I believe it is vitally important for the new administration to seek out the best thinking of the nation's opinion leaders in finding solutions to the critical problems with which we are confronted. Above all, I want ours to be an open administration — open to new ideas — listening and respecting those who disagree with us as well as those who agree with us.
>
> Sincerely, [signed] Richard Nixon[77]

It was not to be!

This is what the media had to contend with until the end of Nixon's term. A further media attack is found below concerning Vice President Spiro Agnew's speech in 1969.

Concerning Vietnam, after a Nixon address on May 15, 1969, Brinkley reported: "The president has now made it clear what he would like to see done in Paris [at the peace talks] and how. The main points of what he said are these: The withdrawal of American and North Vietnamese troops in a year, an international body of some kind to supervise the withdrawal and arrange a cease-fire, and free elections. And that is the base from which this country will negotiate from now on."[78] The war would end (1975) a year after Chet died.

Vietnam was summed up in this statement by Army General William Westmoreland and Navy admiral Ulysses Sharp: "The Vietnam War ... has been the most thoroughly documented, most centrally controlled, most computerized, and most statistically analyzed [was] in history. This was due in part to the necessity to measure progress of a war in which there were no clearly drawn battle lines, no front, no safe rear."[79]

AFTRA Strike

AFTRA, the American Federation of Television and Radio Artists, 18,000 members strong, went on strike against the three major broadcasting networks on March 29, 1967, for 13 days, ending April 10. The major issues were "1) wages and fees for newsmen at network owned TV stations and, 2) announcer staffing on FM radio stations. The strike affected 150 newsmen covering stories in Chicago, Los Angeles, and New York."[80] The networks continued to operate with reruns and network executives replacing performers or newscasters except for Chet Huntley, and later, Frank McGee and Morgan Beatty.

David Brinkley wrote a few words about the strike. Huntley and Brinkley were required to be union members. Brinkley said "the title gives most all of us members the benefit of considerable doubt that we could claim to be artists. [I] seldom paid much attention to the union." It is doubtful Chet gave much attention to it either, until they went on strike. Both men had individual employment contracts with NBC. Their contract "required [them] to belong to the union and pay dues to it, and [they] did, it really had little or nothing to do with us."[81]

Huntley crossed the picket lines at 30 Rockefeller and went to work. In carrying "the Huntley-Brinkley Report" by himself, Chet reported on the strike but "made no mention of his part in the story." To cover for Brinkley during the nine-day strike, Huntley mentioned: "David Brinkley is off tonight."

Huntley had a "30-year colloquy" with AFTRA.[82] He believed AFTRA did not "represent" him and he didn't think news people had to belong to a union with "actors, announcers, singers and dancers."[83] Huntley said AFTRA "is not qualified as a bargaining agent or representative of network news broadcasters."[84] In another story, he said, "AFTRA does not understand the economics of the news operation in TV."[85] He questioned the union's qualifications to serve as the radio and television news broadcasters' bargaining agent. AFTRA was "comprised of entertainers whose problems had no relationship" with news personnel. Chet had attended AFTRA meetings some years before. "Newsmen rarely had the opportunity to participate in discussions, which, he said were dominated by announcers, entertainers and singers." Huntley believed some "40 newsmen at NBC [and] other colleagues at other networks shared his view."[86] "I didn't join AFTRA to become a journalist, and I'll be damned if they are going to push me into anything." Huntley believed "journalists were or should be a kind of priesthood answerable only to their readers and viewers and should not belong to any union and should not join a strike, particularly one having nothing to do with us. If journalists wanted a union they should have one of their own."[87] Chet held a membership card (and had since 1941) because he needed it for "guest television appearances" not "newscaster chores."[88]

Brinkley did not cross the picket lines in Washington — he stayed home — so Chet, as mentioned above, did "the Huntley-Brinkley Report" alone.[89]

Huntley's crossing the picket line created considerable ill-will. The union did not like his action and said "he was liable to suspension or even expulsion."[90] One "unidentified" NBC employee said, "Many of the guys [strikers] think Huntley's position is ridiculous. He talks about newsmen. He's not a newsman. He's a reader. I've never seen him on the street" reporting the news. This interpretation was "unfair."[91] Although Huntley did little writing for the "Report," his radio commentaries and many television specials were all his. Several "Huntley-Brinkley Report" writers refused to work with Huntley when the strike was over, "preferring to transfer to other units."[92]

One night when Chet left 30 Rockefeller, "unknown assailants tried to mug him. Unruffled," Chet continued to report the news and "for years tried to convince news people they needed a separate union of their own, exclusive of actors, dancers, and jugglers. It never got off the ground."[93]

His house was picketed, windows were broken and he received threatening mail and phone calls.[94] The strike was settled on April 10.

According to Nielsen ratings, NBC's audience share went up while Huntley was alone. Meanwhile, over at CBS, the audience share went down! Arnold Zenker, an administrator, replaced Cronkite. At ABC, "a black secretary did so well substituting for [the news anchor] she was hired as a permanent member of their news staff when the strike was ended."[95] Columnist Jack Gould added a touch of humor: "Even some television officials have expressed surprise over how readily viewers have accepted the executive personnel that has been filling in for the striking members of [AFTRA]. Before the strike it was a TV maxim that educators, journalists and clergymen were the easiest to induce to go on TV and the hardest to persuade to get off. After the strike there will be an addition to the group: TV executives."[96]

When Chet and David met in Chicago on April 3 to received the National Association of Broadcasters' 1967 Distinguished Service Award, they were asked about the strike. Brinkley said, "Chet is doing what he thinks is right, and I am doing what I think is correct. We respect each other's views." Chet replied that 150 news personnel on strike should not belong in a union of 18,000 jugglers, singers and dancers. Brinkley, as he came to the roster for his acceptance speech, quipped, "Good morning, Chet. I am usually unable to say anything at all until I've heard a commercial."[97] Chet, dispelling any rumor of their conflicting position concerning the strike, stated, "David and I are too proud to fight — or that I am getting too old."[98] When the strike was over, the union and NBC agreed to a "No reprisal" clause specifying that the union and the network "might not take any punitive or disciplinary action against anyone for their actions during the strike."[99]

Brinkley wrote that both made a mistake: Huntley working; Brinkley striking. The mail from viewers was "hostile." The letter writing audience "assumed Brinkley was striking for money and accused [him] of greed." Huntley's mail "accused him of being so rich and famous [and] he cared nothing for the other and lowlier" union members.[100]

Some sources say this strike and Huntley crossing the picket line cost "The Huntley-Brinkley Report" its lead in the ratings. Frank believed this: "… If some perception of friendship or at least cordiality between Huntley and Brinkley swelled audiences, then it is conceivable the public was put off by what they saw during the strike."[101] Brinkley thought "when the strike was over," and normalcy returned, "the audience's anger would fade." It did not. Their Nielsen ratings began to decline. The duo guessed — though they never knew — that Brinkley "had antagonized the anti-union people ... while Huntley antagonized those who were pro-union, and [the two of them] had managed to antagonize both sides" of their audience. Chet took the decline in stride.[102] Frank said, "No one said so and it may not have been true, but it appeared that Brinkley disagreed with Huntley, that there was a rift."[103] There was no rift.

In October 1967, Huntley was invited to participate in a debate titled "Television of the Unions" in New York's Hilton Hotel. Again he raised the problem of all newsmen being required to be AFTRA members. The new contract also would allow actors and announcers "to qualify when a newscast is to be done," Huntley said. "I'm sure that must be why AFTRA wants newsmen in the union." AFTRA had not defined "newsman" from the spring strike with the networks and it was not defined that night.[104]

Ratings Decline

"The CBS News with Walter Cronkite" during 1967 was making inroads into NBC News' ratings. It seemed NBC's analytical reporting, which CBS was trying to copy, and CBS' Vietnam-based reporters were giving audiences what they wanted. Because of decreased ratings, and with several months of discussions and two weeks of rehearsal, on August 21, 1967, "The Huntley-Brinkley Report" added four "contributing editors" to the report. "NBC officials said assignment of the four newsmen to the show will give them more 'exposure' and will enable them to work on in-depth reports and possible 'open discussions' of major news issues during the course of the program."[105] John Chancellor and Sander Vanocor in Washington, Jack Perkins in Los Angeles and Douglas Kiker in New York became part of what *Variety* called "Huntley-Brinkley and the 4 Horsemen." The magazine complained that because of these additions, "fewer stories are covered and the emphasis is more on remotes than filmed reports." It looked more like a reporter's "roundtable" at various times in the broadcasts. "The Report" became a far more interesting program but the ratings stayed about the same as can be seen below.[106] Brinkley claimed credit for the "contributing editor-round-table" program. He thought it would make the "Report" "more informative."[107]

The mail concerning the change was heavy. One furious viewer from New Jersey "wrote not only to NBC but also to a sponsor, The American Home Products Corporation, vowing that until the new approach was scrapped he would not combat his sinus congestion with Dristsan or shave his face with Aero Shave."[108] Chet did not think much of the "roundtable" format either, saying in a 1970 interview, he was "impatient with 'new' ways to do television news, such as having panels and discussions within news programs. 'There's one good way, and that's to sit a guy down and have him read the news.'"[109]

1967 TV News special

In November 1967, "Just a Year to Go," a "Huntley-Brinkley" 60-minute special, was aired. Its content included the violence that was gripping the United States from such places as Vietnam, Watts in Los Angeles, Detroit and Newark, N. J. Brinkley told the audience:

> We have an unpopular foreign war and something like a domestic cold war at home between the races. Either of them could tear this country apart. But even worse than that, these two dangers have combined to produce a third danger even bigger. It is that a majority of the American people have little or no confidence in their leaders' willingness or ability to deal with these dangers—little or no confidence in the leaders they have now or any they seem likely to get....

With statistical surveys and polls, Huntley and Brinkley presented the situation that had brought on this cynicism: Vietnam opposition continued to rise — the hawks and the doves were screaming. Three elements of the population recommended that America get out of the war, smash North Vietnam and China if necessary, and get out unilaterally.

The race issue was aired too. The duo reported that 88 percent of whites polled thought the summer of 1968 would be more violent than the summer of 1967. Black Americans polled (73 percent) agreed. A majority of whites polled wanted any riots put down by some sort of force, and 25 percent thought the authorities ought to "shoot on sight."

The surveyed Americans showed their hostility concerning President Johnson's handling of Vietnam. A minority thought any of the Republican candidates could do better. The Republican contenders demonstrated their inability with evasive and carefully hedged statements. They did suggest temporary solutions as pretty and fragile as a "rainbow." Incisive and brilliant though it was in presenting the critical stalemate on these issues, the program seemed to have two flaws: it did not look past the 1968 elections, and no tentative solutions were presented by the six newsmen involved in the program: Chet, David, John Chancellor, Sander Vanocur, Douglas Kiker and Jack Perkins.[110]

More Assassinations

"The Huntley-Brinkley Report" was part of reporting the race issues of the 1950s and 1960s. Comments on a documentary "Second Agony in Atlanta" are found in the Appendix below. A September 2, 1963 NBC documentary titled "There Comes a Time: American Revolution '63" was another. The three-hour special was aired without commercials because sponsors did not want to be associated with controversy.[111] NBC News President Bob Kintner, in a June 1965 *Harper's* magazine article claimed this documentary was his idea. He also stated RCA chairman Robert Sarnoff agreed enthusiastically to its creation. Kintner believed Americans "sensed for the first time the depth and continuity of what had previously seemed a spasmodic and puzzling protest."[112]

Segregated churches and church activities were avoided. The producers, to avoid any structural concept, adopted segments presented A-Z by city/state. When the program arrived at "Montana," Huntley told the audience that his home state schools had integrated the few Montanans of color. He stated, "We were a frontier people, or at least our fathers were, and the tradition of judging each man by his merits had by no means died out. Still, in an odd kind of way, the Negro was outside our tradition, a thing apart. In a sense we never really saw him, not the way we saw our friends. We never looked with honesty at Negro[e]s the way we examined the anatomy of a grasshopper, or speculated on the after-hours life of our teacher. We looked, but we had been told what to see. What we were really showing, of course, was ourselves."[113]

Kintner, in the above magazine article, added that NBC had its first black correspondent, Robert Teague, who had reported from an Elizabeth, New Jersey, construction site. A demonstration was going on. He decided to march in the picket line and said that "surprisingly" it was "one of the greatest experiences of his life." Kintner added that this program "may have helped in establishing the national consensus which expressed itself in the Civil Rights Act of 1964."[114]

President Kennedy had civil rights legislation sent up to Congress in early 1963. Attorney General Robert Kennedy and associates brought it to the House of Representatives Judiciary Committee whose chairman, Emmanuel Celler (D-New York), knew civil rights legislation was ready for favorable work in the House. Celler suggested Kennedy visit with Senate Majority Leader Mike Mansfield (D-Montana) and Senate Judiciary Committee Chairman James Eastland (D-Mississippi) about it. Eastland was courteous but not willing to give civil rights any other affirmation. Kennedy visited with Mansfield but he was reluctant to offer any encouragement. Mansfield suggested the legislation could be introduced in 1964.[115] Racial unrest continued in the South during 1963 but it would take Kennedy's successor, Lyndon Johnson, to finally get the Civil Rights Act of 1964 pushed through Congress.

The news televising continued. Eventually, the following sad event was brought to the viewing audience.

Martin Luther King was assassinated on April 4, 1968, in Memphis, Tennessee, by James Earl Ray. King had worked for racial equality since the late 1950s. He was the minister of the Ebenezer Baptist Church in Atlanta, Georgia. Inspiring both blacks and whites to become activists, King believed in non-violent, dignified tactics to make changes in America. Unfortunately, because of his death, rioting broke out in Boston, Detroit, New York's Harlem and, the worst, in Washington, D. C. The sky turned dark with over 700 fires, and smoke obscured the Capitol building. More than 75,000 troops nationwide were called to active duty to keep the peace and patrol various cities' streets. Casualties totaled 3,000 injured and 46 dead, all but five blacks. As Terry H. Anderson wrote, "This [was] because one violent white man slaughtered a nonviolent black man who had called on America to live up to its promise."[116]

Chet said his voice "trembled" when he announced that King had been shot. Television helped bring a calming effect on America by covering the death of a private citizen. Huntley remarked on the loss America felt on the April 9, 1968, "Huntley-Brinkley Report:"

> This country and every person in it suffered a terrible loss tonight, with the assassination of this man.
>
> Again, we are made to look like a nation of killers at a time when our detractors and unbridled critics and adversaries had already advanced that damaging assertion. The perpetrator of this deed brings down upon all of us the painful charge that we Americans are prisoners of violence and destruction and death. What others *think* we are, however, is less important than *what* we are; and we are poorer as a consequence of this, farther away from our national goals, and more prey to complete disaster ... the disaster described in such stark language in the recent report of the President's Commission on Civil Disorders.
>
> Dr. Martin Luther King is victim of the violence he preached against and eschewed. This stirring and gifted voice of restraint is now silenced and we will find it difficult to argue convincingly in behalf of moderation. That is the tragedy of it. Restraint, gentleness, charity ... virtues we so desperately need ... have had a day....

NBC News, by way of a memo from Robert Northshield, decided to present the "minimum amount of riot footage following" King's assassination. They wanted to show the restoration of peace. This was left up to the producer. The producer, in evaluating the stories, had to decide if the violence was "isolated incidents" or a "general trend."[117]

Up to 100,000 people surrounded Atlanta's Ebenezer Church for King's funeral that day.

In King's biographies and related books, the media received surprisingly little attention. The media covered race issues and played an important part in public reaction to the assassination, so the omission is puzzling.

New York Senator and former U.S. Attorney General Robert Kennedy won the California Democratic presidential primary on June 5, 1968. Huntley and Brinkley were in Los Angeles to broadcast the results. When Kennedy was shot, he was walking through the kitchen of the Ambassador Hotel in Los Angeles. The networks had shut down their coverage for the evening. Chet and David had left the studio but returned when they heard what had happened. NBC covered everything from midnight, June 6, just after Kennedy was shot: the death announcement, return of the family and his body to New York, the funeral at St. Patrick's Cathedral in New York and the burial near his brother the late John Kennedy in Arlington National Cemetery on June 7 at 11:04 A.M. Brinkley summed up the event with these words, "When Senator Kennedy went down he was trying to speak for those Americans, including the young, who feel a need to change many aspects of American life. That cause has not been stilled forever because even without him the changes will be made because they have to be."[118]

The media rejected the idea that they were "to blame for any breakdown in the 'governability' of American society." The "governability" problem was based on crises such as Vietnam, the civil rights movement, and the 1968 Democratic Convention that the media naturally covered. Public confidence in American government declined during this decade. This non-confidence caused "attachment to both political parties to weaken, and the political system began a twenty-year period in which not a single president would serve two full terms of office."[119] Brinkley, in a documentary, summarized the decade of the 1960s: "What television did in the sixties was to show the American people to the American people.... It did show the places and things they had not seen before. Some they liked and some they didn't. It wasn't that television produced or created any of it."[120]

The 1970s

NBC publicist Joe Derby mentioned a serious but humorous story that gave Chet an addition to his character.

> Chet and I were in Minneapolis-St. Paul in January, 1970 for some reason I can't remember and two members of the Winter Carnival Committee were driving us somewhere on an expressway. Chet and I were in the back and it was dusk.
>
> Just off the road was a parked car with a woman waving her arms. Chet asked the driver to stop, he did, the woman explained she was out of gas, Chet asked her to hop in and she did.
>
> She explained she was on her way to pick up her husband at work when the tank went dry. She talked all the way nonstop to a filling station never looking at anybody in the car.
>
> At the station Chet got out, did the talking to the station attendant and held the [gas can] for the pumped gas. As Chet stepped into the lighted area around the pumps the woman finally noticed him. She screamed. Then breathlessly got out, "My God — Chet Huntley — my husband will never believe it."
>
> We drove her back to the car, poured the gas in and left. She was speechless all the way back and never really thanked Chet.
>
> Chet would always laugh that wonderful laugh when I would recall the incident with, "I wonder what that gal's husband said when she said 'guess who came to my rescue...'"[121]

In his last interview, with Jack Smith of Smith Syndicate, Chet was asked what his proudest achievement was while on network television news. He proudly stated, "On behalf of the television news industry, not just myself, I'm proudest of the way we measured up to the civil rights issue beginning in 1956. We took the lead in shaping public opinion in favor of that movement."

When asked what the most satisfying story he ever covered was, he said it was his last documentary for NBC. It was about migrant farm workers in Florida titled "Migrant: An NBC White Paper" broadcast on July 16, 1970. Huntley said, "We helped get some new laws and practices put into effect, and workers are a little better off now."[122] NBC producer Martin Carr said it was a show that investigated migrant workers' living conditions. "Some of television's severest critics are the very people who make it difficult for journalists to present a balanced story." Carr's experience was that he found his "work in Florida was looked upon with suspicion almost everywhere I went, and in some cases I met with open and frightening hostility." This hostility came from farm owners and managers.

Huntley was supposed to interview three people "who had cooperated with Edward R. Murrow in making 'CBS Reports: Harvest of Shame'" in 1960. Only one was willing to talk but was too frightened to be filmed. He was also supposed to interview Florida Governor Claude Kirk, but Kirk canceled. Carr closed the article on the documentary with "[b]alance *is* a problem in making a television documentary, especially one that deals with social issues…. I'm alarmed at the way the growing criticism of television news makes it increasingly difficult to gather a story and thereby threatens the public's right to know."[123]

When the program was broadcast, Huntley introduced it and provided commentary at its end. Fred Ferretti in his column stated, "Last night [July 16] Chet Huntley and the producer, Martin Carr, poignantly reminded us that [the migrant worker is] still here. He won't go away."[124] Unfortunately, Coca-Cola Company was alleged to be negatively involved with the migrant workers; that was corrected by NBC, but the meeting between them landed in the *New York Times* anyway.[125] Huntley's part was not affected.

The Republican team of Richard Nixon, former Vice President under President Dwight Eisenhower and the 1960 Republican presidential candidate, and Maryland Governor Spiro Agnew won the 1968 presidential election. Vice President Agnew took broadcast news to task in a speech to the Midwest Regional Republican Committee in Des Moines, Iowa, November 13, 1969. The networks had advanced notice of Agnew's speech so they canceled their Thursday night November 13 schedule. With an audience of 50 million watching, Agnew let loose. For the Republicans the context of the speech was Vietnam and the enormous erosion of popular support for the Vietnam conflict. (This seemed a proper followup on former President Johnson who had decided not to run again because of a "credibility gap" and by "domestic divisions" concerning Vietnam.)

After Richard Nixon was elected President in 1968, he was determined to make "sure that no such thing would happen to them"—the Nixon Administration. (For further interpretation the reader is referred to the letter Nixon wrote to Huntley in the Vietnam section above.) His distrust of the media has supposedly been traced back to his involvement in 1948 in the Alger Hiss-Whittaker Chambers perjury event. In August 1948, a *Time* magazine editor, Chambers, testified before the U. S. House of Representatives Committee on Un-American Activities. He accused Hiss, a former State Department employee, of being a Communist Party secret member in the 1930s. A Soviet agent himself during that decade, Chambers reported receiving State Department documents from Hiss to be turned over to the Soviets. Chambers offered evidence with microfilms of the documents allegedly typed by Hiss on his formerly owned Woodstock typewriter. Representative Nixon (R-California) and a member of the Un-American Activities Committee, became part of this event when Chambers took Nixon to Chambers' farm where he produced the microfilm from a hollowed-out pumpkin. The press, in its coverage, provided "terrible attacks" on Nixon in the form of "nasty cartoons" and "editorials." Both the *New York Times* and the *Washington Post* offered "balanced" reporting on the event. Regardless, according to William Porter, this seemed to be the beginning of Nixon's distrust of the media.[126] Huntley remarked in his last televised interview that "Nixon has had a twenty-five year argument with the media."[127]

Shortly after the 1968 election, President Johnson told Vice President-elect Agnew, "Young man, we have in this country two big networks, NBC and CBS." Johnson also named newspapers, magazines wire services and pollsters. "They're so damned big they think they own the country. But, young man, don't get any ideas about fighting ..." them.[128]

Now to 1969. In the weeks leading up to a speech President Nixon would give, the networks "speculated" on what Nixon would say concerning Vietnam. The White House was not successful in trying to discourage such speculation On October 20, Huntley opened "The Huntley-Brinkley Report" with what one author wrote, "blew the balloon to a massive size."[129] "The week-end featured a barrage of speculation about President Nixon's imminent moves to end the Vietnam War. More troop withdrawals were mentioned. So was a timetable for a program of troop reductions in Vietnam. The United States proposal for a cease-fire in Vietnam was prominently discussed."[130]

A week before Vice President Agnew gave his speech, President Nixon, on November 3, gave a speech on Vietnam on national television. Giving a thorough review of the Vietnam policy, Nixon rejected "an immediate, precipitate withdrawal of all Americans from Vietnam without regard to the effects of that action." He added that the U.S. would "persist in our search for a just peace through a negotiated settlement if possible, or through continued implementation of our plan of Vietnamization if necessary — a plan in which we will withdraw all our forces from Vietnam on a schedule in accordance with our program as the South Vietnamese become strong enough to defend their own freedom."[131]

Brinkley said in his autobiography that NBC had its broadcast day, known as a log, completely scheduled. For example, when a president asks for time for a speech, and he does not use all of a quarter-or half-hour, a news person is assigned that unused time for commentary or discussion. That night on NBC the time fell to Brinkley.

Nixon press aide Pat Buchanan, a 1962 journalism graduate of the

Columbia School of Journalism, a former reporter for the *St. Louis Globe-Democrat* who had never worked for a broadcast news service, and on Nixon's personal staff since 1966, wrote the Agnew speech. When Nixon reviewed the speech, he softened some of Buchanan's words; then Agnew, in some sections, softened it some more.[132] The President acknowledged Agnew had his approval. "Whatever Agnew was engaged in, apart from the fact that he fought with the press, was with my approval."[133]

Agnew, in seven-pages, said in part: on a Vietnam speech Nixon had given a week before, the media had "instant analysis" and "querulous criticism." The "analysis" that night by a majority of the media was "hostile." Network television news decides "what 40-50 million Americans will learn of the day's events in the nation and in the world.... No more than a dozen anchormen, commentators and executive producers settle on the 20 minutes or so of film and commentary that's to reach the public." Television networks "represent a concentration of power over American public opinion unknown in history.... The great networks have dominated America's airwaves for decades. The people are entitled to a full accounting of their stewardship." Agnew did not specify who should follow through on their "stewardship." Agnew did mention David Brinkley. "Do they [commentators] allow their biases to influence and presentation of the news? David Brinkley states, 'objectivity is impossible to more human behavior.' Rather, he says, we should strive for fairness."[134] Frank said Brinkley was "the first journalist to be denounced by name by Spiro Agnew."[135] The Vice President suggested letters and phone calls to the local stations by the public.

The speech caused the networks to condemn Agnew and Nixon. The networks thought the speech was intimidating. NBC reported 1,600 telephone calls against Agnew and 1,900 for him. CBS, on November 25, on their "60 Minutes" program devoted a whole hour to Agnew's speech. As a guest on the program, Brinkley stated that every administration had complained about news coverage. "All that's new is that this time — this time — it came in the form of a threat."[136]

Agnew struck a "responsive chord with many Americans." These people let the networks know what they thought.[137] In his memoir, Nixon said "the networks purposely ignored the wide-spread public support."[138] The Agnew-media confrontation inspired a cartoon. The *Toronto* [Ontario, Canada] *Star* reporting inspired its cartoonist to parody Huntley and Brinkley with President Nixon and Vice President Agnew at two microphones saying to each other, "Goodnight, Spiro; Goodnight Richard." The caption underneath was "Brinkley and Bluntly."[139]

Even congressmen got into the controversy. Representative Samuel

Stratton (D-NY) endorsed President Nixon's war policy and Agnew's views. He said the television news criticism "desperately needed to be brought into the open." Stratton was specific in naming, in part, Huntley, Brinkley and Sander Vanocur and their views on the news. Other politicians agreeing with Agnew included Arizona Senator Barry Goldwater, California Governor Ronald Reagan, U.S. Secretary of Housing and Development Director George Romney and Federal Communications commission director Dean Burch.[140]

Huntley was not quiet! NBC sent Huntley to the network affiliates' convention, and he later reported, "Our stations are furious at us. They agreed with Agnew and are after us. I tried to placate them, of course, but they're mad as hell."[141] Huntley added: Agnew "knew clearly what he was doing. People were disturbed by adverse news, of course. What was the response from the government? 'Let's get those guys,' instead of trying to get rid of the aberrations and the disturbances." Agnew "assembled a big pool of discontent, and there seems to be a willingness to delete many provisions of the Bill of Rights if need be."[142] Julian Goodman, NBC President, added that Agnew's "attack on television news [was] an appeal to prejudice."[143]

Huntley continued on this subject at the 22nd annual George Polk Memorial Awards for outstanding achievement in journalism at Long Island University, March 24, 1970. He "...defended the nation's journalists and criticized government officials for causing 'Americans to deprecate their heritage of the richest and most free and most all-inclusive press in the world and to join a noisy chorus demanding restraints on the right to inquire, the right to speak and write freely.... I can find no record of a time when we in journalism were so assailed and ridiculed.' [He warned that] 'it may take years to undo the damage which has already been done.... I fear that the current assault on journalism is not going to go away soon.'"[144] Chet stated in another interview: "Spiro Agnew is appealing to the most base of elements. All the networks broke their [backsides] putting his famous Des Moines speech on television. We almost created him, for God's sake. ...I resent being lumped in with his Eastern establishment intellectuals.... I've had more cow manure on my boots than he ever thought about."[145] Apparently, Agnew never checked the home states or towns of the three networks' news anchors or reporters. For example, Brinkley was from North Carolina; Huntley from Montana.

In a *TV Guide* article, he said, "We are not about to let Mr. Agnew or the White House staff, or any of the others get away with the old canard that radio, television and press are only inventing these signs of social, economic, political and racial unrest." In another part of that interview, he added, "Journalism's role is not, and has never been, to cheer up, to mollify, to spread joy and to indulge in sycophancy. Journalists were never intended to be the cheerleaders of a society, the conductors of applause. Tragically, that is their function in authoritarian societies—but not in free countries."[146] He told Fred Ferretti, "Every guy who sits down to a typewriter knows Agnew is tapping on his shoulder. Nixon is playing the whole thing like a virtuoso. I have a feeling we haven't heard it all from him yet."[147]

Huntley ended up on the "White House Enemies List." He commented that he probably landed on it because of what Agnew said and a later *Life* magazine article (see below).[148] Huntley did not seem displeased and remarked, "I'll be damned if I know what it's all about."[149]

In June 1970, the Federal Communications Commission "ruled that the networks be required to provide air time, under the Fairness Doctrine, to answer President Nixon's prime-time speeches defending his Vietnam policy."[150]

When asked about the Agnew-media problem one final time, Huntley stated in puzzlement, "I'm at a loss to know why Agnew is making a career out of attacking the press and television. There must be other issues. And, of course, he couldn't do it without Nixon's approval."[151]

In the aftermath of this, in an event which had no parallel, Agnew resigned the vice presidency October 23, 1973, because of alleged financial kickbacks while he was Maryland's Governor and Vice President. America would see the Nixon Administration destroyed by Nixon's misuse of power and he would resign and leave office August 9, 1974.

In June 1970, Huntley was interviewed for *Life* magazine. His comments on President Richard Nixon caused an uproar. It was written that Huntley said: "I've been with Nixon socially; I've traveled with him in his private plane; I've seen him under many conditions. The shallowness of the man overwhelms me. The fact that he is President frightens me."[152] On July 22, in a letter to *Life*, Chet denied that he told Thomas Thompson the last two sentences. Huntley said his actual statement was: "such efforts as the 1968 campaign and the rationale on Cambodia were, in my judgment, rather shallow. I also said that since I had been given the opportunity to know the Presidents, I worried about *all* of them: the power they possess, the decisions they must make, and the tendency of the country to bestow upon them a degree of monarchism. While I am not at all sure that whatever I think is all that important, perhaps it is important to state it is as accurate [sic] as possible."[153]

Life said on July 23,

Chet Huntley's denial of statements attributed to him … is surprising. Mr. Huntley was interviewed by Thomas Thompson, a writer for *Life* Magazine, on board a flight from Tampa [Florida] to New York and in his office at NBC in late June. Mr. Huntley was quite relaxed during the interview and some of his statements were even stronger than those published in *Life*. After reading the account of what he had said, Mr. Huntley may have regretted saying it. But there was no question about the accuracy of what was reported. Mr. Thompson's notes are available if Mr. Huntley wants to see them.[154]

Thompson replied, too:

I am sure he [Huntley] has experienced the cry of "misquote." It sometimes happens when a subject reads his outspoken words in print and suddenly decides that they were not spoken at all. But in this case they were. He is welcome to see my notebook which is filled with his eloquently enunciated words over a 48-hour period. What Mr. Huntley says in the above letter is, like almost everything he told me, a good quote and worth printing.[155]

NBC told a different story. A spokesman stated the "shallowness" statement was made but it was said by another newsman but attributed to Huntley during an informal setting with other news personnel.[156]

In an interview with *Newsweek*, Huntley said he thought *Life* was "interviewing him strictly" about what he would be doing in Montana. Huntley "assumed" the interview was "off the record" when politics became the subject. "I said something with two Martinis that I wish I hadn't said. I never expected to be quoted."[157]

Huntley apologized for the remarks to Nixon in a letter that the Nixon Administration leaked to the press and one newspaper, the *Billings Gazette*, published:

Dear Mr. President,

I want you to know that I am terribly embarrassed about some remarks attributed to me in the current issue of Life magazine. How the reporter had the audacity to make me responsible for the alleged statements is something I cannot understand.

I just hope you know me well enough to appreciate that the statements do not sound like me, and that I am more sorry about them than you will ever know.

Sincerely, Chet Huntley'[158]

No reply from President Nixon was found in the Chet Huntley collection. Huntley and NBC did not release a copy to the press, but an administration's staff member, Ron Ziegler, "leaked it."[159] White House Director of Communications Herbert Klein had heard about the letter but was puzzled why NBC did not publicize it.[160]

The Nixon Administration did have something to say. Lawrence Higby, H. R. Haldeman's assistant, sent a "SECRET" memo to Jeb Magruder, special assistant to Nixon. Higby said,

> We need to get some creative thinking going on an attack on Huntley for his statements in *LIFE*. One thought that comes to mind is getting all the people to sign a petition calling for the immediate removal of Huntley right now.
>
> The point behind this whole thing is that we don't care about Huntley—he is going to leave anyway. What we are trying to do here is tear down the institution. Huntley will go out in a blaze of glory and we shall attempt to pop his bubble.... Obviously, there are many things that we can do such as getting independent station owners to write NBC saying that they should remove Huntley now.
>
> Let's put a full plan on this and get the thing moving. I'll contact Pat Buchanan and forward copies of my correspondence with him to you so that you will know what the Vice President is doing.[161]

Magruder said: "Since the newscaster enjoys a very favorable public image and will apologize for his remarks, claiming to be misquoted, we should not attempt to discredit him personally. Also, since his remarks were expressed as an individual, we would have difficulty attacking his network directly." He also suggested releasing the letter to the press, "along with a gracious reply from the President."[162] Nixon aide H. R. Haldeman wrote in his diary for July 14, 1970, "Back onto Huntley issue, about Chet's bad quotes in *Life*. He denies them to Klein. Gives us a chance further to discredit TV newsmen and a dig at *Life* at same time." On July 25, Haldeman added: "Back on Huntley. Important to destroy him for effect on all other commentators."[163] Nixon's attorney, Robert Finch, said on Metromedia Radio News' "Profile Plus," that Mr. Huntley could say what he pleases when he is retired, but "he is not acting professionally" to say what was attributed to him "as an active member of the media."[164]

Even U.S. Congress members became upset over the "misquotes" about Nixon. Then Senator Robert Dole (R-Kansas) said, "The real Chet Huntley has finally revealed himself to the American people, and he is nothing more and nothing less than many of us suspected—a pat propagandist who has an antipathy for Republicans.... Perhaps his colleague, Mr. [David] Brinkley, will follow his lead."

Representative William Scherle (R-Iowa) said in a House speech, "His retirement comes 16 years too late. [He is] what we've always suspected—a Nixon-hater."[165]

Conservative magazine the *National Review*, edited by William F. Buckley, added its negative comment: "... it occurs to us that all that gallimaufry adds up to is that "1) the people who like Agnew do so because "2) they get their news from the television networks and know that Agnew's criticisms are just, and "3) were always able to see through the shallow impartiality of such as Chet Huntley."[166]

Chet's mother, Blanche, got into the mess, too. In an interview in July 1970, she stated, "I knew the moment I read that paragraph [Nixon's shallowness] that Chet couldn't have said it. He just isn't a profane man. That really made me mad."[167]

Chet and Tippy Huntley, July 31, 1970, as Chet retired from NBC News. Photograph in Chet Huntley Collection. By permission of K. Ross Toole Archives, Maureen and Mike Mansfield Library, University of Montana, Missoula.

Huntley retired before the administration could do anything.[168]

There was a story that the Nixon Administration allegedly tried to block a land exchange of Huntley's Big Sky project to get Chet to "support Republican candidates." However, he did not do "anything to help the GOP, although he did give a $100 contribution to GOP senatorial candidate Henry Hibbard, an old friend." During the 1972 presidential campaigns and election, Huntley said he was never pressured by the White House to "support Republican candidates."[169] More of this incident is found in Chapter IX below.

In another letter to the *Bozeman* [Montana] *Daily Chronicle*, Chet disputed another portion of the *Life* article that said in a visit with former President Lyndon Johnson that "I just kept filling his glass with Scotch, and that we talked about breeding" Hereford cattle. Huntley corrected that by saying, "I never poured Scotch for Mr. Johnson. He poured Scotch for me."[170]

Retirement

By the time Huntley retired he was earning about $300,000 a year, although the *New York Times* said it was half that.[171] However, he deferred payments until after his retirement when the money would show up in his estate.

Brinkley tells a humorous story, time period unknown, about Chet and his twenty-four volume *Encyclopædia Britannica*. Chet noticed these books began disappearing, one at a time, from his shelves over his roll-top desk. The janitors apparently were "stealing them and taking them home." For about a month he watched as they slowly disappeared. When the VASE-ZYGOTE volume was left, "he took it off the shelf and locked it in his desk, saying to Brinkley, 'Now they'll never get a complete set.'"[172]

When *Newsweek* reviewed Chet's book in 1968, the last paragraph said, "There has been persistent talk that Huntley will flip off the switch one of these days and return to his native state...."[173]

In an interview with *New York Times* columnist Fred Ferretti, in 1969, Huntley said the Gallatin River development was "a long range dream for more than five years." Ferretti added, "Mr. Huntley has weathered his storms, but at 57, there are times when he appears weary during his broadcasts." Brinkley stated, "Chet and I have talked about it. It's been developing. I've known for quite some time that he was interested in that Montana resort setup."[174] Chet casually told Reuven Frank early in 1970 (although it is mentioned in the above 1969 interview) that he would not be staying with NBC after his contract expired in August.[175] His reasons according to Frank were, first, that he wanted to start the Big Sky resort; second, that there was "a broadcast company [Horizon Communications] he owned with partners, which, because of FCC rules, he could not expand as a network employee;": third, that he wanted to write; and, fourth that he wanted to "quit while ahead."[176]

NBC officials did not try to dissuade him. Also, NBC had no legal claim on him since he was not joining a competing network.

On February 16, 1970, Brinkley announced Chet was leaving NBC News on August 1, 1970 [*sic*].[177] Chet was to become chairman of Big Sky of Montana Corporation, a yet-to-be-built resort development south of Bozeman, Montana, and northwest of the Yellowstone National Park. Chet was on vacation in Helena, Montana when Brinkley made the announcement (see Chapter IX below). This writer found two additional *New York Times* articles on the above announcement and a story of his last night on the August 1 edition.

Chet and David had broadcast some 4,500, 15- and 30-minute "Huntley-Brinkley Reports" when Chet retired on July 31, 1970.

NBC was perplexed at what to do for the last "Huntley-Brinkley Report." Suggestions included "letting Chet take the whole program with reminiscences; playing the entire second movement of Beethoven's Ninth (the show's closing theme); ... [and] news as usual."[178]

Number three was the final decision. His last day included an appearance with host Hugh Downs on the NBC morning "Today" program. Excerpts from Huntley's and Brinkley's first TV appearance together on August 11, 1956, at the Democratic National Convention in Chicago were shown.[179] The day ended with a farewell party that numbered among many "he had been attending for the past two months."[180] That July 31 broadcast offered the usual daily news reviews. NBC News broadcast two evening news programs, one at 6:30 to the Eastern and Midwest time zones and another to the Mountain and Pacific time zones at 7 P.M. During the 6:30 feed "someone mixed the films up. At the end, an enthusiastic girl associate threw shadows on the screen as she rushed to give Huntley a goodbye kiss." Brinkley observed, "We ended up as we began, with technical foulups."[181] During the 7 P.M. broadcast feed everything was normal.

Then, the time came. During the emotional moments ahead, he bit his lip, brushed his cheek, and spoke of his faith in the common sense of the American people. Huntley said,

> And so this difficult — uh — moment is here. In leaving this post after almost fourteen years, I recommend to you the NBC Nightly News, which begins

tomorrow. It will be in the capable hands of David, John Chancellor and Frank McGee. I will be watching with interest and affection. I might also remind you that American journalism ... all of it ... is the best anywhere in the world. I want to thank the entire staff of NBC, for this nightly broadcast has not been an individual effort, by any means. And as for you ... out there ... I thank you first for your patience, then for your many kindnesses and the flattering things you have said and written. More difficult to take, to be sure, has been your criticism, but that too has been helpful and in most cases valid.

But you have bolstered my conviction that this land contains an incredible quality and quantity of good common sense, and it is in no danger of being led down the primrose path by any journalist.

At the risk of sounding presumptuous, I would say to all of you, Be patient and have courage, for there will be better and happier news one day if we work at it.

And David, thanks for these years of happy association and being such an easy colleague to work with and for all the kindnesses.'

The screen switched to Brinkley who replied, "From now on, when somebody stops me in the street and says, 'Aren't you Chet Huntley?' I'll say, 'No ma'am. He's the one out West on a horse.' I really don't want to say it, but the time has come and so for the last time, Good luck and good night, Chet.

"Good luck, David. And good night for NBC News."[182]

CBS news anchor Walter Cronkite was gracious in his salute.

Since he came out of the West to team with David Brinkley back in 1956, Chet Huntley has been our competitor, and what a competitor. But he also is a colleague and a good friend. Tonight, on that other network, he is saying goodbye to David for the last time on their evening newscast, returning to his native Montana to build a resort and I suspect perhaps to get involved in politics. As he leaves the daily broadcast scene, a giant departs the stage. For journalism and for ourselves we hate to see him go. But that's the way it is, Friday, July 31, 1970. Goodbye, Chet.

Then on videotape, on CBS, Chet appeared saying, "Good night and good luck, Walter."[183]

ABC's Frank Reynolds thanked Huntley "for proving that newscasters can eventually escape without being tarred and feathered" by Spiro Agnew. Reynolds offered "all the best" to Huntley and closed the news "from his fellow horse thieves at ABC."[184]

NBC producer Lester Crystal called Huntley "a pillar of our information age."[185]

That night at a small dinner gathering at Lutèce restaurant, as a retirement present, NBC executives gave Chet a black Tennessee walking horse named Walk-A-Long-Go-Boy. Frank said it was a palomino. He rode it quite often around his Montana resort.

After a short vacation, Chet and Tippy settled in a rented house in Bozeman, Montana.

When Huntley retired, CBS' news audience increased. A CBS senior producer for Cronkite, Sandy Socolow, stated, "All of us—effete easterners—had always assumed it was Brinkley who was drawing the audience with his wit and charm. He was a breath of fresh air, and we'd wait to see what smarty thing he was saying tonight. But lo and behold, when Chet left, the audience left—and they came to CBS."[186]

NBC News decided to use correspondents John Chancellor and Frank McGee as co-anchors on alternate nights along with Brinkley following Huntley's retirement. On August 4, 1970, Brinkley finished a news story, looked up, and stated, "Chet ..." Chancellor replied, "No it isn't," and moved onto the next news story. Chancellor remarked later, "At first, I considered making a little joke of it. But I looked down, saw a hurricane story next and thought, 'Unh, unh, I can't joke going into that."[187] This trio co-anchorship lasted only a year.

VII. Tippy

Chet and David always discussed their work by monitor between New York and Washington beforehand. One afternoon in early 1958 while they were discussing that evening's program, Chet noticed a young lady walking across in the background behind David headed for the parking lot. Huntley asked Brinkley who she was. He told Chet she was Tippy Stringer, the blonde, blue-eyed WRC-TV weather reporter. Chet wanted to know if she was married. David answered, "No." Chet asked to be introduced.[1] In a 1961 interview, Brinkley told it a little differently. "She sat in my lap or something corny like that and I told her who Chet was while he looked on [in] the monitor. The next thing I knew he was taking her out."[2] It was a year of casual conversation before they met in person.[3]

Tippy was the daughter of Mr. and Mrs. Arthur Stringer, born Lewis Tipton Stringer in Illinois, Mr. Stringer had worked for the *Chicago Tribune* as a cub reporter. In 1939, the Stringers moved to Washington, D. C.[4] where he later became an official with the National Association of Broadcasters.

Tippy was a graduate of the University of Maryland.

Chet and "Tippy" were married on March 7, 1959, in Lake Bluff, Illinois, in a Unitarian ceremony conducted by Rev. Russell Bletzer in the home of the bride's brother, Arthur Stringer, Jr. Tippy's sister-in-law, Arthur Jr's. wife, was her matron of honor. Suellen Stringer, Tippy's niece, was flower girl. Chet's best man was Reuven Frank.[5]

Chet and Tippy in their New York home about 1961. Photograph in Chet Huntley Collection. By permission of the Museum of the Rockies and Archives, Bozeman, Mont.

In 1960, they bought and moved into a New York Manhattan East
side "town house" between First and Second avenues on Sixty-ninth
Street. It was an 80-year-old brownstone that was "seventeen feet wide
where each room is as wide as the house."[6] He called it a "'town house'
because that is what it was originally. There [were] about a thousand of
them left.... They started out 100 years ago as fashionable town houses
for rich New Yorkers. But due to economic cycles they became rooming
houses, then tenements and flophouses. In the past 15 or 20 years they've
been gutted and transformed into plush town houses."[7] He rented a garage
for his auto at $45 a month. It was used on the weekends when he and
Tippy traveled 60 miles west to their Stockton, New Jersey, farm (see "The
farm" in Chapter VIII below).

The new Manhattan home was equipped with "compact pieces" that
would not "crowd the room." On the first floor was a kitchen, dining room
and garden. The second floor included a den or study and living room.
On the third was a bedroom and guest room. The den/study was walnut-
paneled with an Italian provincial desk and a fireplace that sold Chet on
the home. The rug was white and came from Morocco. The patio garden
(18 feet by 18 feet, fenced), decorated by Tippy, was paved with slate, illu-
minated by lights with planters, and included a fountain and summer

table and chairs. The dining room was decorated in early American, with French doors that opened into the patio. White walls, full draperies, and off-green carpet described the long and narrow living room. Tippy mentioned that "in a house as narrow [as this one,] our furniture arrangement [was] limited; there [wasn't] much you [could] do about it — which [was] alright with Chet because he [hated] to move furniture." Chet said, "To me, home means relaxation among the familiar things that give a man stability in a constantly changing world. Good books, good conversation, good friends— without such things as these, man can indeed be lonely."[8] In another article it was mentioned that both loved antiquing. Their first marital argument "was about how high to hang a painting." She said, "Chet was a loving husband who gave lip service to [her] doing [her] own thing."[9]

When Chet went overseas a half-dozen times each year, Tippy was along. On these trips Chet and his crew filmed "news on the spot" and gathered information, or filmed a documentary.

VIII. Other Events

Pat's and Blanche's 50th

Pat Huntley retired from the railroad in 1960 because of ill health. His salary was $4,492 a year.

In June 1960 Pat and Blanche Huntley celebrated their 50th anniversary. Family members and 300 friends were in Reedpoint, Montana, to help celebrate. It was a moment in print when the area newspaper said, "Incidently, the senior Huntleys were married in 1910, but not in June. June is the time when all the family could be home, so June is the official date."[1] Pat and Blanche would enjoy 57 years together. In 1966, they moved into St. John's Lutheran Home in Billings. Pat died in 1968; Blanche in 1975.

The Farm

Chet's idea of a weekend was "to sleep late, go without shaving, and read. [He] never [had enough time] to read all" he wanted.[2]

He owned a cattle ranch in Montana and had a part ownership in an Iowa feedlot. In regard to the farm he also owned, Huntley would have conflict of interest commentary problems as will be highlighted below. The Huntleys bought the 230-acre farm and leased another 400 near Rosemont/Stockton, New Jersey, in 1961. The fieldstone farm house was built

121

Pat and Blanche Huntley's fiftieth wedding anniversary, June, 1960, Reedpoint, Mont. (l-r) Chet's daughter, Sharon; Chet; Blanche; Pat; Chet's grandson, Rick Arensmeier; and Chet's daughter, LeAnn. Photograph in Chet Huntley Collection. By permission of K. Ross Toole Archives, Maureen and Mike Mansfield Library, University of Montana, Missoula.

in 1690. The original two rooms were extended to ten and included genuine early American antiques Tippy and Chet wanted. Tippy mentioned in an interview in 1977 that she helped decorate this home. They started with a herd of 40 heifers, a collie named Mac and a basset hound named Sammy on the premises. Their cattle brand was the C Bar T. When the farm was sold, they kept the branding iron and used it as a poker for their fireplace in their Manhattan home and took it with them to Montana.

The Huntleys drove the 60 miles to their farm retreat every weekend they were in New York. At the farm Huntley recharged his batteries to restart his pressure-packed job the following Monday. By the mid-1960s, the farm had increased to 303 acres and the cattle herd to 900 Aberdeen Angus. Huntley invested a half-million dollars in the operation.[3]

A minor conflict arose concerning him in 1964 when he put his name to "Chet Huntley's Nature Fed Beef"—beef from his farm. Critics believed he could not objectively deal with the meat industry because of this connection.[4] He broadcast on March 19, 1964, a commentary against the "importation of Australian beef." The next day, Huntley discussed on his radio program the beef industry's price structure. Huntley told *New York Times* television critic Jay Gould, that "upon reflection perhaps he should have disclosed to his listeners that he now had a private business interest in one phase of the beef industry."[5] Ten days later, the Federal Communications Commission put pressure on NBC concerning his conflict of interest. Huntley and NBC "agreed" to have him withdraw his name on the product, and the advertising/promotion was discontinued. The cattle from his New Jersey farm would be sold on the open market with no mention of his name.[6] "I owned one per cent of a feeding company. Does that mean that everybody who has a piece of stock in a company must issue disclaimers if he is to speak about related subjects?"[7]

He told Edith Efron in 1965, "I know the problems, the despair, the hopes of the farmer. The American consumer simply does not appreciate the American farmer. The U.S. Government wants to get out of the farming business. The farmer wants the Government to get out of it. Everybody wants a free agricultural economy. But how do we do it? It's a great challenge.... I'd like to get the Government out of it and fine some other way to reward the farmer."[8] He may or may not have been able to do something had he decided to run and been elected to Congress. That did not happen, however.

Huntley, on May 27, 1968, in a radio commentary criticized the Wholesale Meat Act of 1967. Chet said, "In New York, this reporter knows, truck drivers and other employees of the wholesale district are now quitting their jobs to become Federal inspectors and they talk openly of the 'fringe benefits.' The fringe benefits are monies under the table in return for that misleading inspection stamp."[9] Iowa Congressman Neal Smith (D-Iowa) requested and received equal time to Huntley's radio commentary. Smith was not happy that Huntley had not revealed his "business links to meat packing companies" and said that he should have aired his association to them at the beginning of his broadcast. Since Betty Furness, President Johnson's advisor on consumer affairs, was mentioned too, NBC News invited her to respond. Huntley replied, in part, "Too much has been made of a relatively small and recent investment in a feed lot company ... my interest in cattle and cattle raising goes back ... to my boyhood in Montana."[10] However, the controversy lingered.

A few months later, Chet said meat inspection requirements are an "injustice to farmers and ranchers, creating ... the impression that the

Chet with a Hereford cow and calf, place and date unknown. Photograph in Chet Huntley Collection. By permission of the Museum of the Rockies Archives, Bozeman, Mont.

new meat inspection law adversely affect[s] cattle growers."[11] Congressman Smith again "objected." The objection was that Huntley, again, had not disclosed that he had "a close corporate relationship" with Edmund Mayer, Inc. of New York, a company "under the jurisdiction of the meat inspection act." The FCC investigated the issue and found that the employ-ees of the Mayer company were also "directors and stockholders in Group 21, Inc. One Alfred Mayer is president" of Group 21.[12] Huntley had sub-mitted in September 1968 to the FCC an affidavit that he owned 2.3 per cent of the shares of Group 21, Inc. (1500 shares). It also listed him as the company's executive vice president. The company operated a feedlot near Everly, Iowa, and he had invested $15,000 in the company.[13]

While in Montana for a speech that same month, Huntley added to the commentary on the issue by saying: "I tried to lift my voice recently on behalf of the cattle growers of this region and last week I felt as though part of the dome of the national Capitol had come down on my benighted head. I keep waiting for some of these guardians of the national welfare and morality to tell me what I might do to raise the price of cattle a few cents. I plan to keep talking about Montana and the Northwest."[14]

Because of the FCC action, NBC issued a new policy that their tele-vision and radio news personnel would be required to "submit a record of private financial investments that might conflict with their journalis-tic responsibilities." If there was a conflict of interest another reporter would be assigned to the story. This was suggested by Senator Philip Hart (D-Michigan), chairman of the Senate Subcommittee on Antitrust and Monopoly. Chet denied that his meat and livestock industries broadcasts "could have benefited him financially." He believed the "same require-ments should apply to Congress and the Federal Communications Com-mission."[15] Commenting a couple of years later, he said, "I don't see Congressmen filing disclaimers. I can't subscribe to that."[16]

Returning to his New Jersey farm, it brought him problems, too. "Incompetent" farm help, repeated vandalism with fence gates being opened that allowed part of his herd to roam, bullet-riddled windows, sand in a tractor crankcase, and stolen tires, gasoline and oil caused him to sell the herd in 1967. The vandalism cost him $100,000. Even with the local Civil Defense patrols on the farm the vandalism continued. That same year, August 1967, the Huntleys sold the farm to Princeton [N.J.] Land Development Corporation.[17] Officials such as the town's mayor, Franklin Ford, county sheriff's officials and New Jersey state police claimed he never informed them of the vandalism. Chet admitted that since the Huntleys were "often away and the house was dark, [it] invited this sort of vandalism." He also said the vandalism was because he was "'an out-sider,' presumed to be blessed by TV's limitless riches."[18] He related in another interview, "sometimes I guess it's just because I'm me [that there are attacks] but it's part of the business."[19]

He sold his Montana ranch and his interest in the Iowa feed lot in

1968.[20] He mentioned he enjoyed his livestock operations "as a hobby, as a business, and as a national political problem." He brightened up and added, "To see growing things is probably the most satisfying piece of business in the world. It doesn't matter whether it's a rosebush or a purebred bull. It's so different from writing or broadcasting. A field of alfalfa is tangible."[21] When he retired from NBC, he would re-enter the cattle raising business.

His Book

Chet wrote his first book in 1965, *Chet's Huntley's News Analysis*, published in 1966. It was an essay on various persons and subjects then in the news. It did not get the publicity of his second book.

During the 1960s, "on rainy weekends,"[22] Chet worked on a book of his childhood in Montana, *These Generous Years.* When Tippy found out he was writing it, she encouraged him to have it published. She found a publisher, Random House, and the rest was history. The book was released September 30, 1968.[23]

Newsweek magazine said, "At his best, NBC's Chet Huntley evokes touchingly the Montana frontier of his boyhood and youth in the century's teens and '20s. The human profiles—especially that of his grandfather— are full of unfeigned tenderness…. The imagery of that marvelous [Montana] landscape embedded itself in [Chet's] imaginations recollected from early childhood — that Huntley is most attractive."[24] In a *New York Times* ad, Random House said, "Chet Huntley recalls a marvelous frontier boyhood when a ten-year-old could catch a runaway horse or a bank robber — and an ice cream parlor had the headiest smell in the world; when life was plagued with locusts and hailstorms, prairie fires and droughts— and curious Indians peered in the windows at night; when nothing was greater than Christmas, the harvest, and the Fourth of July — and three generations could live together with love and laughter; it was a time — perhaps the very last — when it was still possible to enjoy being young."[25] An ad Random House bought in the *New York Review of Books* stated, "If you can't give boyhood, give [book's title and dust cover]…. the famed TV newscaster recalls his Montana frontier boyhood, when life — however hard — seemed infinitely simpler than it does today."[26] *Time* magazine never gave the book a review. It did not make the *Time* top ten books' list. The book made it to number five in the Seattle, Washington, area at the end of December 1968. It went through five printings.

Murray Illson stated, "Mr. Huntley's records it all with loving nostalgia humorously and often movingly — the changing seasons, the smell of the general store,…"[27] Reviewer Marshall Sprague in *The New York Times Book Review* said, "Delightful … His writing … is limpid, unpretentious and honest … Mr. Huntley writes of our tensions today and our fears for tomorrow and compares this untranquil environment with that of 50 years ago, when our present progress in its manifold forms was mere talk."[28] Fawcett Books, which published the paperback version a year and a half later, said, "*The Generous Years* gives the reader an insight into a man who learned early in life the demands for surviving and the love and closeness of a family."[29]

To give him the last word, Chet said, "they were truly generous years in spite of so many things including the vulgarities of weather. Growing up in that time and place you get a certain amount of pragmatism and a highly developed suspicion of orthodoxy. I think it made me the maverick I am, politically, socially. It's fun, I think, to be unpredictable and unlabeled."[30]

Pat Huntley's Death

Chet's father, "Pat" Huntley, died at 79 in Billings, Montana, on September 25, 1968. Chet and Tippy went home for the funeral. Pat was the first to be buried in the family plot in the Sunset Cemetery, Bozeman. In his book Chet paid tribute his father: "Dad was [a railroad man] … not as garrulous, blustering as many [in storytelling] — Dad's humor was more waspish — but he held his own. It became a source of deep satisfaction to me over the years to note that the railroaders genuinely liked and respected Dad. 'Pat' Huntley was the friend and companion of them all."[31] Whether or not "Pat" saw his son's book is unknown.

IX. Big Sky

The first ski resort in western America was developed in 1936 when Union Pacific Railway chairman W. Averill Harriman was needing a "destination that might enhance his railroad's lagging passenger revenues." Ketchum, Idaho, was chosen by UP-hired ski consultant, Austrian Count Felix Schaffgotsch. It became known as Sun Valley.[1] In 1970, Chet Huntley wanted to add one to the list.

What did Chet come home to in 1970? Montana had had a good previous decade. However, the state was in need of a sales tax that did not happen by a two to one vote of the voters in 1971. The population of the state was shifting to the expanding cities from the rural areas. Television and radio were bringing the nation to Montana. The state's citizens were shocked by the crises of the great cities in America. In the decades before the 1960s, Montana was used to seeing many of its young adults leaving the state. By the 1970s the population was seeing appealing reasons to stay. In November 1970, the voters approved a constitutional convention. The new constitution became effective in 1973 after a hard-fought campaign and the Montana Supreme Court narrowly approving the vote. Historian Harry Fritz suggested liberal activism, the new constitution, voters more involved in their democracy and the environmental protection movement kept Montana busy during these two decades.[2] This was what Chet came home to in 1970. Environmental protection would give him a headache in developing Big Sky.

This author has been to Big Sky and is awed by what Mr. Huntley saw and started. There is no way to speculate what Big Sky would have been had Huntley lived for another 10–15 years. Below is a short history of Chet's efforts to bring his dream through its studies and primary construction.

> Just as important as working for the good life is finding a place to enjoy it. A place free from congestion, pollution, ugliness and noise. And full of nothing but wide open spaces, clear skies, sparkling water and breathtaking scenery. If you've been too busy to look for such a place much less find one, you need look no further than Big Sky of Montana [Plaque at Meadow Village Mall].

Chet began thinking about this resort as early as 1964. "It's something I've always wanted to do."

It was "a long range dream for more than five years."[3]

Chet and Tippy, in the summer of 1968, vacationed at the 320 Ranch, some 45 miles south of Bozeman, Montana, and about twenty miles northwest of the Yellowstone National Park boundary. The 320 was owned by Jimmy and Patty Goodrich. Chet confided to the Goodriches that he wanted to "buy a cattle ranch in the mountains. He planned to put together a group of investors who would use the ranch as a tax write-off and a place for vacations." Goodrich mentioned that some west fork, Gallatin River acreage and the Lone Mountain Ranch, north of the 320 Ranch about ten miles, were for sale.[4]

Originally, what is now US Highway 191, the highway from Bozeman to West Yellowstone, was a wildlife and Indian trail that had steep grades and forded the Gallatin River in several places. A survey team was hired by Gallatin County commissioners in 1883 to find out whether or not a road could be constructed from what is now Gallatin Gateway to Yellowstone National Park. The first leg between the Gallatin Valley and Taylor Fork was completed by the summer of 1898. Twelve years later the road was extended to West Yellowstone.

Pat Shane, the Micheners and Andrew Levinsky settled on the West Fork of the Gallatin River in 1890, followed by Ira Dodge, a mountaineer and guide in 1892. Shane's homestead is now the site of the Soldier's Chapel. Nelson Story III received Shane's ranch and provided the land and money to build the chapel in 1952 in memory of his son and other members of a Montana brigade.[5]

The Lone Mountain Ranch was originally the Lytle Ranch which was homesteaded by Clarence Lytle before World War I. Lytle used it for hay production, cattle grazing and as a dude ranch. In 1927 J. Fred Butler, his daughter, Florence, and her husband, Don Kilbourne, bought the ranch

The 320 Ranch, looking east, with the Gallatin River in the foreground, south of present-day Big Sky, Mont. Lyle Johnston photograph, 2001.

for $50 an acre and changed the name to B Bar K Ranch. Objecting to sheep grazing in the West Fork of the Gallatin River drainage because of the damage the animals did, Butler bought 17 sections of the Northern Pacific Railroad land to keep other ranchers from moving sheep over Jack Creek north of Lone Mountain. In the 1940s Butler and his daughter, Florence, died. Bob Turner and Earl Reiser bought the ranch from Butler's and Kilbourne's heirs. It was a camp for young men for a few years. Later Turner and Reiser sold the ranch to Bob Corcoran, a Bemidji, Minnesota, businessman. The Corcorans ran a pulp mill operation on the ranch. In 1955 former Chicagoans Jack and Elaine Hume bought the B Bar K and its 900-plus acres. The Humes, with another partner Tom Boa, renovated the buildings and renamed it the Lone Mountain Ranch where it was used as a dude ranch. In 1962 the Humes and Boa sold Lone Mountain and the 960-acre Crail Ranch to Sam and Florence Smeding.[6] (Frank Crail had established his ranch in 1902.) Chet said, "I didn't particularly look around, I just dropped a word here and there that if some deeded property came on the market that I would appreciate being alerted to it and that is precisely what happened."[7] In another conversation he said, "When I conceived [Big Sky], I had to go out and get some money. I had to find,

Lone Mountain, at Big Sky Resort. Lyle Johnston photograph, 2001.

if you please, an angel." Chet considered "public conscription" and believed it "could have been successful. But a venture of this type ... is not guaranteed ... so it seemed more prudent to me to get some of the bigger corporations to put up the money."[8] He found Chrysler.

The Chrysler Realty Corporation bought the property Corcoran and Smeding had for sale in 1970. Chrysler Realty, a wholly owned subsidiary of Chrysler Corporation, Detroit, Michigan, was a company with $375 million plus in assets that had been incorporated in September 1967. The resort would be developed, financed and operated as an affiliate of Chrysler and fellow investors. Big Sky would be owned 49 percent by Chrysler and 51 percent by other corporate investors; Huntley would be board chair, have stock options and a little over 1 percent. The other corporate investors included Montana Power Company, Northwest Orient Airlines, the General Electric Pension Fund, Continental Oil Company, and the Meridian Investing and Development Corporation of Coral Gables, Florida. Chrysler Realty gave nearly $235,000 to back preliminary studies on a calculated risk basis, and would finance the rest.

Huntley and Chrysler Realty's executive Ed Homer flew to Bozeman and drove to the Gallatin Canyon in May 1969. Homer liked the view. A ski resort consultant, Jean Claude Killy, was hired and his report came back a month later that a ski resort was feasible — one village nine miles west of U. S. 191 at the base of Lone Mountain; the other village down the canyon in a meadow six miles east. The company arranged to buy 8,714 acres at $698,534.[9] Later, as mentioned below in the land exchange section, another 1,897 acres were bought by Chrysler from the Burlington Northern Railway.

In August 1969, Chet was in Helena, Montana, visiting with state officials about his proposed project. He told the media he was back in Montana to "promote interest from outside investors in Montana's resources." Looking for "investment capital for Montana from both corporations and individuals," he hoped those interested were "people who want clear air and water."[10]

Newsweek reported Chet's pending retirement in October 1969. "There's no crunch, now," he declared. "But I don't intend to keel over in this office." The magazine reported "The Huntley-Brinkley Report," NBC's $30-million a year breadwinner, "may be near the end of a thirteen-year reign as the glamour twins of newscasting." A new project on the drawing board was coming together and Huntley was ready to return to Montana as its chairman and promoter. Huntley said, "I haven't the foggiest notion when I'll be leaving. And I have mixed feelings, of course, but I want to go back to Montana. It's country I like and people I like."[11]

In a 1971 interview with E. W. Kenworthy, Chet gave three reasons for wanting this new, simpler life:

1) "I have always loved these mountains and the clean water and the wildlife and the climate";

2) "I was getting weary of that nightly deadline six days a week, living by the clock. You know it's the one profession where you can't be even one second late"; and,

3) "it was a kind of a patriotic thing in a way, I guess, in that the economy of this state is not all that it should be by any means."[12]

On February 16, 1970, Chet, along with Montana Governor Forrest Anderson and Chrysler Realty president Edwin Homer, announced in Helena, Montana, plans for developing a nearly 11,000-acre, year-round resort complex in south central Montana. It would be 40 miles south of Bozeman and approximately 46 miles northwest of West Yellowstone, Montana, the west entrance of the Yellowstone National Park in western Gallatin and eastern Madison Counties.

Bozeman at 4,700 feet elevation, the county seat of Gallatin County, had then a population of 18,000. The Montana State University, where Chet spent a few years as a student (1929–1932), has its home in Bozeman. Gallatin County is a farm and ranch area.

At future Big Sky Resort site, looking west from U.S. Highway 191. Sam Smedling, left; Tippy Huntley, center; Chet Huntley, right. Lone Mountain, the centerpiece of Big Sky, in background. Photograph in Chet Huntley Collection. By permission of K. Ross Toole Archives, Maureen and Mike Mansfield Library, University of Montana, Missoula.

Homer at the time of the announcement, said:

Special thanks are due Governor Anderson and the many state and local government officials who have given generous amounts of their time in helping us plan the Big Sky development. We look forward to a continuing close relationship with these officials as we work out the problems ahead of us to make this a mecca of prestige and enjoyment for recreation oriented sportsmen.

I know that the people of Montana are proud of their native son, Chet Huntley, who brought this area to our attention. But I'm sure that Chet Huntley is also proud of his state and wants to share its grandeur with the rest of the country. He will be the board chairman of the new corporation, the former to develop and operate this new concept in a year-round recreational community.

We will take every step necessary to assure that the land and waters of Big Sky will be as beautiful from now on as they are today.'[13]

Chet added in another interview, "One of our problems will be to convince people that 'we are the banana belt of Montana and that we have just as good weather as Sun Valley.'"[14]

Officially known as "Big Sky of Montana, Inc.," the development would have three features: it would be a summer recreation village, a mountain-type winter resort ski village and a convention center. Surrounded by national forests, the Big Sky area has scenic rugged views. The property's west boundary is dominated by a 11,166-foot peak called Lone Mountain. A large valley, two to three miles wide and nine miles long, is part of the property. To be built at the base of Lone Mountain at 7,500 feet was the ski village. In a natural basin four miles east, a summer recreation village would be created. Two miles further east are the Gallatin River and U. S. Highway 191.

Huntley made mention to Governor Anderson that he (Huntley) would like to be assigned the phrase "Big Sky." Anderson called the Montana Secretary of State Frank Murray and the assignment was done.[15] However, author A. B. Guthrie, wrote Huntley that he originated the phrase "Big Sky" in his 1947 book, Big Sky. Guthrie did not care about Huntley using it but asked that credit be given where due.[16]

Huntley and company made it known that 75 percent of the project would be left in a "wilderness state." There would not be any trails because it might "upset the feeding grounds of the deer, moose, elk, bear, and mountain sheep that roam there." He also stated that $8 million would be used to build a "sophisticated filtration" sewer system.[17] He commented in another interview, "the water [from the system] will be put back into a stream that the Fish and Game Commission will use as a fish hatchery. Water from our secondary settling pool, which is full of nutrients, will be used to irrigate the golf course." The solid waste will be placed in erosion areas that are "50 feet deep ... then we'll sod them in."[18]

According to Huntley the then $19.5 million project would attract visitors from throughout the world "to see its incredible scenery and meet its equally incredible people." A construction crew of 800 would start when snow melted. Several areas of the complex such as roads, an 18-hole golf course designed by Arnold Palmer, a small lake, a half-dozen condominium apartments at the guest ranch location and utilities, would be the initial work. The lake would be surrounded by a residential area for small horse ranches. A nearby dude ranch would be enlarged. Scheduled to open in the spring of 1972 was the summer recreation village. The ski village and convention center would open in the fall of 1972.[19] Telephone service came to Big Sky in November 1972. On December 15, 1973, the ski area officially opened. The delays in opening earlier are discussed below.

Chet, at right, showing pro/golf course designer Arnold Palmer topography of Big Sky Resort. Photograph in Chet Huntley Collection. By permission of K. Ross Toole Archives, Maureen and Mike Mansfield Library, University of Montana, Missoula.

Huntley, on June 30, 1970, announced that Gustav Raaum, former ski jumping champion and president of a skiing community and realty development in Jackson Hole, Wyoming, had been elected Big Sky president and chief executive officer. Raaum would administer and direct the operations, marketing and sales development of Big Sky.[20]

When the Huntleys moved west, they rented a home in Bozeman. Then, Chet and Tippy arranged to build a 7,000-square foot, one-bedroom log home (completed in 1973). It reportedly was valued around $200,000 and was built on a rise in the Hay Meadows section that overlooked the Meadow Village of the resort. In four rectangles, their new home was designed to comprise bedroom, office, living room and kitchen wings. The project, with some help from Bozeman architect Dave Wessel, was Tippy's. She suggested options to Chet after they learned from decorating four houses together. Chet had "a real affection for rural, usable things, natural textures, no tinsel. Everything had to be good of itself, and sturdy," she said. All were "earth tones except ... the fine blue bedroom." The kitchen was the "center of home life" for the Huntleys. Lone Mountain filled the picture window of the big dining room.[21]

A Few Opponents

As this writer was trying to sort out the studies, the opponents and the supporters of Big Sky, a chronological order would evidently not be possible. In the events recorded below, the various problems are highlighted according to subject. Recreational plans will always have their critics and, according to them, "Chet's Project" was going to impact the environment of the Gallatin River area.

Chet said in the *Life* magazine article, "There's a ringleader of the opposition who claims I'm going to bring in marijuana, heroin and naked women." He said he would be bringing in "—besides drop-around friends— ... a profound concern about the currents of American life."[22]

These critics hoped the project could be delayed through U.S. Forest Service appeals. The *New York Times,* the *Bozeman Daily Chronicle* and the *Billings Gazette* put "Chet's Project" in print constantly between 1970 and 1974. The *Times* reporter E. W. Kenworthy stated in 1971, "A numerous band of environmental vigilantes is fighting to halt [Big Sky], not only, they say, because it is being built in a fragile valley but also because it is a dramatic example of what they regard as a deplorable national trend — the corporate accumulation of great natural areas for development."[23] Laurel, Montana, resident James Southworth wrote, in part, protesting:

Chet in front of Big Sky sign. Photograph in Chet Huntley Collection. By permission of K. Ross Toole Archives, Maureen and Mike Mansfield Library, University of Montana, Missoula.

The development is going to bring in all those Dudes and plant them right in one of the last Primitive areas.

And our beloved Forest Service is going to do some land trading again and rest assured that it will be good for us whether we like it or not — because they say so.

I can picture it now, snowmobiles, four-wheel drive vehicles, helicopters, airplanes, skiers, all this mass of people disturbing and disrupting nature in an area that should not be opened up to this kind of easy access.[24]

Billings Gazette columnist Harvey Griffin, an outspoken conservative, wrote on April 7, 1971:

We've had the best of it. So make the most of what is left. See it. Live it. It's your last fleeting sight of a lost world. There'll never be it's like again, not in our time or any other.

Mr. Griffin also wrote:

From the start there have been a considerable number of Gallatin [County] people who have been opposed this Huntley-Chrysler project. They feel the project is entirely too large for this locality and would eventually destroy the open environment that is the chief attraction of the area. As one Bozeman man succinctly put it, "We have a stable community, growing as fast as we wish, based on agriculture and the college. Why risk upsetting it by encouraging the very elements (too many people) we came here to escape, and which could spell the end of a manner of life we highly cherish?"[25]

Montana State University veterinary medicine professor Russell Berg wrote a four-verse protest song that said, in part:

> Now I can't help but wonder will the sun shine again
> After Chet Huntley's Big Sky comes in.

A protest leader, Mrs. Willard Keightley, said, "It's foolish to accept any verbal promises, as much as we like and accept Chet Huntley."[26]

Huntley had mentioned in a March 9, 1970, letter to a travel agent, Robert Stevens, Jr.: "I guarantee you one thing: If I or Big Sky represents a threat to anyone, we will get out tomorrow morning." In a telephone interview, Huntley added: "God bless 'em. They're sure keeping us honest."[27]

An environmental group that claimed 1,500 members, The National Forest Preservation Group (NFPG) with professor Russell Berg as its leader, zeroed its attention on two areas:

1) Big Sky needed additional land: a seven-acre parcel near Meadow Village to complete a proposed golf course fairway; and

2) Big Sky needed three sections of land for the Mountain Village and the ski runs.

These two parcels needed to have U.S. Forest Service approval. NFPG was going to try to block this swap.[28] The swap did happen but it took two years to finally settle. See below.

One story suggested "there is a lingering feeling [in Bozeman] that his resort may haul some bit of the crowded East Coast and its troubles into the remote and spectacular mountain valleys of southwestern Montana." Another mention was made that the Big Sky protest "could be written off as part of the national fever over the environment. Montana has been touched by it and is beginning to look aghast at the results of unregulated copper smelting, paper pulp mills and phosphate plants."[29]

Chet at Big Sky Resort site. Photograph in Chet Huntley Collection. By permission of K. Ross Toole Archives., Maureen and Mike Mansfield Library, University of Montana, Missoula.

Another group, the Montana Wildlife Federation headquartered in Missoula, crossed Huntley's path in the summer of 1970. When Chet said the federation opposed Big Sky, its then director, Don Aldrich, told the media that the federation "neither approved nor disapproved " of Big Sky. The Federation, Aldrich said, is "apprehensive ... because present zoning legislation does not delegate the authority needed to prevent architectural mayhem of the Gallatin Valley for miles on both sides of the recreational development."[30]

As the criticism mounted, Huntley lost his temper. He called the detractors "ninety-day wonder ecologists and smart-aleck editors." Huntley added, they "are marching majestically backward from conclusion to fact." What was wrong with having tourists leave "a few tracks in the snow if they also left their money behind in the state[?]"[31] He mentioned in a panel discussion that "the moment the Big Sky is demonstrating irreparable damage to the environment, I assure you my name will be detached from it."[32] In an interview in 1972, he quipped, "I think these days no matter what you do— you can go out and paint the front porch — someone is going to be complaining that you're lousing up the ecology."[33]

In 1973, Huntley had to "angrily" deny a report that the resort had caused harm to the Gallatin Canyon big game habitat. A Montana State University study, funded by the National Science Foundation, said, "land development had reduced big game habitat and will continue ... if encroachment on wintering areas is not considered." Huntley responded,

> I find nowhere in the study that the Big Sky had hurt the big game area.... Those of us who live and work [in the resort] are convinced that we are seeing additional numbers of animals due to the fact that there are no cattle in the area for the first time in years." He added, "in the future press releases should be viewed with caution.... We have great concern for the Gallatin Canyon. We are sure no damage has or will be done to the area.[34]

A quarter-century later, Bob Ekey, director of the Wilderness Society's Northern Rockies regional office in Bozeman, said, "Big Sky severs the Madison [mountain] range in half, so in terms of elk and grizzly movement, the animals have to run a gauntlet of development. The irony of the resort is: the ecological integrity of the area is the very reason many people move here, which in turn compromises it."[35]

The above comprise merely a sampling of the critics' comments, but they do give the reader a feel for what Huntley and Big Sky were up against.

Further Work on Big Sky

After he retired from NBC and during the time of studies, surveys, land swaps and having his patience tried, Huntley spoke at least twice a week about Big Sky somewhere in Montana, calling it "the greatest thing that ever happened to Montana."[36]

On February 19, 1970, Huntley spoke to the Bozeman Chamber of Commerce and pledged "$15,000 toward a planning study to protect the quality of life in the [Gallatin] canyon. He favored zoning regulations to protect the area from tarpaper shacks and hot dog stands" along U. S. Highway 191 along the Gallatin River.[37] A group tried to form a "Gallatin Real Property Owners" association to "primarily work toward a comprehensive master plan for the canyon that would implement a rural zoning district." Unfortunately, only 15 property owners had signed on and the plan failed because of disagreements on "outside help and need for zoning." A Big Sky Owners Association does now exist.

The U. S. Forest Service gave Big Sky a special permit to "plan ski lifts at Lone Mountain and a highway" into the complex. Kingsbury Pitcher of Santa Fe, N.M., would conduct the ski studies. A two-lane $1.1

million highway would be surveyed by Montana's Highway Department.[38] Huntley mentioned early in the planning that the only "stumbling block" would be the land at the bottom of the three main ski slopes.[39]

On May 25, 1970, surveying began on the 18-hole golf course next to the summer recreation village. However, the course was going to need some land that Huntley and company did not own. Trying to explain the whole process gets a little complicated. A land swap was arranged that caused quite a stir.

The nearly 2,000-acre course needed seven acres for two fairways near the Meadow Village. These acres were part of the United States Forest Service. The Forest Service cannot lawfully sell land. It can exchange it for land of equal or greater value with other owners who will give it up. The Northern Pacific Railroad's successor, the Burlington Northern Railroad, a corporate owner of Big Sky, owned land outside and inside the northwest Yellowstone Park area that it had owned since the 19th century as a railroad land grant. The railroad and the USFS made two land exchanges in June and December 1970. Exchanged by the railroad was 21,479 acres for 10,243 acres. This would allow Big Sky to buy 1,927 acres for the golf course and Mountain Village and the ski slopes. However,

Arnold Palmer designed this 18-hole golf course at Big Sky Resort. Bob Allen photograph. By permission of Bob Allen, Bozeman, Mont.

federal law required the swap be approved by the Environmental Protection Agency. During 1971, Chet was on the phone and writing letters trying to get the ski slope land exchange approved. (By August 1971 the Environmental Protection Agency administrator, William Ruckelshaus, had not commented on the land swap.[40]) In late 1971 Huntley and Big Sky attorney David Penwell traveled to Washington to lobby the Department of Agriculture (the Forest Service is a part of Agriculture) to move on the exchange.

As mentioned in a previous chapter, Huntley landed on the "White House Enemies List" allegedly because of the *Life* article highlighted in Chapter VI above. In an October 19, 1971, memo between Republican National Committee executive Lyn Nofziger and H. R. Haldeman, Nofziger said, "The state [Republican] chairman of Montana tells me Huntley claims to be a Republican and will support and work for whatever Republican runs against Senator Metcalf next year." In addition, the White House aide dealing with environmental matters, John Whitaker, "ordered the Department of Agriculture to quit dragging its heels on Big Sky." Nofziger recommended several "alternatives" for approval by Haldeman:

1) "Give Mr. Huntley all the help we can with the clear understanding that he reciprocate with help to us in Montana";

2) "continue along the course we have been following since Mr. Huntley's intemperate remarks [in the *Life* article]"; [and]

3) "same as No. 2 until we see how Mr. Huntley performs."

Haldeman checked alternative 3 and wrote: "Agree — so inform LN" [Nofziger]. Another notation said, "spoke to JW [Whitaker] and he said he will inform Ag [Agriculture]. That we should be kept posted, but matter will move at normal pace." White House counsel John Dean later stated, "at one point in time, apparently, there was a change of heart on Chet Huntley, and there was a turnaround." The land exchanges were approved within a couple of days.[41] The exchange was not without its critics—1,362 of them — who wrote letters or signed petitions. For a while this held up construction on the two fairways and the Mountain Village.[42] Chet explained that "if the land exchange is nullified, I am certain that the approximate 8,000 acres of Big Sky land will be sold, most likely to multiple purchasers, who will in turn develop it, but with no planning, no sewage system, no water control and no safe-guards of any kinds."[43] With this news, environmentalists again challenged the Big Sky project in the United States Court of Appeals for the Ninth District in San Francisco.[44] The case would be settled in December 1973 but the road funds (mentioned above and below) for Big Sky's highway could not be used.

Back in May 1971 Chrysler and Huntley applied for federal road building funds for nearly seven miles of their road (now Montana state highway 64) west into Big Sky from U. S. Highway 191. New federal laws allowed the development to apply through the offices of Governor Forrest Anderson and the Montana Highway Commission. In the application, Big Sky contributed $288,000 and would build the first three miles. The highway commission earmarked $115,000 for surveying and design.[45] The National Forest Preservation Group sued to stop it. However, the U. S. Department of Transportation approved funding for the road on March 26, 1972. A problem arose concerning an environmental impact statement that had not been submitted by the proper department! The Federal Highway Administration had submitted Montana's Department of Highway's statement. That was against the rules. A federal judge ruled against the funding because the road would benefit a "private enterprise." He did approve funds for the "preparation of the environmental study!"[46] The NFPG won their lawsuit in December 1972 that blocked the use of federal funds.[47] By the end of 1972 Big Sky itself financed and finished the 6.7-mile logging road between U. S. Highway 191, Meadow Village and the ski area.[48]

Environmental impact studies would cause further delays in Big Sky's development. The Environmental Protection Agency was "ill-equipped [with personnel] to process such statements when they did get them," and though the Environmental Protection Act of 1969 existed, the agencies of the U. S. Government "found themselves unaware of the provisions of the acts ... to implement its provisions."[49]

The project ran into zoning problems when it was announced on June 29, 1970, in Helena, that National Science Foundation funds had been cut in half for the economic baseline study to be conducted by Montana State University.

Gallatin Canyon residents were not able to get a zoning district established to "ensure orderly growth near the resort," so the Montana Planning and Economic Development Department had to "seize the initiative." Adding to the problems, the nine-mile road into the resort had problems such as possible rock slides, and the need to "change some of the channel of the West Fork of the Gallatin River."[50]

Montana State University's Center for Environmental Studies began an impact study on the Big Sky area July 1, 1970. Dr. Charles Bradley, MSU professor of earth sciences, directed the National Science Foundation study with other university faculty and students. The two-phase, one-year program was under a $110, 000 NSF grant announced by Senator Mike Mansfield (D-Mont.). Scientific teams would work on 14 projects studying such areas as weather, terrain, air and biological aspects of the canyon including impact on fish and wildlife.[51] An MSU fishing study on the Gallatin River Canyon showed "the fishing pressure is heaviest at each end of the canyon, not the middle near Big Sky and the resort does plan an extensive [trout] stocking program."[52] The study's main concern was rock formations and land slides. "Anything that isn't flat [in the area] is a potential landslide. The slopes are frightfully unstable."[53]

Concerning other environmental issues, Chet said, "Every bonafide environmentalist has given us a very clean and enthusiastic bill of health."[54] Huntley and company had bought all the timber and logging rights on the ten thousand plus acre property for $600,000 to keep clear cutting from happening.[55] Chrysler Realty promised the public that two ecologists would be brought in to "make sure the project does not mess up" the valley.[56]

In 1972 Huntley voiced this response to the assistant professors who had voiced their negativism to the project: "Where you have to fault these guys is that they paid no attention to this land when it was being raped before we acquired ownership. It was a clear-cut case of being denuded — terrible damage from erosion — and the owners had made four deals selling off one-acre plots that were going to be private homes with septic tanks."[57] However, the development slowly began to take shape and some facilities were opened by December 15, 1973.

Planning and zoning for the resort was financed by a Big Sky $15,000 planning study.[58] Huntley projected that those sixteen-square miles (or 22 percent) would be developed. Seventy-eight percent would be left in its natural state.[59]

During the winter of 1970–1971, Lone and Andesite mountains ski trails were inspected. Construction began on the sewer and water systems for the Meadow Mountain Village in the spring of 1971. Water and soil tests were also conducted. By 1971, work on the golf course at Meadow Village was started. In May, work began on the first condominiums, clubhouse and a small commercial center there.[60]

Huntley was part of a three-hour meeting in 1972 which several hundred people attended. Forty people spoke, half were for the resort, half were against. A couple of comments were relevant. One participant spoke in affirmation: "We sat by for years asking for help from the Forest Service and the Highway Department and we got none," said Homer Fisher, a canyon resident. "Big Sky will help with taxes and jobs. I think we all will owe them a lot."[61]

A moment of humor needs to be inserted here. Chet was on a panel discussion with Dr. Wilson Clark and Norman Schoental at the Eastern

Montana College in Billings in 1971. A participant asked Huntley, "What have you done for the protection of the wildlife if Vice President Agnew should play golf on the course?" Huntley quipped, "I don't know about the animals, but I know I'll stand far behind" Agnew.

The attendees knew golf pro Arnold Palmer had looked at and made plans for the project's golf course, so Huntley added, concerning animals, "I'll have to ask him what kind of hazard the Professional Golf Association permits for a moose on the fairway."[62]

The Supporters

Various supporters included the Montana State University Associated Students. The group wrote, "The development of the Big Sky project will have a far-reaching and profound effect not only upon Montana State University but upon the entire state as well." The students "have much to gain from [this] thoroughly planned development."[63]

The *Billings Gazette* editors saw good things in Big Sky and in an editorial on March 2, 1970, said, "...Big Sky of Montana plans two villages

Entrance to Mountain Village, Big Sky Resort. Lone Mountain in center background; Huntley Lodge in left center. Lyle Johnston photograph, 2001.

in the Gallatin Valley. Each will have a sewage plant that is to turn out water clean enough to drink and solids to handle erosion. Game will be taken care of, not primarily for hunting, but to maintain the animals for the interest of visitors.... The economic spillover across the state from the eventual $19.5 million project should be outstanding.... We say welcome to Montana and Billings."

The Bozeman Chamber of Commerce was "delighted" that the project was coming to south central Montana. Most Bozeman-area residents probably agreed. The complex would bring people and money to the area without industrial pollution.[64] Bill Merrick told the author that all of Bozeman's businessmen were behind Big Sky. On several occasions Merrick took businessmen for tours in the project and also did remote KBMN radio broadcasts.[65]

Montana State University's newspaper, the *Exponent*, gave some positive lines for Chet's return to Montana. "Unlike most Montana boys who leave the state and return to Montana, Huntley will not be coming back [when he retires from NBC] empty handed. " Few Montanans have come back to their native state to live, bringing with them millions for a budding recreation industry."[66] The *Bozeman Daily Chronicle* climbed on the bandwagon in an editorial the weekend Chet retired from NBC. Commending Chet, they said, "you might well be the catalyst that changes the way of life in Bozeman and Gallatin County.... We are convinced that you are concerned about the environment and the ecology and that in the long run the obstacles to Big Sky will be removed.... Welcome and good luck."[67] Wanting on the bandwagon, too, *The Park County News* editorialized positively on "Chet's Project": "Let's put out the welcome mat, not 'go away' signs and let's not fence Montana [in].... Chet Huntley deserves to be an appreciated 1970 pioneer[.] ..."[68]

The Montana Fish and Game Commission also agreed that Chet's project was needed.[69]

Montana's senior senator, Mike Mansfield, stated, "I think the project Chet has proposed in the Gallatin Canyon is one which he has looked into all the angles on."[70]

Chet at Big Sky

When the Huntleys moved to their new home in Montana, the new schedule pleased him. Chet was not a skier. He was up at sunrise and outside until Tippy or business called him in. There was not a day, unless he was traveling out of or in other parts of Montana, that Big Sky construction

Chet on leisure ride at Big Sky, ca. 1971. Photograph in Chet Huntley Collection. By permission of the Museum of the Rockies Archives, Bozeman, Mont.

was not being checked on (or mowed — see below), by Chet. When everything was not accomplished for a certain day, "I can say, 'To hell with it,' I can do it tomorrow," he once stated. Huntley would return to New York occasionally for business with the Levine, Huntley and Schmidt Advertising Agency (see below). As part of a speaker's bureau (see Appendix below) he would occasionally deliver speeches for various organizations across the United States.

Yes, the Huntleys missed their New York friends, but they also had new ones in the Bozeman area such as "livestock growers, farmers, members of the legislature, doctors, lawyers, and from the [Montana State University] campus."[71]

He had his radio commentaries to type and tape each Sunday. Interest in foreign and national news kept his attention. His subscriptions to the *New York Times,* the *Washington Post,* the *Economist,* and *LeMonde* continued. Concerning receiving a late newspaper, he said, "I get it [the *Times*] five days late, but you know, that's good enough."[72]

When he was working at the resort and near home, he stated he tried "to get home every evening at 5:30 to watch" the NBC Nightly News with John Chancellor, Frank McGee and David Brinkley. He viewed it "with interest, and sometimes admiration, and sometimes I'm on the verge of writing a critique."[73]

The Huntleys also rode their horses, including his retirement present, "Walk-A-Long-Go-Boy."

The Big Sky development was a wonderful release from the pressure of newscasting. He said, "It's just living with a more relaxed schedule." Tippy knew he was "going to be home for dinner, each night, for certain." "One morning I walked across the highway to the Gallatin River." Baiting the hook on a fishing pole, and casting with a spinner, it did not take long to catch four 10-inch trout. "Then I noticed that I had been standing on the very lip of a spring gushing ice-cold water into the river, and it was packed with watercress. The trout, watercress salad, sourdough bread and a bottle of Napa Valley white wine ..." what a meal![74] When asked about fishing elsewhere in Montana he replied, "The best way to do it out here in Montana, is to go to a small town and into the first bar and buy the bartender a drink, and you'll find a place to fish, I guarantee you."[75]

On a friend's Montana ranch 75 miles away, he "boarded" his small herd of registered Herefords. He stated, "We split up the proceeds."[76]

When Chet was chairing a board meeting, Great Falls, Montana, architect Phil Korell said, "meeting after meeting, he was the peacemaker. He wanted to be as kind to that valley as he possibly could be, but he also wanted other people to share it." Korell and fellow architect Eric Iversen designed Meadow Village's Western-style buildings.[77]

Huntley was out promoting Big Sky a couple of times a week somewhere.[78] He was called on as an after dinner speaker often, whether at the resort, or in other parts of America.

A story by Chrysler Realty project manager Mike Foley is told of a visitor stopping in the Big Sky complex office and asking if Chet Huntley really was involved in the day-to-day operation.

"He doesn't really come here, does he?" the visitor asked.

The receptionist proved the visitor wrong by calling out to a man mowing the grass, "who obliged her by turning his head her way. It was Huntley himself."[79]

When asked in 1972 about Big Sky and it possibly having too many people for any wilderness area, he replied, "We're faced with a paradox ... one we've got to learn to live with. On the one hand, we want city people to see Nature at its finest so they will be inspired to help us safeguard the great heritage we have. On the other hand, we're legitimately worried about too many people spoiling it all."[80]

Big Sky, Montana's two villages: West Fork Meadows on right; Meadow Village on left. Looking south from Chief Joseph Trail. Lyle Johnston photograph, 2001.

During his few years getting Big Sky started, he developed at least two brochures that were made available to the public. One was titled "The Best of Two Worlds at Big Sky." It ran as follows:

The Best of Two Worlds at Big Sky.

Do you enjoy shining mountains towering over dark green conifer forests? Are you a nature lover who yearns for fresh air, sparkling water, clear skies, and the grandeur of unspoiled natural wonders?

OR do you require all the modern comforts and conveniences and a certain sophisticated flair along with your magnificent scenery?

BIG SKY offers you the best of both of these wonderful worlds ... and in extraordinary abundance.

Man or woman, child or adult, you can spend a beautiful day walking in scenic splendor or horsebacking into the flower-filled mountain meadows. You can ski the spectacular slopes, play a set of tennis, or soak up sun at the pool. How about a steak cookout in the evening?

OR would you rather browse among the smart shops and dine at one of the fine restaurants?

BIG SKY ... an exciting year-around recreation area planned for fun in an atmosphere of harmony between man and his environment.

Signed, Chet Huntley

Big Sky Dedication

Big Sky was dedicated at the Black Otter Lodge and at the Mountain Village Mall among lumber piles and other construction materials on March 23, 1974, three days after Huntley died. The theme was "Chet Huntley's Dream — Now a Reality." More than 200 people including Tippy Huntley and Chet's mother, Blanche, were present and introduced. The last two received standing ovations. Dignitaries attending were Montana Governor Tom Judge, Washington State Governor Dan Evans, astronaut Gene Cernan, Miss Montana Debbie Reber and a number of other officials who were invited.

Tippy said a "Chet Huntley cultural center would be established" from the memorial funds received. "It would be for the study of the arts, humanities, and the environment."[81]

Big Sky Resort president Gustav Raaum said, "the event marked a renewed sense of dedication for those concerned."[82] He remarked that Chet "'wanted to show off Montana' and to create a family place to relax."[83] Eighteen slopes were served by four lifts.

Events during the three-day weekend included a national men's 50-

kilometer cross-country ski championship and the women's 15-kilometer Samsonite race. The Governor's Cup downhill ski race was canceled when Montana's Governor, Thomas Judge, "slipped in the parking lot and broke a bone in his right ankle."[84]

Chet was there in spirit.

The resort would eventually cost $30 million to build.

The aftermath of Huntley's dream is highlighted in the Epilogue below.

X. Other Interests and Honors

As he neared retirement from NBC Huntley had financial interests in three radio stations in New York State: WRIV, Riverhead, and WALK-AM and FM in Patchogue on Long Island. Also, the following television stations were part of the Horizon Communications' umbrella: KPAT, Berkeley, California, WKOW-TV, Madison, Wisconsin, WXOW-TV, LaCrosse, Wisconsin, and WAOW-TV, Wausau, Wisconsin. He owned 23.9 percent of Horizon's stock. However, they were not listed in his estate inventory.

In September 1970, Chet went back to work as a newsman when he began broadcasting a daily five-minute, syndicated radio commentary for his co-owned Horizon Communications.[1] He typed and recorded his commentaries on cassette, and mailed them for broadcast. The five-day-a-week program ran until March 20, 1974. His last commentary is found in the Appendix below. Bill Merrick told this author about the evening Chet provided commentary on election night 1972.[2] The photograph of that night is on the next page. When Chet mailed his weekly commentary as a backup, he always brought one to KBMN radio to wire to New York. In late 1972, Bill invited Chet to come back on election night. Chet was not sure he could. About 8 P.M. election night Chet strolled into the station,

Chet provides commentary on election night, November 7, 1972, KBMN radio,
Bozeman, Mont. Clockwise from below fire extinguisher, Milton VanderVen-
ter; unknown woman; Chet Huntley; Hal Phelps; (standing) William Merrick,
station owner; unknown woman; Ruth Stuckey; unknown woman. Photograph
from and by permission of the Gallatin County Historical Society, Bozeman,
Mont.

said hello, put in an ear device and for four hours offered annotations on
the national, regional, state and local candidates. About midnight Chet
bid everyone a "good evening" and went home.

Huntley's entering politics had been raised in 1964, 1968, 1969 and
in 1970 as he was getting ready to retire from NBC and in a 1971 interview. "Six years ago [1964] there was talk that it was going to be Mike's
[Mansfield's, U. S. Senator, D-Montana] last term. I did poke around, and
found out that Mike changed his mind and was going to run. That settled it for me. You'd be an idiot to run against Mansfield in Montana."[3]

In an interview with William Whitworth in the New Yorker magazine in 1968, Huntley told the public that he had "thought about returning to Montana and entering politics." Huntley said, "I would have to
make up my mind by 1972. I'd be sixty by then. I wouldn't want to use a

Senate or House seat as a form of relaxation, and I don't know how much this trade [newscasting] is taking out of me. Sometimes I feel it's taking my very blood. Of course, the people of Montana would be justified in saying, 'What goes here? What makes this guy think he can come back and claim elective office.' But if I had a fighting chance, and if I didn't have to hurt anybody, and use elbows and claws, I might try it." He added that he could run in either political party.[4] He told the media in Helena in 1969 that he "once toyed with the idea of seeking" Mansfield's seat, but Huntley said, the senator "does not plan to retire and intends to seek office again."[5] In December 1970, Chet had to "emphatically" deny that he was going into politics for "governor, senator, congressman, county clerk and recorder." He quoted Civil War general William Sherman, "If nominated, I will not run and if elected I will not serve."[6]

Chet said, "delegates from both [Republican and Democratic] parties twisted my arm to become a candidate.... I said I wasn't interested."[7]

He told E. W. Kenworthy in 1971, repeating, that he was not running for the Montana Democratic senatorial nomination. "I've just ruled it out absolutely. It would have been attractive to me, 10, 15, 20 years ago. But here I am — 59 years old, and I think it's a little late in the day to take on a new career of that nature. Furthermore, I think a state is better served by a Senator if he has a chance of staying on a while and getting some seniority." The governorship, then? "No, I'm a poor administrator."[8]

Politics would not take him to Washington. Huntley had come home to Montana to stay and to give his all to build Big Sky.

As mentioned above in Chapter III, Chet had narrated several Department of Defense films. In 1970, CBS put together a telecast for February 23, 1971, a film titled '*The Selling of the Pentagon.*' Chet was shown "narrating a film on the Navy's role in Vietnam." It was still in distribution, but by then (1971) Huntley might "disagree with the intent of the film" he had narrated.[9] Chet was "encouraged" to sue CBS over being included in the film. He refused to do so, and commented in a speech in Midland, Michigan, later that year that he had made military "recruiting" films. He added,

> Now, I am disturbed, however, by the use the Pentagon frequently will put these films and other efforts to. They put them into another context and tried to indicate that Walter Cronkite or David Brinkley or I have been given an unlimited and unreserved endorsement to everything that the Pentagon may be doing or may be planning and such is not the case. [Engaging in] a hard sell piece of advertising [is what the military is doing] — or I suppose you could say propaganda. Much too much money is being spent on this whole enterprise. We just don't need the military coming on so strongly engaging in that hard sell.[10]

There was no mention of his trying to sue to keep the government from using in the future any portion of any film he had narrated. He told a *Denver Post* reporter that he would do "no more Pentagon public relations because of the film."[11]

In March 1972 Huntley helped form the Levine, Huntley, Schmidt Advertising Co., in New York with Harold Levine. However, the *New York Times* columnist Philip Dougherty did not think much of the association. The ad agency was "not-so-famous," which Dougherty did not explain. Chet stated he would be in New York for various business reasons 60 to 90 days a year.[12]

Levine said,

> ...from that time until his untimely death, Chet attended client meetings, visited with prospects and addressed industry conferences.... If Chet Huntley had not become a journalist, he could have been a successful advertising man. He wrote [succinctly], and had a unique understanding of the consumer. I recall him telling our staff in the very beginning, "if you show respect for the consumer, the consumer will respect your message and your client's product."[13]

Levine added that "because of his special contribution to the world of broadcast journalism and his unique contribution to our agency,"[14] a lecture program was created. NBC News and Tippy Huntley gave their blessing. The lectures were to be held on the New York University campus. The theme of the lecture series was "that each year an outstanding journalist would be invited to speak on whatever topic relating to the press they wished to discuss." The series was open to "all university students in addition to guests from the print and broadcast media."[15]

He later advertised by voice and in person for American Airlines. Traveling to Los Angeles, he would spend three days at a time taping the commercials. This "raised the eyebrows of fellow journalists."[16] His motive: "Having logged millions of miles, I believe American is pushing frontiers back for all of us by making travel less costly and more efficient. Sure, I've taken flak from newsmen who think I've sold out, but I just don't buy that." He earned $300,000 for being American's ad man.[17]

One critic of the airline commercials was Alan Kriegsman. He wrote:

> I don't know about the rest of the folks out there in television land, but I find it mind blowing when Chet Huntley comes on to do his little bit for American Airlines.
>
>   Here he is, regarded by millions before his retirement as Mr. News, the personification of "objectivity," a symbol of journalistic authority and incorruptibility. All of a sudden we're called upon to accept him as a peddler, to put as much faith in his sales pitch as we once did in his reportage....

It's quite another thing when Huntley starts pushing an airline. His area of competence isn't aeronautics, it's news. We're supposed to be taking his word because in his former profession it was his business to distinguish fact from falsehood, to search out the truth.[18]

During 1972 he traveled to New York to tape a documentary for the bicentennial of the United States.[19] With American Airlines as sponsor, he narrated an NBC television series, "The American Experience." He stated, "I decided they [American Airlines] really were out to further and advance the art of transportation. And I wanted to get something going on behalf of the Bicentennial."[20]

NBC presented the first "American Experience" special, "The Fabulous Century" on October 21, 1972. Chet and actor Walter Brennan narrated this "fervent, glistening and superficial" special that "all but raised the flag atop Mount Rushmore." The subjects dealt with "sketchily or merely mentioned," were 18th century frontiersman Daniel Boone, 18th century statesman/inventor Benjamin Franklin, 19th century Army officer George Custer, silver king Horace Tabor and 20th century aviator Charles Lindbergh. *New York Times'* columnist Howard Thompson called "The Fabulous Century" "an incredible banal rhapsody of patriotism clichés in radiant color."[21]

Doyle Dane Bernbach, Inc., American Airlines' ad agency, conducted a poll in 1972 that placed Chet second among Americans who were when asked, "Which newscaster do you believe the most?" Walter Cronkite came in first. American Airlines vice president Tom Ross added, "It is important that this business becomes more believable. Chet Huntley is believable."[22]

Over the years, Chet thought about writing a memoir of his 1930s radio days; but he never got around to it. He also contemplated, but never wrote, a memoir of his television years that would help people really know what went on behind the stoic face and delivery."[23]

On April 7, 1973, Chet delivered a speech before the National School Board Association Convention in Anaheim, Ca. He recognized the same school problems that America had in the late 20th century and at the beginning of the 21st century. Huntley said,

...the tremendous and incredible social changes occurring in this country have had an impact on our schools far beyond that [sic] affecting any other institution but the school or the school system does not have the equipment to cope with this impact of social change.

[One change is] the incredible mobility of the American people [that]

creates school problems because of your raw product ... the pupil ... comes in a baffling variety of grades and standards of quality.

[Another problem is that the school board] is trying to be all things to all people and therefore not good for any particular group of individual. [They are to be] a baby sitting establishment and child-care center, ... required to be an entertainment center, ... [and provide] for the morality of the younger generation.

[I was] frequently appalled when [I] visited a modern urban or suburban school.... . What are we trying to [do with the audiovisual equipment] train or produce a whole generation of fifty million radio announcers and cameramen? In scores of schools I see electronic equipment the likes and qualities of which we never enjoyed at the National Broadcasting Company.[24]

This speech, in its entirety, is printed in the "Appendix below.

During 1973 Chet gave several what would be final interviews and tours of the resort. One was with Rita Shaw about Big Sky, recorded on November 11. Another interview with Dick Hawkins of Portland's KATU-TV included both discussions of the resort and his retirement from broadcasting. Titled, "Whatever Happened to Chet Huntley?" It was broadcast in December 1973. In February 1974 he was interviewed by the Smith Syndicate. Some of this information has already been highlighted.

XI. Death

In nearly every picture of Chet Huntley between his retirement and his death, we find a cigar, cigarette or pipe in his mouth or nearby. In an interview with Don Schanche in the May 1972 *Today's Health* magazine, it was written that "he smokes, and the dry cough with which he punctuates every couple of sentences regularly reminds him that he ought to quit." Chet responded, "I've tried several times, most recently a couple of years ago." He frowned, then laughed. "To hell with it. I enjoy it," he said, and then lit another cigarette. He told Schanche that he "hoped smoking cigarettes at Big Sky [was not] quite as harmful as it [was] in a city like New York, because the air you breathe between puffs [at Big Sky] is about the cleanest in the world." Chet added, "we checked our pollution levels very carefully, and found that we are as clear as Point Barrow, Alaska. Believe me, that's clean."[1]

Chet turned 62 on December 10, 1973. That same year he was diagnosed with lung cancer. Chet entered a hospital in Billings December 28.[2] On January 5, 1974, he underwent surgery followed by chemotherapy. In a note to fellow University of Washington student Senator Henry "Scoop" Jackson (D-Wash.) after the surgery, he wrote "I have a fight on my hands, but I don't plan to be here forever."

He chaired his last Big Sky board meeting on February 16. The Big Sky organization realized he might not be around much longer and scheduled a dedication of the resort for March 23.

In late February, he was interviewed by telephone by Jack Smith. Part of that interview concerned his proudest achievement and most satisfying story.[3]

Gustav Raaum, Big Sky president, mentioned that Huntley had lost weight and seemed to be doing well.[4] In early March, Chet was asked about his health and replied, "The doctors seem to be not without hope."[5] On March 7, Chet and Tippy celebrated their 15th wedding anniversary. Tippy mentioned in a letter to James Farley that Chet was "working and reading and thus stimulated until a very few days before his death."[6] His last radio commentary, "Regarding American Youth," was broadcast on March 20.[7] It is found in the Appendix below.

On March 19, he slid a sheet of paper in his 1950 Royal typewriter and tried typing a daily radio commentary. It was not completed. The next morning, Wednesday, March 20, at 2:20 A.M., Chet died of abdominal cancer in his home at Big Sky. His body was taken to Billings for cremation. In a private ceremony[8] on July 6, his ashes were buried under a small stone in Sunset Cemetery in Bozeman that reads:

Chester R. Huntley

December 10 1911

March 20 1974

He was survived by Tippy; and his mother, Blanche of Billings; two daughters, Mrs. Sharon Arensmeir then of Ft. Collins, Col., and Mrs. Leanne Khajavi then of San Francisco; three grandchildren; and three sisters, Mrs. Marian Turner of Billings, Mrs. Peggy Schutes, Colorado Springs, Col., and Mrs. Wadine (James) Cummins, Rapid City, S.D.

A memorial service was held at 6 P.M., Monday, March 25, at the Big Sky Mountain Village Mall and officiated by Rev. Lyle Onstad of the Hope Lutheran Church in Bozeman. Another service was held at noon, Tuesday, March 26, in NBC's studio 6b, 30 Rockefeller Center, New York. See below.

Vice President Gerald Ford said, "Our world, so much in need of able communicators, will miss his unique abilities which did so much to bring broadcasting and journalism to its present position of influence."[9]

Fellow news anchor David Brinkley said on the March 20, 1974, "NBC Nightly News":

> Most pleasant to think about was that wherever we traveled around this country we both ran into younger people, college age and older, who said: "You know I grew up with you guys. You were part of my youth, part of my education and part of my life.' He certainly was touched by that. He had that to think about and the knowledge that he always told them the truth

as far as he knew it.... I guess we and television grew up together. Now that part of it is over, and I believe Chet had every right to think he had left the American people something useful, honest and of permanent value.... And for myself, I guess I can say for one more time, Good night, Chet.'

Former Montana Governor Forrest Anderson said Huntley was "one of those rare people who left Montana and became successful and came back with a decision to do some development in our state and with the necessary backing to do something about it."[10]

Huntley's 1950 Royal typewriter. Photograph by Bruce Selyem. Used by permission of the Museum of the Rockies Archives, Bozeman, Mont.

NBC Nightly News co-anchor John Chancellor was quoted in the Phoenix *Arizona Republic* obituary of Chet: Huntley was "one of the most important people in the history of journalism in this country. I have always believed that his success was based to a greater extent on the fact that television ... displays character. The inner man is finally perceived by the viewer. And by the millions, they perceived Huntley to be honest, hard working, honorable, courageous, warm, patriotic and decent."[11]

CBS' Walter Cronkite reran the end of the last "Huntley—Brinkley Report," including their final "Goodnights," and added his own commentary.[12]

President Richard Nixon wrote to Tippy, "While words can have little meaning in the face of your great loss, we [Pat and I] hope that happy memories will lighten your burden, and that God's blessings will give you strength and comfort in the days ahead."[13]

In a letter to Tippy, Former Vice President Hubert Humphrey said, "After watching and listening to Chet for so many years on television, we [Muriel and I] felt very close to him. We loved him as a man and like so many Americans we admired and respected him for his professional qualities."[14]

"Scoop" Jackson wrote to Tippy "I always admired him for his great courage, integrity and high degree of professionalism."[15]

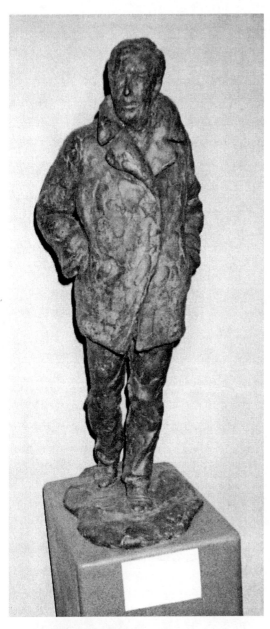

Chet Huntley in Bronze, by Derek Wernher. Archived at K. Ross Toole Archives, Maureen and Mike Mansfield Library, University of Montana, Missoula. Lyle Johnston Photograph, 2001.

The *New York Times* ran a tribute editorial saying,

In American broadcasting a special niche is reserved for television's anchormen — the familiar and trusted journalists who deliver a summary of the world's day crisply and objectively. Because tens of millions of viewers see the network news programs nightly, every story and every raised eyebrow is watched carefully by public and Government.

For nearly fifteen years Chet Huntley delivered the news professionally. If he smiled, the world was alright temporarily; if he grimaced, one could almost hope for a brighter touch by his partner, David Brinkley. The Huntley-Brinkley Report on the National Broadcasting Company stations was a turning point toward maturity and sophistication in television news. Huntley, before he retired, wrote his own "epitaph" in a biographical statement: "He had a great respect, almost an awe, of the medium in which he worked. He regarded it as a privilege, not a license."[16]

The *Times* did not announce the following memorial service, however, or print a follow up story.

At the March 26 half-hour memorial, in the NBC Rockefeller Center in New York, attended by an estimated 375 friends and colleagues, Huntley was remembered as a man who interpreted and helped "American people know and understand the world we live in." David Brinkley described Huntley as a "good and honest man" who, right or wrong, always "spoke honestly what he believed, which is a great deal to say of anyone." Brinkley declined to say farewell to Huntley, closing his remarks with: "It was a good job, Chet, and thank you."[17]

NBC producer Reuven Frank commented, too:

> I remember how rarely he got angry, how easy it was to tell he was angry. He did not hide his anger or cherish them. He did not know how to be devious. He was bad at getting rid of pests, refusing favors, at saying no. Bill McAndrew once said to me, if Chet was a woman, he would always be pregnant. He was always doing something for somebody.
>
> He was without envy — at the peak of his fame he was unpretentious. He never told me the inside story of anything. He was the easiest man I ever worked with, he liked to work, and his physical capacities were prodigious. He would fly all night, and work 12-15 hours the next day, and help carry the gear and be gracious to everybody, and still be going when the rest of us had given out. He knew everybody he worked with, and never kept himself apart from them.
>
> We who worked with him, especially in those early days, came from all over, but we were mostly city boys. He taught us about the West, his attitudes, his absolute openness, his optimism.'[18]

His daughters, his former wife Ingrid Huntley and Tippy were present for this remembrance.

His estate was valued at nearly $2 million in stocks, bonds, life insurance, miscellaneous assets, NBC deferred payments and jointly owned property.[19]

In 1977, various speeches and newscasts, newspaper articles, photos, family history, Big Sky materials, tapes, both reel to reel and cassette, a three-foot tall bronze by Derek Wernher and other assorted memorabilia were given by Tippy to the University of Montana, Missoula. The Museum of the Rockies in Bozeman received various photos, his Royal typewriter, two bronze sculptures by Wernher, his 1960–1961 Emmy and plaque, and his Montana State University honorary degree of laws and various cartoons about the duo.

Epilogue

Financial problems began plaguing the Big Sky partners after Huntley's death. With $20 million invested by 1976, the resort was in red ink. Three other economic factors helped suggest finding a new owner: the Arab oil embargo hurt travel for skiers and tourists causing them to stay closer to home; there was a national recession; and real estate sales dropped. These factors cost 200 Big Sky employees their jobs.

In 1975 the Big Sky board called for an accounting on the construction to date. The decision was made to sell. The Big Sky Resort was sold in 1976 to Boyne USA, a Michigan company with a record for managing ski resorts. The CEO, Edward Kirchner, bought Big Sky for 40 cents on the dollar. Boyne paid $1 million down and assumed about $7.5 million in debt.[1] Boyne did not buy the Lone Mountain Ranch which they later regretted. The Lone Mountain Ranch portion of the resort, still owned by Chrysler and partners, was sold in 1977 to Vivian and Bob Schaap.

As reported in a 1999 *Great Falls Tribune* article, the resort would be plagued with problems. Sadly, growing pains have included "patchwork planning, litigation and spillover development." Chet Huntley was spared the "indignity of his brainchild [as it began] to flounder." As the above newspaper's sub-headline said, "ski resort eclipses developer's down-to-earth dream." He could never have envisioned the litigation, spillover development and patchwork planning. Gallatin County commissioner and a former Big Sky Homeowners' Association executive Bill Murdock believed Huntley "would be disappointed by the magnitude of sprawl that 'looks like one big subdivision'" from the air. Real estate developer Jerry Pape said Huntley "would be rolling in his grave."[2] For other examples, problems, such as electricity usage, developed by 1974. Montana Power Company had only one transmission line into the resort until 1988. Outages were frequent. By the mid-1980s the sewage lagoons were leaking 30-60 million gallons of partially treated sewage. A new ski run behind and above a home owner's site caused an avalanche during the 1990s. This had been an attorney's "heyday." In 1997, Bozeman lawyer J. David Penwell said, "Big Sky is the best thing that ever happened to us."[3]

Another problem that plagued both Big Sky partners and Boyne, Inc. was Deerlodge Condominiums. Among the first condominiums built at Big Sky, they were of poor and unsafe construction and were finally torn down after a lawsuit and settlement.[4]

As the reader may remember from above, Huntley said the sewage treatment plant would be a closed system and not reach the Gallatin River. The sewage lagoons received a "cease and desist order" from the State of Montana in 1990. The state wanted two requirements satisfied:

1) drain and line ponds and rebuild a more sophisticated sewage plant (which was done), and

2) develop a long term plan for waste (20 years).

However, the state "caved in and set a precedent" for Big Sky to discharge sewage into the Gallatin River, "without even requiring Big Sky to fix the current piping system that was built with very poor construction methods."[5] In 1996, the resort went online with a new sewer system. The residents in 2002 approved $16 million sewer and water system bonds, including for a sewage treatment plant. This, along with spraying the effluent on the Yellowstone Club golf course, nine miles away, will help keep the treated sewage out of the West Fork of the Gallatin River.[6]

Big Sky's population numbers around 1,000 year-round residents and 1,400 seasonal residents. The unincorporated community has an excellent chamber of commerce, a U. S. post office, a physician, a school, shopping mall, realtors by the dozen, restaurants, shops and hundreds of homes. A new zoning law was approved for the Gallatin County portion of the resort in 1996. Property covenants and public transportation are handled by elective district committees. Developments include Meadow Village, West-fork Meadows and Mountain Village. The entrance to Big Sky is at 5,900 feet in elevation. Meadow Village is at 6,200 feet and the Huntley Lodge area is at 7,500 feet. The resort built the $18 million Shoshone Condominium Hotel and the 43,000 square foot Yellowstone Center in 1990. In

2000, the Summit Hotel Condominium, for $45 million, was constructed.[26] Today, the resort has eighteen lifts that carry snowboarders and skiers up to 4,350 feet. Over 100 runs are spread over 3,500 acres. The Lone Peak Tram that hoists skiers to 11,150 feet was built in 1995. This gives skiers the most vertical drop (4,180 feet) of any U. S. ski area. These runs total 80 miles.

In early April 1999, the resort celebrated its twenty-fifth anniversary. Events included "the '70s-theme anniversary party complete with images of the past, two 'Carving for a Cause' days with a portion of [ski] lift ticket proceeds being donated to local nonprofits, another successful Jimmie Heuga Snow Express for multiple sclerosis, the second annual Thrash and Bash Cross Games, the 21st annual Dirt Bag Day and Ball and the US Snow Cross Grand Nationals."[7]

Big Sky resort has had airline service (Northwest, Delta, Horizon and Big Sky) through the Bozeman/Big Sky Airport for several decades. United Airlines from Denver International was added on November 1, 2000.[8]

Credit must be given to the Boyne USA Resort company for their persistence in working through the problems and bringing Big Sky to the world-class resort that it is. To make it both year-around friendly, it involves the people from top to bottom. Everett Kirchner, Boyne USA CEO, Steven Kirchner, the youngest son and present overseer of Big Sky, Art Tebo, present CEO of Big Sky, John Kirchner, former Big Sky CEO, Scott Bowen, former mountain manager, Taylor Middleton, co-general manager, and John McGregor, co-general manager, and Brian Wheeler, development director and real estate director, must all be given credit for their work. Mention needs to be made of the thousands of workers who helped bring Big Sky to fruition and continue to provide the expertise for its operation.

Everett Kirchner died at 85, in January, 2002.

This author highly recommends Rick and Susie Graetz' booklet *Big Sky — From Indian Trails to the Tram,* and Phyllis Smith's book *Bozeman and the Gallatin Valley — a history* for a more comprehensive, yet less controversial telling of the Gallatin Valley, Bozeman and Big Sky story.

Regardless of the problems we have read about, Chet Huntley started a resort in a beautiful, breath-taking location. It is a place where Lone Mountain is the centerpiece.

Tippy continued to live in their Big Sky home she helped design. She did some public speaking on widowhood in the years after his death. The resort also needed her and she helped them promote it.[9]

In 1976, Tippy ran as a Republican candidate for the Montana U. S. House of Representatives but was defeated.[10]

Chet and Tippy. Photograph in Chet Huntley Collection. By permission of the Museum of the Rockies Archives, Bozeman, Mont.

Big Sky officials named a ski run after her called "Tippy's Tumble." Today, she no longer owns property or lives at Big Sky. She sold the Huntley home and now lives in California.

The Huntleys and actor William Conrad were friends of many years. Tippy fell in love and married Mr. Conrad after his wife died in 1979. He died in 1994.

Her involvement with the Chet Huntley Memorial Lectures, mentioned above, continued.

In early 1975 Huntley, so far the only broadcaster to be elected, was honored with eight other Montanans when they became part of Montana's

Hall of Fame. Their photos were unveiled in the Montana state capitol building in Helena. Others honored were actor Gary Cooper, Montana U.S. Senator Mike Mansfield, professor H. G. Merriam, Crow Indian chief Plenty Coups, businessman T. C. Power, artist Charles Russell, scientist Harold Urey and Methodist minister William Van Orsdel.[11]

So, here was Chet Huntley. He wrote in 1966, "Journalists do not write conclusions. Historians do."[12] This writer offers this short conclusion.

Chet made his mark in radio and television broadcast news. He helped pioneer a news broadcast that worked for nearly 14 years. "The Huntley-Brinkley Report" has not been successfully duplicated even though CBS and ABC tried it, even with male-female teams. Huntley was a person who made his mark and became a news correspondent's mentor. A man who never forgot his Montana roots was Chet Huntley. In his last years he wanted to do something special for his native state. He did and it would have been curious to see his involvement into the 1980s. We will not see such a personality walk this earth again. Thanks Chet, and, again, "Good night."

Appendix A.
Documentaries
and Awards

Chet Huntley filmed and narrated countless documentaries and radio commentaries. A complete list is not available. Some have already been mentioned. A few more will be highlighted in this segment to give the reader a final taste of his work.

"Outlook," "Chet Huntley Reporting" and "Time Present"

This Sunday afternoon, 30-minute magazine program was enjoyed and filmed "the way we wanted to," Reuven Frank wrote. The program, with the above name changes during its seven-year run, began on April 1, 1956, and ran until September 17, 1963. "Outlook" took on various themes such as segregation, disposing of nuclear waste, layoffs, college commencements, independence in Algeria, Israel's first wheat crop, and the San Andreas fault, to name a few. Frank stated that with "Outlook," "we started covering the civil rights movement very heavily on the show...."

171

We covered the story on the news, too, and were very bitterly resented throughout the South, where we were known as the Nigger Broadcasting Company."[1]

When the first program was scheduled to be broadcast "live" April 1, 1956, it drew the smallest audience of its time period ever. April 1 was Easter Sunday. Huntley was looking out the window at 30 Rockefeller Center down on 50th Street. He marveled at the crowds lining up to watch "The Glory of Easter" in Radio City Music Hall. He stated, "Why aren't those people at home watching television instead of outside on this glorious afternoon?"

The first five minutes of "Outlook" were reserved for weekend news. None of the networks had weekend news programs. The program used four reporters and cameramen stationed in Philadelphia, Chicago, Kansas City, and Los Angeles. Each reported on items mentioned above as well as school budgets, and milk strikes. NBC's vice president for television programs, Pat Weaver, said, "I think you have a hit."

New York Times columnist Jack Gould saw "Outlook" as "the silliest news show of the season."

Huntley and Frank were justifiably proud of the program. However, two things killed it. One was Sunday football, and the networks going from 15- to 30-minutes newscasts in September 1963.[2]

"The Second Agony of Atlanta"

Brinkley stated news coverage was decisive. "These same things have been happening for years[,] certainly since the Supreme Court decision of '54. But until the last few years there wasn't any national television news of any importance. I think television has made a great difference to the Negroes themselves. They look at news a great deal because they are in it."[3] In 1965, NBC News President Bob Kintner wrote a three-part *Harper's* magazine article on newscasting. "Many Southerners believe rather resentfully that television has *created* the civil rights movement." As mentioned above, Huntley was proud of what NBC News did to help move America toward integration.

One program was the following. In 1958 NBC News and Huntley developed a television documentary titled "The Second Agony of Atlanta." The program, on school integration in the South, was broadcast on February 1, 1959. During the first 52 minutes Huntley provided information that hopefully would sustain the federal law and keep Georgia's schools open. NBC presented both sides of the issue. The program made light of the "unwholesome control" by the extremist, the bigot and the segregationist. It reported that Atlanta was willing to desegregate but the surrounding county's schools were not. "Second Agony" presented a Northside High School PTA meeting where integrationists and segregationists had their say. When the program visited McKee's Beat, a nearby hangout for white children, there was vocal evidence of mostly segregation statements. When the program visited Amo's drugstore, across the tracks, the Negro children spoke of inclusion.

Segregationist and bigot Carter Pittman was also interviewed. He thought it was impossible that Southern schools could be integrated. Then Atlanta mayor William Hartsfield and Atlanta *Constitution* editor Ralph McGill spoke against the NAACP and the problem they were causing. They also stated that a private school system would be folly should the city decide to close their free school system.

During the last five minutes, Huntley suggested that the National Association for the Advancement of Colored People (NAACP) and the "militant Negro leadership" could see desegregation happen faster if they stayed out of it. Huntley recommended new Negro leaders could achieve greater progress. This caused a furor with the NAACP leadership. NBC offered time the following week. NAACP executive director Roy Wilkins spoke, telling the audience that the organization was not "extremist," as Huntley had told the audience the previous week. Wilkins also refuted several other points, including one that the NAACP was "trying to speed integration [and not] to block it."[4]

It is of note that a 1997 book on American TV news of racial minorities[5] did not mention NBC or any documentaries concerning desegregation!

"Winds of Change"

In April of 1960, NBC News telecast "Winds of Change" about Africa. In one portion of the 60-minute program Huntley commented about the South African racial crisis. The South African Foreign Minister, Eric Louw, complained that Huntley "spoke of terror and bloodshed." Louw added that Huntley had "described South Africa's policy of apartheid [racial separateness] as going beyond segregation and flirting ... with slavery." Louw wanted NBC and a sponsor, Caltex, to "calm down" Huntley. Caltex [Texaco Oil Company] said it would try, but a statement from NBC News director Julian Goodman said, "The sponsor [Texaco] has never, quite rightly attempted to concern itself with the editorial content of 'the

Huntley-Brinkley Report.' The N. B. C. News policy is to permit its commentators to express opinions within the context of their assignments and the framework of fact. Mr. Huntley's comments have always been fair, but we must accept the inevitable fact that any expression of opinion cannot please everyone." Louw was also upset with *Time* magazine and United Press International (UPI) over their "reporting of South Africa's apartheid policy."[6]

"The Ramparts We Keep"

Another 1960 documentary was this 30-minute film. Featuring the cooperation of four branches of the U. S. military, the program featured Huntley narrating, with segments by the then Secretary of Defense Thomas Gates, President Eisenhower, and the joint chiefs of staff. A propaganda film that was a possible recruitment film, it suggested that the armed forces genius was the soldier. Pictures of American soldiers operating equipment, helping in Hong Kong with Chinese refugees, and working with Taiwanese kindergarten children were shown. Even though the military were operating in outer space, Huntley told the audience, "We still face the need for defending the Free World's ramparts on Earth." He suggested a human and traditional method: "The nuclear soldier may look different from today's soldier, but [that soldier] must have the same patriotic fighting spirit and more specialized training." Parts of this film would be incorporated into a 1971 film that has already been mentioned previously, in Chapter X.

"The Many Faces of Spain"

This 60-minute 1961 NBC special was written and narrated by Huntley. It is one of the few foreign documentaries reviewed. The film was an "enlightening" overview of Spain's pageantry, citizens, cities, church influences, and its farmers. Huntley and crew filmed the program near the Civil War bastion of Alcazar at Toledo, at a fish bar in Madrid and at a Valencia festival. He caught the Holy Week parades and demonstrations in Seville, and a tour of Barcelona. Also, included were shots of a bull fighter finishing off the bull and a flamenco dancer. Spain's dictator Francisco Franco was presented as a sportsman, ruler and "functionary." *Variety* (magazine) called it "multi-faceted, ... vivid captured, ... and unfortunately subjected to a once-over-lightly treatment" in its "broad" nature.[7]

Bob Kintner stated that NBC's documentaries averaged 11.5 million viewers.

Awards

Beside the awards mentioned above, Huntley received from the Alfred I. duPont Foundation: "Best Commentator of 1956" based on the coverage of the 1956 political conventions and campaigns; Overseas Press Club of America: "Best Radio or TV Interpretation of Foreign Affairs: 1957 and 1958"; the Robert Sherwood Award: 1958; University of Southern California School of Journalism and Alumni Association: "Distinguished Achievement —1960"; "Golden Mike Award: 1960"; "TV Guide Award — 1960"; Woodrow Wilson Memorial Commission: 1962; Boston University Sigma Delta Chi: "Outstanding Broadcast Journalism —1965"; "Order of the Grizzly Award," University of Montana, Missoula —1966; "Man of Year Award for broadcast journalism" (for both Huntley and Brinkley) by Pulse Research, 1964; National Association of Broadcasters: "Distinguished Service —1967"; Broadcast Advertising Club of Chicago: "Award of Merit —1968"; American Hungarian Studies Foundation: "George Washington Award —1970"; Institute of Human Relations: "Mass Media — 1970"; International Radio and Television Society, Inc.: "Broadcaster of the Year Citation and plaque: 1970"; and posthumous: International University of Communications, Master of Arts, 1974.

When Huntley and Brinkley met in Chicago, April 3, 1967, to accept their NAB award mentioned above, they had several things to say:

Brinkley said he wanted to see more public time given to "nonnews programs before taking them off the air" by broadcasters. "In making program decisions, I think we often are too quick to brandish a Nielsen in the air to prove that a good program is a failure. A program we think is good should not be canceled until it has a fair chance of finding its audience, and 13 or 20 weeks are not enough. We've canceled good programs on the assumption that the public didn't like them when in fact most of the public had never seen them."

Huntley said news broadcasters need to "delve more, analyze more, reflect more and weigh more. In our sometimes zeal for shooting film with interesting facades and lovely landscapes, and in our fear of dullness or the low rating we arbitrarily rule out a long imposing list of awesome subjects and conclude that they were just not meant for television or radio. What an incredible confession of weakness."[8]

"The Huntley-Brinkley Report" won two Peabody Awards in 1958 and 1960 and eight Emmy Awards for "TV News." The Peabodys were for "Outstanding Achievement in News." Chet, in 1969, won an individual award for his contributions to television news. Concerning the Emmys, he was nominated as "Best News Commentator" (1956), nominated and won (1958-1959), nominated (1965-1966), and nominated for "Coverage of West German Elections" (1969-1970). "The Report" was nominated for "Best News Commentary" for "News coverage of the Integration in Little Rock and other Southern Cities" and "News coverage of the first Russian Sputnik, the U. S. Satellite launching efforts and Vanguard failure" in 1957. Their broadcast won the award for "Outstanding Program Achievement in the Field of News" from 1959 to 1964. They were nominated for "Individual Achievement in News Documentary" in 1966 and for various documentaries in "Immediate and On-the-Spot Coverage." These included: "Coverage of the Milwaukee Open Housing Crisis, Father Groppi, Demonstrations and Riots," and "The Police Chief Executing VC [Viet Cong army officer] During Tet Attack" (1968). In 1964-1965, the program was nominated for "Outstanding Program Achievements in News, Documentaries, Information and Sports," with "NBC Convention Coverage" of the Democratic and Republican conventions.

For "News and Commentary," they were nominated for "Coverage of Hunger in the United States" (1968-1969); in "Outstanding Achievements on Special Events," they were nominated for "Chicago Democratic Convention Coverage" (1968). Their last nomination (1969-1970) was for "Regularly Scheduled News Program." The "Distinguished Service Award" was given in 1967 by the board of the National Association of Broadcasters. They were the first duo to receive the award.

Chet was also a recipient of the Sigma Alpha Epsilon in Media award in 1968; the "Robert F. Kennedy Memorial Award in Journalism" (1970) for his last NBC special, "Migrant"; the Demolay Award in 1970; and, in 1971, he went to Seattle, Washington, to receive from the University of Washington the "Summa Laude Dignatus" award.

In 1977, the Old West Trails Foundation conferred a posthumous award for his work with the Old West Trails "in fulfillment of his vision of a major resort complex in the Old West Region." The award was accepted by Chet's sister Wadine in Rapid City, South Dakota.

Both men were the 30th and 31st inductees into the Academy of Television Arts and Sciences Television Hall of Fame on January 8, 1989.

Through the years, Huntley received honorary doctorate degrees from Montana State University, Bozeman, Boston University and Franklin and Marshall College, Lancaster, Pa.

He was elected the first member of the Montana Broadcasters' Association Hall of Fame housed at Montana State University. Huntley is the only broadcaster in the Montana Hall of Fame honored in the State Capitol building in Helena.[9]

In 1962–1963 "David Brinkley's Journal" won an Emmy for "Outstanding Program Achievement in the Field of News Commentary or Public Affairs." None of Chet's commentary programs won an Emmy although he won individual awards as reported above.

The duo also received the Alfred duPont Award for "News excellence."

His last documentary was for the University of Chicago titled "The Quiet War." The 26-minute film was about cancer research.

Chet left the public many documentaries and several sound recordings. These include the 1960 "Best of Washington Humor." His participation comprised spoken introductions for the humor of John Kennedy and others (Cameo Records, C 144). In 1963, 1964 and 1965, he and Brinkley provided intros for the top news stories of those years (RCA Victor LOC 1088, LOC 1096, and LOC 1122). In 1964, he provided analysis for "The Kennedy Years—1956-1963" (Longines Symphonette Recording Society LW 125-127). When Winston Churchill died in 1965, Huntley provided intros and commentary for an RCA record titled, "Winston Churchill— the memory of a man" (LM 2723). With Wernher Von Braun, he narrated a 1969 RCA long-playing record about the space program titled "One Small Step: the Voyage of Apollo 11" (X4RM 1283). A three L.P. set and book titled "Wall Street Speaks to Chet Huntley" with interviews with Robert Burkholder, Louis Engel, Malcolm Forbes, and Edmund Tabels was also produced. With Glen Seaborg, the narrated a double record album, "Century of the Atom —1895-1971" in 1971.

Dadan, Inc., manufactured a board game titled "NBC-TV News with Chet Huntley" in 1962.

In 1999, the *New York Post*, on its web site, polled its readers concerning influential people. Chet and David were listed 15th. He was listed in the century-end Montana newspapers among the "100 Montanans of the 20th Century."

When *Life* magazine commissioned a book titled "Our Century in Pictures" in the late 1990s, Chet Huntley, David Brinkley and Ed Murrow, were the only featured journalists for the 20th century.

Appendix B: Selected Speeches and Radio Commentaries

In looking over Mr. Huntley's speeches and commentaries found in his collection in the K. Ross Toole Archives, the following analysis can be offered. He wrote using as simple and as concise sentences as possible. His speeches ran from 10 to 20 pages double-spaced, in large type (16 point size). Many were written on his 1950 Royal typewriter. A few had the appearance of being typed by someone else or on a regular typewriter. His margins were an inch to an inch and a half on the left to nearly no margin on the right side of the paper. There was very little margin at the top and, give or take a fraction, a half-inch margin at the bottom. He began his commentaries with a date, a year and number for day such as January 1, 1974: 74-01. His opening and closing while at NBC was "This is Chet Huntley, NBC News." His post-retirement opening and closing was "This is Chet Huntley."

Many speeches in the University of Montana collection did not have a title or date. Some that were published were titled and slightly edited, which is not to say that all of them did not have some written additions, deletions or corrected phrases or words.

No more than two doubled-spaced pages made up his news analysis "think pieces." The last five months of these were titled. His last two weeks of commentaries, where edited, showed signs of his cancer. At times, his written corrections/additions/deletions were a little shaky, especially his E's. A tape of his daily commentaries for the week of March 18, 1974, presents a strong, but slightly slowed speaking voice with a word correction in each.

A letter of confirmation concerning one speaking engagement listed his fee of $1,500, with travel expense, food and lodging paid.

Here are a few of his speeches and a few commentaries.

• 1 •

"A Word for the War"[1]

(Broadcast over the CBS Radio Network, 6 December 1942)
(*Italics* are Mr. Huntley's emphasis)

He who writes in a modern, major radio station today is fortunate. Here at CBS in Hollywood, hundreds of thousands of words pour in over hi-speed news teletype machines every day; foreign correspondents in all the friendly and allied capitals are only as far away as the telephone or loud speaker. We communicate with the world by cable, wireless, telegraph, telephone and air mail. Senators, Congressmen, administrators, and diplomats are no strangers to these studios. Fighting men in uniform on their way to and from the fronts are interviewed here; as are the best minds of our day.

So it would be difficult, indeed, to be long associated with a modern radio station and not make a few observations. That is what this talk is … a few observations. It is apparent to me that all of us have long been searching for a slogan for this war. We have been waiting for a word or a phrase which will sum up the background of the war, the reasons for it, the nature of the fight, and what we stand to win or lose. We are looking for the lowest common denominator for this war; the nutshell that will contain its principles, its tenets, and its why and wherefore.

Being, perhaps, only a few months the senior of the average-aged American man in uniform, and from talking to hundreds of civilians and service men alike, I think I know what the majority of both groups are thinking about this war. I think I know why and for what many of my friends are fighting. I have the temerity to suggest a word which will cover most of these thoughts, feelings, hopes and ideas ... just one word.

First, consider some things for which and because of which most of us are *not* fighting:

We are not at war because we were attacked at Pearl Harbor just a year ago. We are not at war because of [Adolf] Hitler, [Italian dictator Benito] Mussolini, or the Japanese war lords. Nor are we at war because of something that happened in Manchuria in 1931 or in China in 1937. Nor are we fighting because of events which transpired in Abyssinia in 1935, in Spain, in Austria, Czechoslovakia, Poland, the Low Countries, or France.

No, we are at war because this world was and is sick of an old and perfidious malady. We are ill and the crisis is here.

What is this disease gnawing away and reproducing itself in bright cities, in spacious office buildings, in the majestic chambers of Congresses and Parliaments, amid all our technological wonders?

I propose to call it *irresponsibility*! It's the irresponsibility comprised of weakness, soft living, easy morals, degeneracy, and the attitude of "anything goes." For all that is wrong with us, for all that brought us where we are today; I suggest the word irresponsibility. But let us state it affirmatively! For all the things we hope to win, for all the things we hope to bring to a bright new world of tomorrow, I suggest the word responsibility.

Today, a ruthless barbarism is turned loose against civilization. In former times this barbarism came from the dark geographical areas of the world, from the dark forests, the dark river bottoms, the dark plains about which civilization knew little or nothing. Today, it comes from the dark corners of men's minds, from perverted thought, from twisted reasoning.

I have no fear, however, of this barbarism. We can eventually and with great sacrifice of blood and heroism stamp it into the earth. But what of this great enemy? What of this disease? What can we do about it?

Consider for a moment the old civilizations of Babylon, Alexandria, Carthage, Rome, and Athens. In each case the barbaric assault from without was preceded by the silent gnawing from within; paving the way for defeat, slavery, oblivion.

Responsibility!

Let us examine a few responsibilities to determine the state of our well-being.

There is the responsibility of political leaders and representatives.

How much longer must we countenance "log-rolling" legislation, political patronage, hi-powered lobbying, selfish and partisan riders attached to important bills, and the hesitancy of Congress to face vital issues in the proximity of election time. The irresponsibilities of this group are legion, but my generation now in uniform has no inclination to accept them as an undesirable part of the game of politics. With what misgivings must oppressed and enslaved peoples look at the recent filibuster in the United States Senate on the anti-poll tax bill. If you are inclined to *accept* these omissions of duty then I suggest you read an article entitled "TWELVE MEN AGAINST THE NATION" in the November *Reader's Digest*; wherein, it is pointed out that twelve Western Senators are denying precious silver to the war machine.

We have been called a nation of experts, for nowhere else has specialization been so demanded or so abundantly supplied. In the laboratory, in the hospital, in control towers, on the bridges of ships, and in the cabs of locomotives we allow only the expert to enter and pull the levers, twist the dials, and press the buttons. The qualifications are highly regarded in all but our political master control rooms, and there we allow the most unqualified amateur to enter and throw the switches, pull the levers, and twist the dials.

Thus, a good example of irresponsibility of our politicians comes home to the voter, where it belongs. How wisely do we caste our ballots? How often do we avail ourselves of the material gladly supplied by such agencies as the National League of Women Voters? Finding on the ballot no candidate of whom we do approve, how often do we make a concerted effort to elect a fellow citizen whom we do endorse?

What of responsibility of the press? In the last two presidential elections the people of this nation have elected a chief executive in spite of the opposition of an overwhelming majority of the newspapers of the country. I do not intend to imply that in order to be responsible or in order to lay any claim to distinction a newspaper must print in its columns only that which its readers want to see there. But I do maintain that a responsible press should reflect in its pages some of the hopes, the wishes, the aspirations, and the thinking of its readers. A responsible newspaper does not carry news, editorials, feature stories, and lead lines reflecting only the thinking of the editor or publisher.

My generation is fighting, too, for the re-establishment of responsibility in the church. Thousands of us have realized the need for a workable religion but knew not where to get it. We have seen the paradox of living with God from eleven to twelve on Sunday morning and living with Satan the rest of the week. We would admire the church having enough courage to fearlessly announce the ethics of God and Christ as the only true pattern for living. We would respect the church that will brutally lay down to us a strict code of behavior, cease compromising itself, risk the loss of its missionary money by which we have attempted to *civilize* the "Heathen Chinese"; risk the loss of its million dollar facades, its gold plate and velvet drapes.

But the congregation also has a responsibility that may be extended to the whole population. Sooner or later we must start believing in something. We have tried a form of nihilism and found it wanting. Regardless of how we may, from time to time, rebel against the written laws of civilization; still they have served mankind pretty well for five thousand years. It's time we paid them some respect. Whether it be the law of Confucius, the Golden Rule, or the Ten Commandments, we must accept some pattern by which to shape our lives.

Business and industry has great responsibilities in the future. Business and industry must come to realize that this world is a far cry from that of the golden twenties. Responsible men in these occupations might well prepare themselves now for two great stipulations the post-war world may well make of a great nation: one, the elimination of unemployment; Two, the guarantee of minimum standards in food, clothing, shelter, medical care, education, and old-age insurance for all the population. We might well plan to establish a new and higher level of well being, below which no man may fall regardless of ill health, misfortune, or lack of education. For him with the ambition, the leadership, the enterprise there can still be room at the top; complete with super limousines, super penthouses, super mink coats, and super blondes, if need be. Responsible business and industry will cease regarding government in the economic control tower as the certain loss of freedom, but come to look upon it as the possible guarantee of one. Free enterprise and freedom from want must be made compatible.

Labor is charged with the responsibility of soon eliminating from its ranks the labor boss and racketeer. Wise and intelligent leadership must be supplied to the labor organizations. Opportunism must be renounced, the laborer must come to understand some of the problems of management, and the working man must realize that harmony demands giving as well as receiving.

We are further charged with the responsibility of learning how to respect other races, other religions, other minority groups. In so far as racial tolerance and understanding is concerned, we had best begin realizing that the white man is outnumbered on the face of this earth by almost four to one. There is unrest among the colored races of all the continents.

They will have none of a war in which, after victory, the white man will again assume his self-appointed "burden". With intelligence and unending patience we must attack our own problem of the American negro.

For the establishment of responsibility we can look with greatest hope toward the schools and the teacher; the teacher who could rightfully be the highest rewarded professional in our national life, with, of course, the qualifications raised to suit the remuneration. There is none in this generation of mine who chooses to fight or die in a "phony" war. And it is a "phony" war if we are fighting it because [of] Hitler or because we were attacked at Pearl Harbor.

What kind of a war is this, that if a[n] Austrian house painter [Hitler] had been killed in the streets of Munich, the war might have been averted? What kind of a war is it, that if [Idaho Senator William] Borah had made a different speech in the Senate, the war might have been averted? What kind of war is this, that if the French had met Hitler in the march on the Rhineland, the war might have been averted? What kind of a war is this that it started so by accident?

If I must fight and die in a war, I want it to be a war with significance. I want it to be a war in which the final victory will re-establish responsibility the whole world over. Responsibility! That's my word for it! For the lack of it we run the awful risk of defeat, slavery, and oblivion. Accepting it, honoring it, and doing something about it, we stand the glorious opportunity of making this world a finer place in which to live; so fine, that on some future day we can perhaps tug gently at the garments of God and, with [a] reasonable degree of pride, say, "Look what we have done!"

• 2 •
"Resolved That —"²

(ABC Radio Network, 3 January 1955)

This is Chet Huntley, ABC News, Los Angeles.

A set of New Year resolutions for a journalist — particularly a radio-television journalist — might go something like this:

RESOLVED: To take a walk each morning around a given issue or problem or controversy and report on all the aspects seen or heard — all 360 aspects, if there be that many.

To show some improvement this year in learning how to depreciate my own opinions.

To stop and think at least thirty minutes before offering one of my own opinions in a broadcast.

That if my opinion must be used, to label it as just opinion with the biggest verbal sign or billboard I know how to make.

To remember, at least once a week, for the next fifty-two weeks, that Providence, unfortunately, did not endow me with complete wisdom or infallibility.

To practice faithfully throughout the coming year to learn how to utter those noble and refreshing words "I was wrong," just in case that uncomfortable situation should arise.

To narrow down almost to infinity, or to keep to a minimum, the number of your fellow citizens to whom you would deny the privilege of being heard, if you had the power. Rather, to remember that they don't deserve silencing—just answering.

To remember that "success" in the profession of journalism is, to be sure, measured by your actual and potential rendering of service; but it's also restrained by the fact that the bigger you are, the bigger and more serious your mistakes.

To remember that only a William Jennings Bryan and a few others seemed to produce their best effort in the first draft, and Bryan never got to be President. In other words, give strength to cut and edit and rewrite.

To face the East each morning and thank Mr. [Cyrus] Sulzberger for the New York *Times.*

To be more decent to my sponsor ... To do some more thinking and wondering whether television is a medium for the reporting of day-to-day news or whether it's more exclusively suited for the documentary.

To waste no more time in search of the "gimmick" or "gadget" for the so-cute and so-contrived television show.

To become a better and more persistent gadfly on the hides of my bosses throughout the coming year in a campaign which is mottoed "There's no such thing as too much news."

To live with the annoying proposition that a little insecurity may be good for a journalist.

And finally—when all the rules, the prohibitions, the restrictions, and points of policy have been violated, to ask only this: a fair and respectable rating on those good questions, "Is he fair, is he decent, and does he have a shred of integrity?"

A set of resolutions and entreaties of this nature by all engaged in the business of buying or selling or giving away ideas might cause even journalists to make some contribution this year to our chances of enduring the uncertainties and confusions with more natural composure and inner strength, unwanted by the exertions of emotional brawls.

This is Chet Huntley, ABC News, Los Angeles.

• 3 •

"Peace"[3]

(Delivered at a national peace luncheon in the Hilton Hotel, March 5, 1969,
the speech received six applause interruptions)

This Convocation, this dedication to an effort in behalf of peace, does not occur by accident. It does not take place in limbo. It is the product of something — of hope, of work, of financial investment and the conviction by a great number of men and women that world peace is a valid and attainable objective.

I suggest there is present in this country and perhaps in the world a new dedication to peace, a new determination to achieve it. For example, how to realize peace was very much an issue in our recent political year, and the pledges which were made in behalf of it were certainly not frivolous. The national desire for peace and the frustrations accruing from its absence had tremendous impact on the political decisions and political events of last year. Recently we read the excellent report of a committee working under the auspices of the American Association of the United Nations. The central thrust of that report was, again, a call for a greater constituency in behalf of peace and a convincing argument in behalf of the premise that it can be had.

Recently, again, I believe some of the distinguished senators and congressmen present here today were petitioned in Washington by the leaders of a new women's organization boasting 50,000 members, founded in Beverly Hills, California, dedicated to work in behalf of peace and demanding that a federal department for peace be created and that it be given Cabinet status.

I would point out that although the volume of American and worldwide student unrest is frequently so high that it's difficult for us uninitiated to comprehend all that's being said, yet it is clear that the call for peace runs strongly through all the talk, all the literature, all the chants, all the music and all the turmoil of our young. This determination of millions of the world's young to achieve and maintain peace is indeed one of our greatest hopes and our finest assets.

Peace has had no greater champion anywhere than the men and women of our and foreign scientific communities. Peace and education are virtually synonymous. It was Senator Fulbright who said in a 1966 speech in Stockholm, "Education is a slow-moving but powerful force. Far from being a means of gaining national advantage in the traditional game of power politics, international education should try to change the nature of the game, to civilize and humanize it in the nuclear age."

Another encouraging development of these post-war years has been the quickening interest in peace and the investment in its pursuit in American businessmen and industrialists, and our artists, and indeed most of the artists of the world, have been splendid ambassadors for peace. And there are many others, groups and individuals, and we need them all.

The quest for peace is never the exclusive project of one group, one profession or one people. It would be most difficult, I believe, to determine who makes or who can make the finest contribution to it. The will to international peace can and does come from the most humble sources and from the most unstudied, unpremeditated acts. It can germinate from a smile or the clasp of a hand, and it can come from those who have no great names nor [sic] reputations. We also know it can be nourished by kings and presidents and by ministers and lawmakers. But I have seen peace advanced by an American handing a ball-point pen to a Russian. I have seen and heard it generated from the trumpet of Louis Armstrong. Our scientists, who converse with Soviet and other foreign scientists, have a tremendous capacity for the promotion of peace. Students and youth are tremendous forces for peace, and we might well consider ways and means to export more of our own, for modest periods of time, and to import all we can. The Fulbright Scholarship plan has been a tremendous peace instrument.

Yes, I think there is a quickened interest and a renewed determination in behalf of peace. We all recall, I am sure, those buoyant and bright days of 1944 and early 1945 when the organization of peace fascinated us. Even in small American towns and American communities you could find citizen organizations working on peace formulas, writing charters, constitutions, preambles and by laws. But then peace slipped by us. It was not to be — not yet. And many of us, I think, grew cynical. Indeed, the temptation was there to regard peace as an idle dream and a delusion.

But hopefully that spate of cynicism is coming to an end. Perhaps more of us are coming to comprehend at last there is actually no alternative to peace except despair — no alternative except despair and ultimate ruin, and that is not consistent with the nature of man. Peace is not one of several choices. It is the only choice. But it is one that mankind has to make. So it is mandatory, my friends, that we believe in it, that we work for it and that we invest in it.

Now, it is my happy privilege to introduce the distinguished Senator from Arkansas, J. William Fulbright, Chairman of the Foreign Relations Committee.

To a standing ovation, Senator Fulbright got up to speak, but a group of demonstrators (see Chapter VII) interrupted the luncheon and Senator Fulbright never spoke. Mr. Huntley analyzed this meeting with a radio commentary printed next

• 4 •

"Harmony"[4]

("Perspective," NBC Radio Network, 7 March 1969)

I had my first genuine encounter the day before yesterday with young demonstrators and hecklers. It's not the most comfortable or satisfying experience, to be sure; but more than that it is sad. It's sad to see young Americans behave so badly and to alienate those who otherwise could be their best champions.

The occasion here in New York on Wednesday [March 5th] was a convocation in behalf of the quest of peace ... involving students, educators, religious leaders, businessmen, community leaders, and so forth. It is significant to note that the theme of world peace runs so strongly through all the current student movement, although the din is sometimes so strong that it's difficult to hear it. As Sen. J. William Fulbright began to speak, some 50 or so young dissidents began shouting, drowning out the Senator, waving North Vietnamese flags, and tossing pigs heads on the lectern. Throughout the remainder of the program they kept up a running disturbance, heckling and trying to dissuade Senators Javits* and McGovern* from speaking, and shouting occasional vulgarities.

The most compelling reaction is one of almost disbelief that these young people could be so ignorant of who their best friends are. It leads one, as a matter of fact, to the conclusion that they want no friends, they want no allies and they are not interested in improving or building. They seek to destroy.

It must be borne in mind constantly that these young Americans constitute a very small minority. There were perhaps almost a thousand other students in the hall. But the student majority made no attempt whatsoever to register its disapproval of the behavior of the small dissident group. One had the feeling that the larger group of youngsters were waiting to determine on whose side they might be.

One young dissident was finally invited to speak for the others. He refused that status, denying that he spoke for anyone but himself. But he delivered a two or three minute tirade against the establishment and departed with the warning that he and his fellows were going to bring it down around our heads.

That word "establishment" is getting over-used here of late but it seems to be escaping the attention of our American young people that the establishment is not as tough or as unyielding as they make it. It is quite likely that the establishment … whoever or whatever it is … would resist any and all efforts of direction and change of policy from within. It is changing now. It is young Americans who have entered business and industry in recent years who are now guiding and leading our corporations into social activity of all kinds.

But the dissident minority insists that it happen all at once.

This is Chet Huntley, NBC News.

*Senator Jacob Javits was a U. S. Senator from New York; Senator George McGovern was a U. S. Senator from South Dakota.

• 5 •

"The Silent Majority"[5]

(printed in the *New York Times*, November 5, 1970, 47)

It is quite likely that a majority of my fellow citizens in this pleasant little town [Bozeman, Montana] might qualify as members of the "silent majority," although I am not sure that they would cheerfully acknowledge it.

Labels are not universally employed in these Rocky Mountain states, perhaps because the population is sufficiently thin and stable to preclude the social and political scientists lumping people into convenient blocs. Besides, there prevails here a remarkable degree of personal independence. If labels there must be, unorthodoxy and unpredictability are as attractive as any.

I think I subscribe completely to the premise that abhorrence and fear of our big cities (plus a compassion for them) increase in proportion to the distance away from them. I sense that some of my old friends look at me and wonder how it is that I am not an alcoholic, not on pot, not maimed, or a dealer in pornography after the years I have lived in the big city. There is a kind of mute and inarticulate fear that these beautiful mountain valleys might one day become refuge centers for the escapees from the nation's urban centers.

There is little sympathy for the protesters, the pickets, the marchers and the shouters of slogans and obscenities. There is total rejection of the violence and those who recommend it.

But this is not "backlash" country. That word disappeared from our political lexicon in 1968 when it became highly uncertain whether George Wallace had done more damage to the Republicans than to the Democrats.

So we were given the phrase "the silent majority," and for all its possible inaccuracies and its vagueness, it was better than most political slogans.

The candidates for "the silent majority" in this lovely land are those who have sickened because of the despairing life style of American cities, the abrasiveness of strident voices and high-pitched decibels of protest. Perhaps the bombing or burning of a government or university building is remembered longer here.

Moderately long hair on boys and hippie attire on campuses tend to be overlooked and forgiven as inexplicable rites of those parading the April of their years. The ranchers, tradespeople and professionals of this community live at peace with the 8,000 college students of Montana State University.

In this rather self-confident community there can be little appreciation of city frustrations and complexities. It has been discovered, recently, that the number of state boards and commissions had increased over the years to more than 160. That is too many, and the Governor [Forrest Anderson] has considerable support in his current effort to reduce that number to about twenty.

Crime and criminals in this region are usually punished. After all, the vigilantes of Montana territorial days were obvious[ly] extralegal and the road agents at Virginia City probably did not enjoy the presumption of innocence until their guilt was proved. But the vigilantes got the job done.

My fellow citizens of Bozeman would agree, I think, that there "is still a lot of good about America." There is—out there. It is all around—on every horizon.

Racial bigotry is not evident. There is an "Indian problem" but it does not feed on racial prejudice. The Indian and his neighbors are frustrated over an inability to find the Indian's proper and rewarding place in American society. We are working at it.

In terms of party politics, the Montana "silent majority" seems not to be the exclusive property of either the Democrats or Republicans. The President and the Vice President are applauded when they assail campus violence, obscenity, revolution and assorted crime. But on the other hand, the anxieties and concerns of Montana people did not manifest themselves this year in a massive voter movement against the solid Democratic identity of the state's delegation to the present Congress.

• 6 •

"Tourism"⁶

("Tourism" is a title assigned for this book. The original, untitled speech appeared to be a combination of three speeches at unknown Montana location[s] possibly for presentation for Big Sky Resort —ca. 1972)

I thought it might be appropriate to talk this evening about this beloved state of ours ... its present and its future.

I must confess that I am somewhat puzzled and perturbed to come home after many years and to discover Montana has such a severe problem in finding sources of revenue for the services which state government is now called upon to render to its citizens. How is it that even in the despair and the sometimes hopelessness of the Great Depression of the early '30's, we found it easier to raise sufficient tax revenue than we seem to find it today?

We are, of course, learning what Europeans learned many years ago ... the danger and the pain of economic inflation. Now we can understand the pain of economic inflation. Now we can understand and appreciate to what extent inflation is truly a thief in the night who robs, not only widows and pensioners, but who robs state governments, county governments, school systems, hospitals, financial institutions, and whole groups of people.

I think we need not look too hard to discover who is the culprit in bringing this curse of inflation upon us ... the record is pretty clear on that. First, there was the military establishment ... the hierarchy of those thousands in the Pentagon who advised a President of the United States that if he would go all out he could win a quick war in Vietnam ... so quickly and so easily that he would not be forced to impose any war time emergency regulations or impose new taxes to pay for, the sources of billions to be spent. The President was persuaded that with half a million men in Vietnam, the victory would be won so quickly that dislocation would not occur.

The President, or course, can be blamed for accepting this erroneous advice.

Then there was [Ohio] Congressman Wilbur Mills, chairman of the Ways and Means Committee who wasted 18 months in his own private argument with the President before moving to enact the new taxes which the President had finally requested as a brake against inflation.

Finally, there is organized labor which in 1966 refused to heed the federal wage-price guidelines and set out to secure in new contracts whatever could be obtained. The excessive labor contracts put some companies out of business. In New York City we say labor recklessly and heedlessly put no less than 4 major newspapers out of business. We have seen wages increases of unprecedented proportions. It is going to take this nation many years to work itself out of dislocation brought about by excessive short-term increases in the cost of labor. You may have heard Secretary of HUD [Housing and Urban Development], George Romney, declare recently that building costs have cost up over 50% since he has been in office.

So, inflation is one of our problems in this state ... a problem which we share with every other state in this nation.

But that isn't all.

While inflation has mounted, our state government has been required to render more services. But back at the ranch, meanwhile, there was little or no growth or expansion to provide the tax revenue required for these services.

The population has not increased to any appreciable degrees. There are fewer agricultural units or ranches in the state than there were 25 to 50 years ago. There are no new industries. Consequently, property taxes have reached their limit and [there] is precious little flexibility in the income tax. Automobile licenses are very costly. Gasoline is heavily taxed ... so are luxury items. Taxes on alcoholic beverages are so high that they now have a problem with illicit bootleg traffic from neighboring states where the beverage taxes are lower. We are staring eyeball to eyeball with the sales tax.

So what do we do?

It appears to me there are two ways out of this unhappy impasse.

It seems to me that we have been carrying the burden of a very expensive luxury having to do with the manner in which we govern ourselves in this state. Frankly, we have too much county government. I don't see how 56 counties in this state, with some 700 thousand people, can be justified, unless we acknowledge that it is a nostalgic luxury.

Efficiency and economics can, in no way, justify the presence of two layers of government, for example, in Silver Bow County.

Modern communications ... I mean all of it from the automobile to the computer and the telephone and radio ... could quite simply make 25 counties suffice for the present 56. As long as we resist amalgamation we defeat all the potential profit and benefit of new commercial technology.

To be sure, we get nostalgic about the fine old courthouses and the county jails and all the rest. But they cost money ... and they cost a lot of it. It is comforting to [know] the clerk and recorder by his first name.

And to be sure, no county employee is going to volunteer stepping aside and giving up his job in order to make an amalgamation of counties possible. But it seems to me that we have so little choice and it is something which we must consider very seriously as we set about drawing a new constitution for our state.

There are other functions of government which could be amalgamated and combined far beyond a reduction of county government. How much does it cost, do you suppose, for a computation and preparation and mailing out of property tax notices? One part-time computer located in any part of the state could make out those tax notices at negligible cost.

So much for reorganization and simplification.

I believe a number of years ago with the conviction that this state of ours could do with some expansion of its commerce. I noticed that our population growth rate just was not there. It was all too evident we were in need of additional means if we were to do all the things that a viable state economy requires ... if we were to build roads, educate our children, construct hospitals, provide for the general health, and offer some police protection to our communities. It was evident that, at considerable expense, we were continuing to educate our young people, only to see them take that education and put it to work in other sections of the nation. I could see our farms and ranches becoming larger and increasingly automated, but fewer in numbers. It did not appear that mining or forestry offered a brilliant future for the state. It was also evident that even if heavy industry were to locate in Montana, we might not want it, seeing the problems it creates.

Big Sky Resort is going to be a major recreation area of which we, I know, will be proud and hopefully the people of Montana will also point to it with some pride.

I was quite aware that 100 per cent of the people of Montana might no agree with my concept or these hopes and dreams. But I was confident then, and I am doubly confident now, that if we can communicate ably and effectively with our fellow Montana citizens we may yet convince them that a few hundred thousand visitors per year in this state will do little damage and might indeed yield some advantages.

I hasten to add that what opposition there is to Big Sky is very modest

and not very numerous as far as I can tell. On the other hand, we are forever indebted to the thousand of citizens of this state who have made us
feel welcome and who have indicated great enthusiasm for the project. I
won't attempt to read a list of groups and individuals, for I would leave
someone out.

In making public the plans for Big Sky, I was determined to hold
nothing back and to make public every detail of the specifications. I have
the feeling that a few people can't quite believe that and are convinced that
we must be hiding something. I assure you we are not. There are no tricks,
no hidden aces. We are convinced that secrecy is too difficult to maintain
and it has a way of backfiring.

It is self evident that some of the future of the state lies in tourism.
It is an industry with a future. It is clean. It does not require vast services
from the state or from counties. It require no special favors.

Furthermore, the development of tourism and the second-home concept in Montana offers an opportunity to show off the beauties of this
state [of] which we are understandably proud.

• 7 •

"The Best of the Democratic Tradition"

(Delivered before the National School Board Association Convention, Anaheim, California, April 7, 1973)

As I sat down to reflect upon and outline what I might say here today,
I asked myself what qualifications I might have which would permit me
to talk about education. What do I know about this complex, exasperat-
ing, and sometimes controversial subject? I was educated in the public
school systems of Montana and Washington State. I am a taxpayer and
therefore a kind of patron of the school systems in my county and in the
State of Montana. Some of my best friends and associates, such as Harold
Levine of the School Board of Freeport, Long Island, New York, are school
people. As a practicing journalist, required and trained to observe and listen and inquire, I have invested a few hundred thousand words on the
subject of education. I am the father of two children, both of them educated, for the most part in the public school system of California. I am
interested in education. Frequently, I find myself wishing that somehow
I could take the modest degree of learning which I now possess and start
all over again. I do not subscribe completely to the notion that education
is the one panacea for all the ills and dilemmas of this world [but they]

are not going to be solved or relaxed without education. And, finally, I do most sincerely believe that learning is one of the most exciting, rewarding, and joyous experiences of humankind.

It is altogether possible that you are not going to take kindly to all that I have to say here. But if anyone came to this convention in search of applause he is wasting everyone's time. In view of what is going on among all the various organizations in the education [system], shifting alliances and ruptured groups and new associations, bruised feelings can be nothing new to this crowd. Perhaps you might be interested in what one observer sees going on in many school systems. I will not talk about any particular school system.

My major feeling toward you school board people is that of great sympathy. In general terms, it seems to me, that the tremendous and incredible social changes occurring in this country have had an impact on our schools far beyond that affecting any other institution, but the school or the school system does not have the equipment to cope with this impact of social change. Education does better in a stable climate in which changes occur slowly. There is no need to give you people a complete list of these problems and difficulties stemming from social change, but let me cite several of them:

The incredible mobility of the American people creates school problems because your raw product ... the pupil ... comes in a baffling variety of grades and standards of quality.

For the first time in our national history, education is forced to compete with other programs for financing.

The phenomenon of the suburb and the consequential phenomenon of the inner-city ghetto have laid some hellish problems on the steps of the schoolhouse.

And there is a problem which I would like to talk about particularly and it largely explains why I sympathize with you. You are charged by the voter, the citizen, your constituency with the responsibility for an institution which is all things to all people and therefore not good enough for *any* particular group of individuals. Your constituents insist that you operate a baby-sitting establish-ment and child-care center. In thousands of American communities you are required to operate the entertainment center: athletic contests, movies, dances, drama, band concerts, drill teams, art exhibits, ceramic displays and so on and on. You are charged with the duty of providing a church, for many of your constituents insist that the *school* is responsible for the morality of the younger generation, and there are those who would also make the school a temple of prayer. You maintain a health center in the name of the school. Your schools are restaurants. They are job-training centers. You are frequently required to provide marriage counseling. You often run psychiatric wards. And there are some who even expect you to educate.

Surely, no one believes seriously that you (school board) people have *deliberately* perpetuated this wasteful and hapless confusion. But personally, I wonder why you have failed to say to your voters, "To hell with it ... we shall be party no longer to this travesty in the name of education." Your patience and your determination to stay with it are incredible.

I would guess that most Americans still think of their school as an *enduring* institution. It has always been there, therefore, it will always be there. It is prominent. It is identifiable. It is convenient. What better place to go to in search of all these desires.

But there is another reason, I think, why the school has become all things to all people. There are some who like it that way. In trying to satisfy all these disparate demands upon the school, systems have, naturally, failed to please anyone completely; and the confusion has provided the opportunity for an army of new professionals ... the school administrators ... whom I would call "the educationists" as opposed to "educators." The mentor, the instructor ... the educator ... all are gone, replaced by clerks, classroom chairmen or moderators. The true teacher wants no part of this confusion, this charade, and she has left the profession. Were those *teachers* we have seen in recent years on the picket lines or in mass meetings, shouting obscenities and the vulgarities of the fish market?

It seems to me that an argument which has been raging (here) in California tends to contain just about the entire malaise of education. It says it all. The California legislature, a few months ago, passed legislation calling for teacher accountability. In practice, it is clear that this process would entail a young educationist coming around to the teacher every so often, putting her through a series of questions, perhaps observing her in class, and determining her future. What a desperate and futile effort that is to establish a kind of alchemy and cause gold to be produced from tin cans ... to cause a non-educating system to educate.

Is it seriously suggested that a gifted and dedicated teacher ... left free to teach ... is not accountable, is difficult or impossible to identify or evaluate? A gifted and dedicated teacher has always been accountable ... accountable to the student ... not to the superintendents, not to principals or vice principals, and not to poll takers or Bachelors of Psychology. A teacher's accountability used to be measured in terms of the quality of the product ... the degree of learning of her charges. There was no problem in finding, detecting, and identifying a fine teacher. You simply surveyed the academic abilities of his former students.

Now those who have replaced the teacher are accountable to something else and by a different process. They are accountable no longer to students, but to lawyers and ranks of administrative personnel and to "the system." The dedicated teacher who has tried to cope with this system has been told by administrative personnel, "Come on. Don't make waves. Just fill out the forms and get your reports in on time." Faculty, today, is accountable to an incredible system of forms, charts, and questionnaires which rival the paper shuffling proclivities of the federal bureaucracy. Teaching has been reduced to filling spaces on pieces of paper with names and numbers. School systems have deserted education, but they do have records ... millions of tons of records!

I am frequently appalled when I visit a modern urban or suburban school. Take, for example, the audio-visual equipment. What, are we trying to ... train or produce a whole generation of fifty million radio announcers and cameramen? In scores of schools I see electronic equipment the likes and quantities of which we never enjoyed at the National Broadcasting Company.

Next, visit the dining facilities of many of our schools. Here again I have seen all the equipment for food preparation and distribution which many a first class hotel or restaurant would envy. Who among us could quarrel too strenuously with the concept of the hot lunch program for needy children? But how did that program get fastened on the school? We know. The school is convenient. It was the one place where we could find youngsters and catch them all in one place at one time. It is not just the hot lunch program which is aware of the school's convenience. If we wish government to administer a hot lunch to needy and underprivileged children, did anyone ever think of proposing that government do it or hire someone other than the school system to do it? I have the feeling that specialists in food catering services might be more efficient at this task then school administrators.

And what about the non-under privileged student? What is the origin of this rigid rule that he, too, must have access to a hot lunch served in the school cafeteria or lunchroom? Is the brown paper bag really all that bad, that unwholesome, that unhealthful? Or what about the lunch bucket? Or are the brown bag and the lunch bucket inconvenient or even humiliating? What is so heartless about the non-under privileged student patronizing Joe's pizzeria across the street or a lunch counter on wheels parked at the curb or on the playground? I do believe we have wasted millions of dollars of unnecessary kitchen and dining equipment in our schools. In view of the coin-operated food machines available today, I don't understand the rationale for expensive food equipment. But apparently mama wants to be certain that Johnny's little belly is full, no matter that his head is empty. Does this explain how you find yourselves in the restaurant business?

I am saddened and dismayed when I examine the list of activities for which academic credit is now given in some school systems. Is your school system giving academic credit for football and basketball and tennis? How about pottery making or flower arranging? Drama? Glee club and band? And what about monitoring? In many school systems credit is given for monitoring ... that's a messenger service in which the student interrupts classroom such-and-such to tell teacher Smith that he'll have to take the bus to get home today. Academic credit is frequently given for participation in student government, and student government is nothing more than a thinly disguised popularity contest. Academic credit is given for contribution to the school paper, for cheerleading and pom pom waving, for making announcements over the closed-circuit radio or television system. A credit for monitoring is given the same value as a credit for trigonometry or for the ability to write a sonnet.

Academic credit is given for these activities which we used to pursue *after* school hours for the sake of pride, for publicity and recognition, for the pursuit of excellence, or for the sheer joy of it.

In the past fifteen years or so we heard much about *innovations* in education. They came along by the score. As I recollect, the Ford Foundation alone spent $31,000,000 dollars on educational innovations. What happened? Perhaps I have been asleep. But I cannot recall a single innovation that became a permanent program. Can you name one?

It is this pedestrian record of the innovative programs which says to me that I may well be what was known recently as a reactionary in so far as education is concerned. In view of the innovations which seem to have failed, in view of all that has happened, in view of all the changes, and in view of the quality of the school's product ... the student or the graduate ... the 3 R's do, indeed have a greater appeal and attraction. And are we really certain that the innovations in teaching the 3 R's are all that fruitful?

I suspect that any attempt to concentrate on the 3 R's in today's school systems is going to draw the fire of the professional educationists, and they maintain a tough lobby! I cite Dr. Kenneth Clark, who, a few years ago as head of the Washington, D. C. schools, called for a minimization of all other programs in favor of teaching Washington youngsters how to read. He said that if a youngster cannot read of what value is anything else? As I recall, Dr. Clark lasted about a year. He was ordering heresy to the professionals.

Examine the hypocrisy in a school system which denies college qualifications to a gifted student because he lacks a credit or two in physical education or student activities; but which will excuse a poor student from school so he can take a job with the tacit understanding that he will return and continue his education. That, of course, is nothing more than aiding and abetting his dropping out until he reaches an age safely out of reach of compulsory education. But that practice is widespread.

Perhaps that is one innovation we might consider seriously. Why burden the high school with the poorly-motivated student? Perhaps there is something to be said for ending compulsory education at the end of eighth grade, for what can the high school do for the poor student other than tolerate him? What do the impressive records of your school systems tell you ... how many students in your system were rescued in high school after failing in primary school?

It is impossible to condemn you people who struggle on school boards. I sorrow for you. The "don't make waves" people have tended to run away with education and they have tended to hoodwink the public.

A very able Stanford graduate working on his doctorate thesis once said that if we could educate the school boards of the nation we would have all the problems solved. I buy that only partially. Perhaps if we could toughen up our school boards and then rally to their defense when the vitriol begins to fly ... perhaps that is the secret!

I will briefly paraphrase the keynote speaker of the 1956 Democratic convention, I believe it was, in Chicago: "How long ... oh how long ... do we tolerate nonsense?"

• 8 •

"Regarding American Youth"[8]

(Broadcast March 20, 1974)

This is Chet Huntley.

Since I shall be talking about youth for the next few minutes, it occurred to me that perhaps the more effective way to communicate any message I might wish to get across would be to do the "streak" this evening through the Big Sky Meadow Village. We haven't had a streak yet so you can understand how intellectually and culturally deprived we all feel.

If anyone thinks I'm going to waste my perfectly good spleen by permitting myself to get upset about campus streaking, he's very wrong. Youngsters are marvelous in the manner in which they can zero in unerringly on the most senseless. We keep thinking that the consumption of gold fish cannot be equaled or excelled in senselessness, or that crowding into telephone booths or cars will establish a recognized and all-time world record. But year after year they are back with something new.

Already it has started ... neurotic assignment editors sending reporters out to discover and bring back the explanation ... the reason, the motivation, the purpose of streaking. What are youngsters trying to say to us by streaking? These particular youngsters are trying to say more to us than they have been saying for years ... which is very little. Probably there are some others who have something of significance to say. But the streakers are saying no more than "it's great fun and of immense satisfaction to violate a minor law or ordnance, now and then, particularly if it has something to do with nudity." There is something rather hilarious about the half-dozen or so naked kids racing through a crowd which is fully dressed. Perhaps this is it ... it remains blissfully or uproaringly [sic] senseless.

More seriously ... are these counterparts of the American youth who were, only a few years ago, breaking up serious meetings, staging riots, trying to change the administration of colleges, threatening to bring the government of the United States to a standstill?

I suspect that was a special group which finally achieved the high degree of its anger and its dudgeon at the Democratic National Convention in Chicago in 1968. That was another special group which fed its anger and threatened to storm the Pentagon. Where have all those groups gone?

It is somewhat easier to trace the end of the civil rights brotherhood movement. After the Democratic Convention of 1964 in Atlantic City, many of the blacks told their white brothers that they wanted no more white help ... that they, the blacks, would try to do the rest of it on their own.

Apparently American youth is adjusting without undue damage to the new facts of American life ... less mobility as a consequence of the gasoline shortage, a genuine pinch in which the cost of living or going to school is becoming unbearable. But it is very difficult to find evidence of serious thinking coming from the campus or the schoolyard. If streaking [is] the best that contemporary American youth can do, [what then] with the changes which are affecting all Western economies and Western governments[?]

Streaking is yet another of those phenomena, I suppose, which youth must explain away or disavow before anyone will take them seriously.

This is Chet Huntley.

Notes

(These notes are an extension of the permissions page.)

Preface

1. Theodore White, *America in Search of Itself — The Making of the President, 1956–1980* (New York: Harper and Row, 1982), 1–2. Reprinted by permission of HarperCollins, rights owner, ©1982, all rights reserved.

I. Chet Huntley — the Man

1. Edith Efron, "The Travels of Chet Huntley," *TV Guide* (19 June 1965), 8. This excerpt used by permission from TV Guide Magazine Group, Inc., © 1965, renewed 1993, all rights reserved. Hereafter cited as "The Travels of Chet Huntley."

2. Barbara Matusow, *The Evening Stars* (Boston: Houghton-Mifflin Co., 1983), 92. This excerpt reprinted by permission of Houghton-Mifflin Co., ©1983, all rights reserved. Hereafter *The Evening Stars*.

3. "Chet Huntley," in *Current Biography Yearbook 1956* (New York: H. W. Wilson, 1957), 291. This excerpt reprinted by permission of H. W. Wilson, ©1957, renewed 1985, all rights reserved. Hereafter *Current Biography*.

4. "Chet Huntley," in *Current Biography*, 291.

5. "Chet Huntley," in *Current Biography*, 291.

6. Florence Trout, "Tippy Today," *Bozeman* (Mont.) *Daily Chronicle* (7 August 1977), 22. This excerpt © 1977 and all related articles below reprinted by permission of *Bozeman Daily Chronicle*, © various, all rights reserved.

7. Barbara Matusow, *The Evening Stars*, 91.

8. Donald Freeman, "Chet Huntley's Eye on the Past," *San Diego* [Cal.] *Union* (27 December 1968), B7.

9. Aline Mosby, "Aline Talks to Chet," *Billings* [Mont.] *Gazette* (1 January 1967), 29. This excerpt © 1967 and all related below reprinted by permission of *Billings Gazette*, copyright owner, © various, all rights reserved.

10. Edith Efron, "The Travels of Chet Huntley," 8. This excerpt reprinted by permission from TV Guide Magazine Group, Inc., © 1965, renewed 1993, all rights reserved.

11. Barbara Matusow, *The Evening Stars*, 91.

12. Edwin Newman, "Critic-at-Large," NBC Radio (20 March 1974). This excerpt, ©1970, and all related excerpts ("The Huntley-Brinkley Report," news commentaries) below reprinted by permission of National Broadcasting Company, Inc. (NBC) © various, all rights reserved.

13. John Chancellor, "Comment on the News," NBC Radio (20 March 1974).

14. Hugh Downs, letter to author (20 January 2002).

15. Bill Ewald, "First Team," *Newsweek* (13 March 1961), 56. This excerpt, ©1961, and all related articles below reprinted by permission of *Newsweek*, © various, all rights reserved.

II. The Early Years

1. Michael Malone, Richard Roeder and William Lang, *Montana — A History of Two Centuries* (Seattle: University of Washington Press, 1976, 1991), Chapter 10 — "The Homestead Boom." Passim. Reprinted by permission of University of Washington Press, © 1976, 1991, all rights reserved.

2. Chet Huntley, [A tribute to Pat Huntley] (date unknown), possibly delivered at the Huntley's 50th anniversary, June 26, 1960, Reedpoint, Mont. Copy in Chet Huntley Collection. This excerpt and those mentioned below as part of "Chet Huntley Collection" are reprinted by permission of rights owner, K. Ross Toole Archives, Maureen and Mike Mansfield Library, University of Montana, Missoula, Mont. Hereafter cited as Chet Huntley Collection.

3. "A Family Affair," *Wisconsin — Then and Now* (July 1971), 6. Reprinted by permission of Wisconsin Historical Society, ©1971, renewed 1999, all rights reserved.

4. *Proceedings, Helena Convention on the Northern Pacific Land Grant* (Helena, Mont., 1888), 14–15.

5. Chet Huntley, *The Generous Years — Remembrances of a Frontier Childhood* (New York: Random House, 1968), 21. Reprinted by permission of Random House, ©1968, renewed 1996, all rights reserved. Hereafter Chet Huntley, *Generous Years*.

6. Chet Huntley, *Generous Years*, 28.

7. Tippy Huntley, "A Spirited Montanan — Mrs. Blanche Huntley" (manuscript), 1975. Copy in Chet Huntley Collection.

8. News Item, *Jefferson Valley News* (Whitehall, Mont.) (19 August 1943). Hereafter *Jefferson County News*. The *News* ceased publication in 1976. This excerpt and all JVN stories noted below are reprinted by permission of Jefferson Valley Museum, Whitehall, Mont. and Montana Historical Society, Helena. All rights reserved.

9. Louis Renz, *The History of the Northern Pacific Railroad* (Fairfield, Wash.: Ye Galleon Press, 1980), 229.

10. Chet Huntley, *Generous Years*, 22.

11. Chris Gosgriffe, "Chatting About Chet," *Billings Gazette* (July 1970).

12. Huntley family genealogy. Copy in Chet Huntley Collection.

13. Don Spritzer, *Roadside History of Montana* (Missoula, Mont.: Mountain Press Publishing Co., 1999), 30. Reprinted by permission of Mountain Press Publishing Co., ©1999, all rights reserved.

14. Chet Huntley, *Generous Years*, 51.

15. Chet Huntley, *Generous Years*, 66.

16. Chet Huntley, *Generous Years*, 49.

17. Chet Huntley, *Generous Years*, 50–51.

18. Chet Huntley, *Generous Years*, 52–53.

19. Tippy Huntley, "A Spirited Montanan — Mrs. Blanche Huntley."

20. Chet Huntley, *Generous Years*, 100–101.

21. Chet Huntley, *Generous Years*, 90–91.

22. Chet Huntley, *Generous Years*, 91. The Huntley school was moved to Saco and located in the town park as part of the town museum.

23. Tippy Huntley, "A Spirited Montanan — Mrs. Blanche Huntley."

24. Chet Huntley, *Generous Years*, 111.

25. Callie Allison, "A Tribute to Chet Huntley," *Jefferson Valley News* (28 March 1974), 7.

26. Roy Poindexter, *Golden Throats and Silver Tongues — The Radio Announcers* (Conway, Ark.: River Road Press, 1978), 33.

27. C. Howard MacDonald, *Voices in the Big Sky, The History of Montana Broadcasting* (Bozeman, Mont.: Big M Broadcast Service, 1992), 3. Hereafter: *Voices in the Big Sky.*

28. Tippy Huntley, "A Spirited Montanan — Mrs. Blanche Huntley."

29. Chet Huntley, *Generous Years*, 134.

30. Thomas Thompson, "Chet Heads for the Hills," *Life* (17 July 1970), 33. This excerpt and related excerpts below reprinted by permission of *Life,* ©1970, renewed 1998, all rights reserved.

31. Tippy Huntley, "A Spirited Montanan — Mrs. Blanche Huntley."

32. H. Roger Grant, *Living in the Depot — The Two-Story Railroad Station* (Iowa City: University of Iowa Press, 1993), 39–41, 43–46; H. Roger Grant and Charles Bohi, *The Country Railroad Station in America* (Boulder, Col.: Pruett Publishing Co., 1978), 70.

33. Irv Letolsky, "Good-by, Chet," *Minneapolis Tribune TV Week* (14–20 December 1969), 7. Hereafter "Good-by, Chet."

34. Chet Huntley to Ronald (last name unknown), Northern Pacific Railroad Telegram (17 June 1924). Copy in and by permission of Jefferson Valley Museum.

35. John Garraty and Mark Carnes, "Chet Huntley," *American National Biography* (New York: Oxford University Press, 1999), 11: 548. Reprinted by permission of Oxford University Press © 1999, all rights reserved.

36. Roy Millegan, Whitehall, Mont., letter to author (20 March 2001).

37. *Trail* (1929 yearbook), Whitehall High School, Whitehall, Mont., passim. Reprinted by permission of Jefferson Valley Museum, Whitehall, Mont.

38. William Whitworth, "Profiles— An Accident of Casting," *New Yorker* (3 August 1968), 37. This excerpt and all related below are reprinted by permission of author William Whitworth, © 1968, all rights reserved. Hereafter "Profiles."

39. Grace Kenfield, "Chet Huntley Has Interesting Career," *Big Timber Pioneer* (7 July 1960), 1. Reprinted by permission of *Big Timber Pioneer* ©1960, renewed 1988, all rights reserved. Hereafter "Chet Huntley Has Interesting Career."

40. Bill Brewster, "Speaker Had Distinct Superiority," *Billings Gazette* (19 February 1970), 4.

41. Bill Brewster, "Speaker Had Distinct Superiority," 4.

42. *Montanan* (Montana State College, 1932 yearbook).

43. Chet Huntley, "The Sound of Beauty," in Enid Haupt, ed., *In My Opinion (the Seventeen Book of Very Important People)* (New York: The MacMillan Co., 1966), 124.

44. Fred Ferretti, "Chet Gets Ready To Say 'Goodbye, David,'" *New York Times* (5 July 1970), D-13. Hereafter "Chet Gets Ready …" This article, © 1970, and those related below are reprinted by permission from the *New York Times,* © various, all rights reserved.

45. Chet Huntley, *Generous Years*, 176.

46. Harry Skornia and Jack Kitson, eds., *Problems and Controversies in Television and Radio* (Palo Alto, Cal.: Pacific Books, publishers, 1968), 358.

47. News item, *Jefferson Valley News* (Whitehall, Mont.) (13 October 1932).

48. Virjean Hanson Edwards, University of Washington (Seattle), assistant registrar of records, letter to author (5 December 2001).

III. The Early Radio and Television Years

1. Thomas Thompson, "Chet Heads for the Hills, 36.

2. C. Howard MacDonald, *Voices in the Big Sky*, 75; Gwenyth Jackaway, *Media at War—Radio's Challenge to Newspapers, 1924–1939* (Westport, Ct.: Praeger, 1995), 15–16, 25–26. Reprinted by permission of Greenwood/Praeger Publishing Co. © 1995, all rights reserved.

3. J. Liston, "At Home with Chet Huntley," *American Home* (September 1961), 17.

4. William Whitworth, "Profiles," 37.

5. Grace Kenfield, "Chet Huntley Has An Interesting Career," 1.

6. "Calm Controversialist," *Newsweek* (19 April 1954), 54. This excerpt, © 1954, and related articles below are reprinted by permission of *Newsweek*, © various, all rights reserved.

7. Fred Ferretti, "Chet Gets Ready...," D-13.

8. "NBC News Biography Release," (Chet Huntley) (8 August 1968).

9. Irv Letofsky, "Good-by, Chet," 7.

10. Michael Murray and Don Godfrey, eds., *Television in America* (Ames, Ia.: Iowa State University Press, 1997), 366. Reprinted by permission of Iowa State University Press, © 1997, all rights reserved.

11. News item, *Jefferson Valley News* (8 November 1934).

12. Workers of the Writers Program, *Washington — A Guide to the Evergreen State* (Portland, Ore.: Binfort and Mort, 1941), 92, 93, 221. Reprinted by permission of Binfort and Mort, © 1941,renewed 1969, 1997, all rights reserved. Hereafter Workers, *Washington*.

13. Workers, *Washington*, 242–252, passim.

14. Workers of the Writers Program, *Oregon — End of the Trail* (American Guide Series) (Portland Ore.: Binfort and Mort, 1940), 68, 73, 106, 139, 207, 213. Reprinted by permission of Binfort and Mort, © 1940, renewed 1968, 1996, all rights reserved; Jeff Kisseloff, *The Box — An Oral History of Television — 1920–1961* (New York: Viking Press, 1995), 9. Reprinted by permission of Susan Bergholz Literary Services, rights owner. © 1995, all rights reserved. Hereafter *The Box*.

15. Fred Ferretti, "Chet Gets Ready...," D-13.

16. William Whitworth, "Profiles," 37.

17. Letter from Chet Huntley to Dr. and Mrs. L. R. Packard, in *Jefferson Valley News* (12 July 1939).

18. "Chet Huntley recognized as outstanding newscaster," *Jefferson Valley News* (12 July 1951).

19. B Marchand, *The Emergence of Los Angeles — Population and Housing in the City of Dreams — 1940–1970* (London, Eng.: Pion Limited, 1986), 60–70, passim.

20. Chet Huntley, *Generous Years*, 101.

21. "Chet Huntley" in *Current Biography*, 290–291.

22. Grace Kenfield, "Chet Huntley Has An Interesting Career," 1.

23. Chet Huntley, interviewed by Lee Cade, in "Montana's Recreation Potential Enormous," *Montana Farmer-Statesman* (3 May 1973), 14. This excerpt reprinted by permission of *Montana Farmer-Statesman*, © 1973, renewed 2001, all rights reserved.

24. Harry Skornia and Jack Kitson, *Problems and Controversies in Television and Radio*, 361.

25. Estelle Edmerson, "A Descriptive Study of the American Negro in United States Professional Radio, 1922–1953," (master's thesis, University of California, Los Angeles, 1954), 108; C. Howard MacDonald, *Voice in the Big Sky*, 119–120.

26. "Chet Huntley" in *Current Biography*, 290.

27. Lynn Bowman, *Los Angeles: Epic of a City* (Berkeley, Cal.: Howell-North Books, 1974), 328; J. Fred MacDonald, *Don't Touch That Dial* (Chicago: Nelson-Hall Press, 1979), 334, 349.

28. Barbara Savage, *Broadcasting Freedom — Radio, War, and the Politics of Race, 1938–1948* (Chapel Hill: University of North Carolina Press, 1999), 180, 181, 183; interview with Chet Huntley, in Edmerson, "Descriptive Study of the American Negro in United States Professional Radio," 108.

29. Irving Fang, *Those Radio Commentators* (Ames, Ia.: Iowa State University Press, 1977), 13. Reprinted by permission of Iowa State University Press, © 1977, all rights reserved; Edward Bliss, *The Story of Broadcast Journalism* (New York: Columbia University Press, 1991), 305. Reprinted by permission of Columbia University Press, © 1991, all rights reserved; Michael Beaubein and John Wyeth, Jr., *Views on the News: The Media and Public Opinion* (New York: New York University Press, 1994), 12. Reprinted by permission of New York University Press © 1994, all rights reserved; Erik Barnouw, *The Golden Web — A History of Broadcasting in the United States,* volume II —1933–1953 (New York: Oxford University Press, 1968), 222. Reprinted by permission of Oxford University Press, © 1968, all rights reserved. Hereafter *The Golden Web ... II.*

30. Erik Barnouw, *The Golden Web ... II*, 258–259.

31. Irving Fang, *Those Radio Commentators*, 13; Edward Bliss, *The Story of Broadcast Journalism*, 305; Michael Beaubein and John Wyeth, Jr., *Views on the News: the Media and Public Opinion*, 12; Erik Barnouw, *The Golden Web ... II*, 259.

32. J. Robert Nash and Stanley Ross, *Motion Picture Guide* (Chicago: Cinebooks, 1985) (10 volumes), I:212.

33. John Dunning, *Tune in Yesterday: The Ultimate Encyclopedia of Old-Time Radio — 1925–1976* (Englewood Cliffs, N.J.: Prentice-Hall, Inc., 1976), 102; Robert Brown, *Manipulating the Ether — The Power of Broadcast Radio in Thirties' America* (Jefferson, N.C.: McFarland and Co., Inc., 1998), 152. Reprinted by permission of McFarland and Co., Inc., © 1998, all rights reserved.

34. J. Robert Nash and Stanley Ross, *Motion Picture Guide*, III:1129.

35. J. Robert Nash and Stanley Ross, *Motion Picture Guide*, I:1112.

36. Howard Thompson, reviewer, *New York Times Film Reviews* (19 August 1949), 12:5.

37. J. Robert Nash and Stanley Ross, *Motion Picture Guide*, VI:2434.

38. Patricia Hanson, *American Film Institute Catalog of Motion Pictures produced in the United States — Feature Films —1941–1950* (Berkeley, Cal.: University of California [American Film Institute] 1999) (2 volumes), M–Z, 1684. Reprinted by permission, University of California and American Film Institute, © 1999., all rights reserved.

39. Bill Ewald, "First Team," 37.

40. John Garraty and Mark Carnes, "Chet Huntley," *American National Biography*, II:549.

41. Bill Ewald, "First Team," 56.

42. "Chet Huntley," *Current Biography*, 291.

43. Chet Huntley, "Goodnight All!" *TV Guide* (1 August 1970), 10. This excerpt reprinted by permission from TV Guide Magazine Group, Inc. © 1970, all rights reserved.

44. Edward Bliss, *The Story of Broadcast Journalism*, 268.

45. Bill Ewald, "First Team," 56.

46. John Cogley, *Report on Blacklisting*, in *Blacklisting — Two Key Documents* (New York: Arno Press and the New York Times, 1971), 88.

47. John Garraty and Mark Carnes, "Chet Huntley," *American National Biography*, II:549; "Lady from Altoona," *Nation* (16 January 1954), 178:3, 4. Reprinted by permission of *Nation*, © 1954, renewed 1982, all rights reserved.

48. "About Time," *New Republic* (25 January 1954), 130:4, 3–4. Reprinted by permission of *New Republic*, © 1954, renewed 1982, all rights reserved.

49. Michael Beaubein and John Wyeth, Jr., *Views on the News*, 11.

50. Edward Bliss, *The Story of Broadcast Journalism*, 305.

51. A. M. Sperber, *Murrow— His Life and Times* (New York: Freundlich Books, 1986), 336.

52. J. Robert Nash and Stanley Ross, *Motion Picture Guide*, III:789.

53. "Mau Mau" (review), *New York Times Film Review* (14 July 1955), 19:1.

54. J. Robert Nash and Stanley Ross, *Motion Picture Guide*, II:533.

55. Barbara Matusow, *The Evening Stars*, 91.

56. J. Fred McDonald, *Television and the Red Menace— The Video Road to Vietnam* (New York: Praeger Publishers, 1985), 46. Reprinted by permission of Greenwood/Praeger Publishers, © 1985, all rights reserved.

57. "TV-Radio," *Newsweek* (19 April 1954), 54.

58. John Garraty and Mark Carnes, "Chet Huntley," *American National Biography*, II:549.

59. Gwenda Blair, *Almost Golden: Jessica Savitch and the Selling of Television News* (New York: Simon and Schuster, 1988), 49. Hereafter: *Almost Golden*.

60. Reuven Frank, *Out of Thin Air: the Brief Wonderful Life of Network News* (New York: Simon and Schuster, 1991), 91. This quote and those related below are used by permission of author, Reuven Frank, ©1991, all rights reserved. Hereafter: *Out of Thin Air*.

61. Fred Ferretti, "Chet Gets Ready…," D-13.

62. David Brinkley, *David Brinkley* (New York: Alfred A. Knopf, 1995), 98. Reprinted by permission by Alfred A. Knopf, a division of Random House, Inc., © 1995 by David Brinkley, all rights reserved.

63. Gary Gates, *Air Time* (New York: Harper and Row, 1978), 77.

IV. "The Huntley-Brinkley Report"—1956–1970

1. William Porter, *Assault on the Media: The Nixon Years* (Ann Arbor, Mich.: University of Michigan Press, 1976), 7. Reprinted by permission, University of Michigan Press, © 1976, all rights reserved.

2. David Brinkley, *David Brinkley*, passim.

3. Gwenda Blair, *Almost Golden*, 49.

4. Thomas Morgan, "Crisis, Conflict and Change in TV News," *Look* (7 November 1961), 52; Barbara Matusow, *The Evening Stars*, 74; Reuven Frank, *Out of Thin Air*, 92.

5. David Brinkley, *David Brinkley*, 100, 101.

6. Reuven Frank, *Out of Thin Air*, 110.

7. David Brinkley, *David Brinkley*, 100, 101.

8. Fred Ferretti, "Chet Gets Ready…," D-13.

9. David Brinkley, *David Brinkley*, 100, 101; Reuven Frank, *Out of Thin Air*, 98.

10. David Brinkley, *David Brinkley*, 102.

11. David Brinkley, *David Brinkley*, 99.

12. Chet Huntley in interview with James Fixx, "An Anniversary Talk with Huntley and Brinkley," *McCall's* (magazine) (XCIV:1) (October 1966), 56. Reprinted by permission of *McCall's* magazine, © renewed 1996 by Gruner & Jahr USA Publishing, all rights reserved.

13. Chet Huntley in interview with James Fixx, "An Anniversary Talk with Huntley and Brinkley," 56.

14. David Brinkley, *David Brinkley*, 100.

15. Paul Gardner, "Anniversary Time for a Top Team," *New York Times* (15 August 1965), 13; Chet Huntley in interview with James Fixx, "An Anniversary Talk with Huntley and Brinkley," 56.

16. NBC News coverage of the Democratic Convention (11 August 1956).

17. Jack Gould, "TV: New Convention Look," *New York Times* (17 July 1956), TV-radio, 2.

18. Sig Mickelson, *The Decade that Shaped Television News (CBS in the 1950s)* (West-

port, Ct.: Praeger Publishers, 1998), 208. Reprinted by permission of Greenwood/Praeger Publishers, © 1998 all rights reserved. Hereafter: *The Decade That Shaped Television News.*

19. Susan and Bill Buzenberg, *Salant, CBS, and the Battle for the Soul of Broadcast Journalism — The Memoirs of Richard S. Salant* (Boulder, Col.: Westview Press, 1999), 38. Reprinted by permission of Westview Press, © 1999, all rights reserved.

20. Maury Green, *Television News — Anatomy and Process* (Belmont Cal.: Wadsworth Publishing Co., Inc., 1969), 285. Reprinted by permission of Wadsworth Publishing Co., Inc., © 1969, renewed 1997, all rights reserved.

21. Theodore White, *America in Search of Itself*, 171.

22. Zachary Karabell, *Rise and Fall of the Televised Political Conventions* (Cambridge, Mass.: Harvard University Press, 1998), 5

23. Reuven Frank, *Out of Thin Air*, 111–112.

24. Av Westin, *Newswatch — How TV Decides the News* (New York: Simon and Schuster, 1982), 36. Reprinted by permission of Simon and Schuster, © 1982, all rights reserved. Hereafter: *Newswatch.*

25. Reuven Frank, *Out of Thin Air*, 112.

26. Eric Newton, ed., *Crusaders, Scoundrels, Journalists* (New York: Times Books, 1999), 256.

27. Reuven Frank, *Out of Thin Air*, 112.

28. Jack Gould, "TV: Spotlight on the News," *New York Times* (30 October 1956), 75.

29. Howard Prouty, ed., *Variety Television Reviews* (New York: Garland Publishing Co., 1985), V:1953–1956 (31 October 1956), no pagination. This excerpted review, © 1985, and others related below are reprinted by permission of *Variety*, all rights reserved.

30. Howard Prouty, ed., *Variety Television Reviews*, V:1953–1956 (31 October 1956).

31. Fred Ferretti, "Chet Gets Ready…," D-13.

32. Thomas Thompson, "Chet Heads for the Hills," 33.

33. Robert Goldberg and Gerald Goldberg, *Anchors — Brokaw, Jennings and Rather and the Evening News* (New York: Birch Lane Press, 1990), 74.

34. Barbara Matusow, *The Evening Stars*, 79.

35. Reuven Frank, *Out of Thin Air*, 118.

36. Barbara Matusow, *The Evening Stars*, 73.

37. David Brinkley, *David Brinkley*, 108.

38. Joe Derby, "The Huntley-Brinkley Bandwagon," *Electronic Age*, 29:3 (Summer 1970), 26. By permission of National Broadcasting Company, Inc. (NBC), © 1970, renewed 1998, all rights reserved. Cited below as "The Huntley-Brinkley Bandwagon."

39. Reuven Frank, *Out of Thin Air*, 122.

40. Av Westin, *Newswatch*, 36–37.

41. Reuven Frank, *Out of Thin Air*, 95.

42. Reuven Frank, *Out of Thin Air*, 117.

43. Reuven Frank, *Out of Thin Air*, 169.

44. Lawrence Laurent, "Chet Huntley's Goodbye," *Washington* [D.C.] *Post* (31 July 1970), C-8. This excerpt and those below used by permission of the *Washington Post*, © 1970, renewed 1998, all rights reserved.

45. Paul Byers, ed., "The Huntley-Brinkley Report," in *Encyclopedia of World Biography* (Detroit, Mich.: Gail Research, 1998), VIII:50.

46. "The Rugged Anchorman," *Time* (1 April 1974), 44. This excerpt, ©1974, and those below reprinted by permission of *Time*, © various, all rights reserved.

47. Gary Gates, *Air Time*, 77; Thomas Fensch, ed., *Television News Anchors* (Jefferson, N.C.: McFarland and Co., Inc., 1993), 25. Reprinted by permission of McFarland and Co., Inc., ©1993, all rights reserved.

48. Gary Gates, *Air Time*, 144.

49. Lawrence Laurent, "Chet Huntley's Goodbye," C-8.

50. Robert Goldberg and Gerald Goldberg, *Anchors — Brokaw, Jennings and Rather and the Evening News*, 30, 68.

51. Robert Goldberg and Gerald Goldberg, *Anchors — Brokaw, Jennings and Rather and the Evenings News*, 33.

52. David Halberstam, *The Powers That Be* (New York: Alfred A. Knopf, 1979), 388.

53. Peter Collier and David Horowitz, *The Kennedys — An American Dream* (New York: Summit Books, 1984), 285.

54. Barbara Matusow, *The Evening Stars*, 74.

55. David Brinkley, *David Brinkley*, 110.

56. Robert Goldberg and Gerald Goldberg, *Anchors — Brokaw, Jennings and Rather and the Evening News*, 67.

57. Michael Kaufman, "Chet Huntley, 62, Is Dead; Gave News to Millions," *New York Times* (21 March 1974), 44.

58. "The Evening Duet," *Time* (19 October 1959), 92.

59. Edwin Diamond, *Sign Off, the Last Days of Television* (Cambridge, Mass.: MIT Press, 1982), 70. Reprinted by permission of MIT Press, ©1982, all rights reserved.

60. Walter Cronkite, phone interview with author (15 March 2002).

61. David Halberstam, *The Powers That Be*, 422.

62. David Halberstam, *The Powers That Be*, 422.

63. Joe Derby, "The Huntley-Brinkley Bandwagon," 26.

64. Aline Mosby, "Aline Talks to Chet," 29.

65. Thomas Thompson, "Chet Heads for the Hills," 33.

66. J. Liston, "At Home with Chet Huntley," 17.

67. William Whitworth, "Profiles," 38.

68. Robert Goldberg and Gerald Goldberg, *Anchors—Brokaw, Jennings and Rather and the Evening News*, 133; Marc Gunter, *The House that Roone Built* (New York: Little Brown and Co., 1994), 63. Reprinted by permission of International Creative Management, Inc., rights owner, ©1994, all rights reserved.

69. Daniel Hallin, *The Uncensored War: The Media and Vietnam* (New York: Oxford University Press, 1986), 11–12. Reprinted by permission of Oxford University Press, © 1986, all rights reserved.

70. Telstar satellite broadcast, NBC Television Network (23 July 1962).

71. Edward Bliss, Jr., *Now the News: The Story of Broadcast Journalism,* 305.

72. Theodore White, *America In Search of Itself*, 174.

73. Howard Prouty, ed., *Variety Television Reviews*, VIII:1963–1965 (11 September 1965).

74. "Now One Full Hour of News on 4" (NBC News ad), *New York Times* (9 September 1968).

75. Jay Gould, "TV: ? Hour of Huntley and Brinkley," *New York Times* (10 September 1963), 79.

76. Howard Prouty, ed., *Variety Television Reviews*, VIII: 1963–1965 (11 September 1963).

77. Gary Gates, *Air Time*, 104–105; "CBS and NBC: Walter vs. Chet and Dave," *Newsweek* (23 September 1963), 62.

78. Kendall Hoyt and Frances Leighton, *Drunk Before Dawn: The Behind the Scenes Story of the Washinton Press Corps* (Englewood Cliffs, N. J.: Prentice-Hall, Inc., 1979), 337.

79. David Brinkley and Chet Huntley, "How They Survived 10 Years of TV — And Each Other," *New York Times* (23 October 1966), Section II:19.

80. Lawrence Lichty and Malachi Topping, *American Broadcasting* (New York: Hastings House, 1975), 422, 423. Reprinted by permission of Hastings House/Daytrips Publishers, © 1975, all rights reserved.

81. Paul Gardner, "Anniversary Time for a Top Team," 13.

82. Lawrence Lichty and Malachi Topping, *American Broadcasting*, 424.

83. "NBC News to tell it in Color, Every Day, starting in Fall," *New York Times* (15 August 1965), 49; NBC Biography (David Brinkley) (8 August 1968); Lawrence Lichty and Malachi Topping, *American Broadcasting*, 426.

84. Howard Prouty, ed., *Variety Television Reviews*, VIII:1963–1965 (17 November 1965).

85. Robert Goldberg and Gerald Goldberg, *Anchors — Brokaw, Jennings and Rather and the Evening News*, 217.

86. Barbara Matusow, *The Evening Stars*, 79.

87. Marie Torrie, "Chet Huntley," *New York Herald-Tribune* (29 March 1956).

88. Paul Gardner, "Anniversary Time for a Top Team," 13.

89. "The Rugged Anchor Man," *Time*, 44.

90. Barbara Matusow, *The Evening Stars*, 94.

91. "A Look at Chet Huntley," *Bozeman Daily Chronicle*, 2.

92. William Whitworth, "Profiles," 43.

93. Interview with Bill Merrick, Bozeman, Mont. (10 July 2001).

94. David Brinkley and Chet Huntley, "How They Survived 10 Years of TV — And Each Other," Section II:19.

95. Jeff Kisseloff, *The Box*, 389.

96. Paul Gardner, "Anniversary Time for a Top Team," 13.

97. "A Look at Chet Huntley," *Bozeman Daily Chronicle*, 2.

98. Paul Gardner, "Anniversary Time for a Top Team," 13.

99. Chet Huntley in interview with James Fixx, "An Anniversary with Huntley and Brinkley," 176.

V. Political Conventions

1. David Brinkley, *David Brinkley*, 96.

2. Bob Doyle in Jeff Kisseloff, *The Box*, 379.

3. David Brinkley, *David Brinkley*, 97.

4. Paul Gardner, "Anniversary Time for a Top Team," 13.

5. "Huntley-Brinkley Chronicles," (advertising section), *New York Times* (4 August 1968), II:13.

6. Jack Gould, "Routine Show," *New York Times* (19 August 1956).

7. Jack Gould, "Elections on Television," *New York Times* (9 November 1958), television/radio, 17.

8. Chet Huntley, "How to Watch a Convention," *New York Times* (11 July 1960), 54.

9. Jack Gould, "TV: Nonpolitical Rivalry," *New York Times* (11 July 1960), 55.

10. Gary Gates, *Air Time*, 101.

11. Sig Mickelson, *The Decade that Shaped Television News*, 220.

12. "Television — The Viewer's Choice," *Time* (25 July 1960), 42.

13. Hollis Alpert, "TV's Unique Tandem: Huntley-Brinkley," *Coronet* (February 1961), 165.

14. Hollis Alpert, "TV's Unique Tandem: Huntley-Brinkley," 165.

15. Av Westin, *Newswatch*, 37.

16. "First Team," *Newsweek* (13 March 1961), 54. Hereafter "First Team."

17. "First Team," 54.

18. Theodore White, *The Making of the President — 1964* (New York: Atheneum Publishers, 1965), 378 note.

19. Tom Wicker, "Miller Suggests Secret Service Provide a Guard for Goldwater," *New York Times* (12 August 1964), 18.

20. David Brinkley, *David Brinkley*, 161–162.

21. David Brinkley-Chet Huntley, "How They Survived 10 Years of TV — and Each Other," II:19.

22. Reuven Frank, *Out of Thin Air*, 220; "In the Cow Palace: Toads and Brinklies," *Newsweek* (27 July 1964), 50.

23. David Brinkley, *David Brinkley*, 162.

24. "Palace Warfare," *Newsweek* (6 July 1964), 48.

25. David Brinkley-Chet Huntley, "How They Survived 10 Years of TV — and Each Other," II:19.

26. Gene Shalit and Lawrence Grossman, *Somehow It Works* (New York: Doubleday and Co., 1965), 39. Reprinted by permission of Random House, Inc., rights owner, © 1965, renewed 1993, all rights reserved.

27. David Halberstam, *The Powers That Be*, 424.

28. "Cronkite out; Trout, Mudd in," *Broadcasting* (3 August 1964), 62, This excerpt ©1964, and all below reprinted by permission of *Broadcasting and Cable*, all rights reserved; "Mudtrout on the Hook," *Newsweek* (7 September 1964), 77–78.

29. Reuven Frank, *Out of Thin Air*, 223.

30. Reuven Frank, *Out of Thin Air*, 229.

31. "Huntley-Brinkley Chronicles," II:13.

32. David Halberstam, *The Powers That Be*, 427; Reuven Frank, *Out of Thin Air*, 227; Gary Gates, *Air Time*, 116.

33. "Mudtrout on the Hook," 78.

34. Reuven Frank, *Out of Thin Air*, 229.

35. "NBC convention coverage" (advertisement), *Broadcasting* (27 July 1964), 17.

36. Gene Shalit and Lawrence Grossman, *Sometimes It Works*, 211.

37. Barry Goldwater, letter to Chet Huntley (January 10, 1973). Original in Chet Huntley Collection.

38. "Huntley-Brinkley Chronicles," II:7.

39. Barbara Matusow, *The Evening Stars*, 78.

40. Gene Shalit and Lawrence Grossman, *Somehow It Works*, 26.

41. Barry Goldwater, *With No Apologies* (New York: William Morrow and Co., 1979), 207. Reprinted by permission of HarperCollins Publishers, rights owner, © 1979 by Barry Goldwater, all rights reserved.

42. John Chancellor and Walter R. Mears, *The News Business* (New York: Harper and Row, 1983), 22. Reprinted by permission of International Creative Management, Inc., owner, ©1983, all rights reserved.

43. Reuven Frank, *Out of Thin Air*, 279.

44. Thomas Thompson, "Chet Heads for the Hills," 33.

45. William Small, *To Kill a Messenger — Television News and the Real World* (New York: Hastings House, 1970), 208. Reprinted by permission of Hastings House/Daytrips, Publishers, ©1970, renewed 1998, all rights reserved; "The post-convention uproar," *Broadcasting* (9 September 1968), 45.

46. Reuven Frank, *Out of Thin Air*, 279.

47. "Chet Huntley Reporting," NBC Radio (28 August 1968); "How deep the scars of Chicago?" *Broadcasting* (2 September 1968), 25–26.

48. William Small, *To Kill a Messenger*, 208, 214.

49. "News chiefs would do it all over again," *Broadcasting* (9 September 1968), 48.

50. Reuven Frank, *Out of Thin Air*, 286.

51. Neil Hickey, "Television in Turmoil" (first of four parts), *TV Guide* (8 February 1969). This excerpt reprinted by permission from TV Guide Magazine Group, Inc., © 1969, renewed 1997, all rights reserved.

52. "FCC Gives Networks 20 days to Reply to Chicago Complaints," *New York Times* (14 September 1968), 61.

53. "F.C.C. Questioning of News Coverage Disputed by N.B.C.," *New York Times* (29 October 1968), 94.

54. "Six Straight" (advertisement), *New York Times* (30 August 1968); same ad in *Broadcasting* (9 September 1968), 32–33.

55. Lee Cades, "Montana's Recreation Potential Enormous," *Montana Farmer-Stockman*, 14.

56. Edward Bliss, Jr., *Now the News*, 249.

VI. The 1960s: The Space Program, Vietnam, Assassinations, and Media Problems

For background information on President Eisenhower, the author is indebted to Stephen Ambrose's Eisenhower, *2 vols. (New York: Simon and Schuster, 1983, 1984). For information on the 1960s, the author is indebted to Daniel Boorstin's* The Landmark History of American People, *2 vols. (New York: Random House, 1987), revised edition.*

1. "The Evening Duet," 92.
2. Chet Huntley, *Chet Huntley's News Analysis* (New York: Pocket Books, 1966), 99. This excerpt reprinted by permission of Simon & Schuster, rights owners, ©1966, renewed 1994, all rights reserved.
3. Chet Huntley, "In the Huntley Manner," *New York Times* (3 May 1964), Television/Radio 12.
4. Reuven Frank, *Out of Thin Air*, 168
5. Gary Gates, *Air Time*, 4–5.
6. David Brinkley, *David Brinkley*, 155–156.
7. William Manchester, *The Death of a President* (New York: Harper and Row, 1967), 190, 354. This excerpt reprinted by permission of HarperCollins, rights owner, ©1967, all rights reserved.
8. William Manchester, *The Death of a President*, 530.
9. William Manchester, *The Death of a President*, 443.
10. Gary Gates, *Air Time*, 5.
11. Gene Shalit and Lawrence Grossman, *Somehow It Works*, 211.
12. NBC News coverage of the Kennedy Assassination (22 November 1963).
13. "The Huntley-Brinkley Report," NBC News (22 November 1963). Hereafter "the Huntley- Brinkley Report."
14. Robert Shayon, "Mileage in Morality," *Saturday Review* (28 December 1957), 24.
15. Reuven Frank, *Out of Thin Air*, 234, 235.
16. "Live from Space," *Newsweek* (14 June 1965), 72.
17. NBC Special Report, "Tribute to Astronauts" (31 January 1967), 3–3:30 P.M.
18. Reuven Frank, *Out of Thin Air*, 290.
19. Edward Bliss, Jr., *Now the News*, 367, 368, 369.
20. Thomas Thompson, "Chet Heads for the Hills," 36.
21. "The Huntley-Brinkley Report" (7 February 1964).
22. J. Fred MacDonald, *Television and the Red Menace— The Video Road to Vietnam*, 169. Hereafter *Television and the Red Menace.*
23. Todd Gitlin, *The Sixties— Years of Hope— Days of Rage* (New York: Bantam Books, 1987), 242. This excerpt reprinted by permission of Bantam Books, a division of Random House, ©1987, all rights reserved.
24. Charles A. Bailey, *The Vietnam War According to Chet, David, Walter, Harry, Peter, Bob, Howard and Frank: A Content Analysis of Journalistic Performance by the Network Television Evening News Anchors 1965–1970* (Ph.D. dissertation, Madison: Univerity of Wisconsin, 1973), 151. Hereafter: Charles Bailey, *The Vietnam War According to Chet.* This is the best interpretation this author has found concerning this subject.
25. Charles A. Bailey, *The Vietnam War According to Chet*, 139; William Whitworth, "Profiles," 56.
26. David Schoenbrun, *On and Off the Air* (New York: E. P. Dutton, 1989), 173.
27. "The Huntley-Brinkley Report" (9 September 1963); Harold Chase and Allen Lerman, eds., *Kennedy and the Press— The News Conferences* (New York: Thomas Crowell Co., 1965), 487–488.

28. William Porter, *Assault on the Media*, 6.

29. George Kahin, *Intervention — How America Became Involved in Vietnam* (New York: Alfred A. Knopf, 1986), 142.

30. William Porter, *Assault on the Media*, 6.

31. Berma Saxton, "Huntley Raps US Foreign Policy Critics," *Billings Gazette* (15 June 1965), II:13.

32. Lee Cades, "Montana's Recreation Potential Enormous," 14.

33. Barbara Matusow, *The Evening Stars*, 94.

34. Chet Huntley, "Emphasis," NBC Radio (28 February 1968).

35. Chet Huntley, "Good Night, All!" *TV Guide* (1 August 1970), 10–11. This excerpt reprinted from TV Guide Magazine Group, Inc., © 1970, renewed 1998, all rights reserved.

36. Chet Huntley to David Frost, "What Do You Think the Kids Want?" in *The Americans* (New York: Stein and Day, 1970), 186, 187.

37. Charles A. Bailey, *The War According to Chet*, 353.

38. J. Fred MacDonald, *Television and the Red Menace*, 176, 177.

39. "The Huntley-Brinkley Report" (10 September 1965). The best chapter on news coverage on Vietnam is in David Farber, ed., *The Sixties* (Chapel Hill, N.C.: University of North Carolina Press), 1994, "That's the Way It Was," Charles Pach, Jr.; the most complete coverage is in David Hallin, *The Uncensored War: The Media and Vietnam*.

40. "The Huntley-Brinkley Report" (23 November 1965).

41. "The Most Intimate Medium," *Time* (14 October 1966), 58.

42. "The Huntley-Brinkley Report" (10 January 1966).

43. "The Huntley-Brinkley Report" (8 July 1966).

44. David Hallin, *The Uncensored War*, 161.

45. "The Huntley-Brinkley Report" (13 May 1967).

46. Robert Dallek, *Flawed Giant — Lyndon Johnson and His Times — 1961–1973* (New York: Oxford University Press, 1998), 453. Reprinted by permission of Oxford University Press, ©1998, all rights reserved. Hereafter: *Flawed Giant*.

47. "The Huntley-Brinkley Report" (18 July 1967).

48. Robert Dallek, *Flawed Giant*, 473; David Barrett, ed., *Lyndon Johnson's Vietnam Papers* (College Station, Tex.: A & M University Press, 1997), 450–451, passim.

49. Robert Dallek, *Flawed Giant*, 481.

50. David Steigerwald, *The Sixties and the End of Modern America* (New York: St. Martin's Press, 1995), 110, 109. Used by permission of Palgrave Global Publishing, rights owner, © 1995, all rights reserved.

51. David Burner, *Making Peace with the 60s* (Princeton, N.J.: Princeton University Press, 1996), 206–207. Reprinted by permission of Princeton University Press, ©1996, all rights reserved.

52. "The Huntley-Brinkley Report" (21 October 1967).

53. David Steigerwald, *The Sixties and the End of Modern America*, 111.

54. Chet Huntley, "To the Protestors of the War, Burning of Draft Cards, Profanity and Flag Burning," speech. Original in Chet Huntley collection.

55. "Outburst by Hecklers Silence Senator Fulbright at Peace Luncheon," *New York Times* (6 March 1969), 16.

56. Glen Altschuler and David Grossvogel, *Changing Channels* (Urbana, Ill.: University of Illinois Press, 1992), 179. Reprinted by permission of University of Illinois Press, ©1992, all rights reserved.

57. "The Huntley-Brinkley Report" (31 January 1968).

58. "The Huntley-Brinkley Report" (2 February 1968).

59. "The Huntley-Brinkley Report" (12 February 1968).

60. Peter Braestrup, *Big Story* (Boulder, Col.: Westview Press, 1977) (2 volumes), I:306.

61. "The Huntley-Brinkley Report" (15 February 1968).

62. Associated Press release (21 February 1968).

63. Peter Braestrup, *Big Story*, I:307.

64. "The Huntley-Brinkley Report" (16 February 1968).

65. Don Oberdorfer, *Tet!* (Garden City, N.Y.: Doubleday and Co., 1971), 242.

66. Allen Matusow, *The Unraveling of America— A History of Liberalism in the 1960s* (New York: Harper and Row, 1984), 391. This excerpt reprinted by permission of author, Allen Matusow, ©1984, all rights reserved.

67. Davis Hallin, *The Uncensored War*, 169.

68. Kathleen J. Turner, *Lyndon Johnson's Dual War: Vietnam and the Press* (Chicago, Ill.: University of Chicago Press, 1985), 223. This excerpt reprinted by permission of author, Kathleen Turner, ©1985, all rights reserved.

69. Kathleen J. Turner, *Lyndon Johnson's Dual War*, 223.

70. William Small, *To Kill a Messenger*, 124.

71. Liz Trotta, *Fighting for Air* (Columbia, Mo.: University of Missouri Press, 1991, 1994), 172–173. This excerpt reprinted by permission of the University of Missouri Press, ©1991, 1994, all rights reserved.

72. George A. Bailey, *The Vietnam War According to Chet*, 327, 329.

73. Robert Dallek, *Flawed Giant*, 500; David Brinkley reported this story on CNN's "Larry King Live" (2 December 1996).

74. Kathleen J. Turner, *Lyndon Johnson's Dual War*, 317: note 112.

75. Lyndon Johnson, *The Vantage Point* (New York: Holt, Rinehart and Winston, 1971).

76. William Porter, *Assault on the Media*, 59.

77. Richard Nixon, letter to Chet Huntley (18 January 1969). Original in Chet Huntley Collection. This excerpt reprinted by permission of K. Ross Toole Archives, Missoula, Mt., Nixon Presidential Papers Staff, National Archives, and Richard Nixon Library, Yorba Linda, Cal.

78. David Hallin, *The Uncensored War*, 185.

79. Ulysses S. G. Sharp and William Westmoreland, *Report on the War in Vietnam* (Washington, D.C.: U. S. Government Printing Office, 1964), 1.

80. Les Stobel, ed., "TV-Radio Strike," *Facts on File Yearbook* (New York: Facts on File, 13–19 April 1967), XXVII:124–125. Used by permission of Facts on File News Service, © 1967, renewed 1995, all rights reserved.

81. David Brinkley, *David Brinkley*, 214.

82. "Networks take on AFTRA strike," *Broadcasting* (3 April 1967), 92.

83. "Cancer Claims Chet, Who Swapped TV for Big Sky," *Des Moines* [Ia.] *Register* (21 March 1974), 2.

84. Les Strobel, "TV-Radio Strike," XXVII:125.

85. "Rusk Planning to Honor Picket Line in TV Strike," *New York Times* (31 March 1967), 75.

86. "Networks take on AFTRA strike," 93.

87. "Rush Planning to Honor Picket Line in TV Strike," 75; David Brinkley, *David Brinkley*, 215.

88. "Executives on Air in TV-Radio Strike," *New York Times* (30 March 1967), 47.

89. David Brinkley, *David Brinkley*, 215.

90. Executives on Air in TV-Radio Strike," 47.

91. William Whitworth, "Profiles," 38.

92. Barbara Matusow, *The Evening Stars*, 95.

93. Liz Trotta, *Fighting for Air*, 50–51.

94. Fred Ferretti, "Chet Gets Ready…," D13.

95. Reuven Frank, *Out of Thin Air*, 247.

96. Jack Gould, "TV: Strike and Rating," *New York Times* (1 April 1967), 43.

97. Robert Dallos, "Huntley and Brinkley United— Briefly," *New York Times* (4 April 1967), 87.

98. "Chet— David: reunion in Chicago," *Broadcasting* (10 April 1967), 74.

99. Robert Dallos, "Huntley and Brinkley United— Briefly," 87.

100. David Brinkley, *David Brinkley*, 216.

101. Reuven Frank, *Out of Thin Air*, 248, 249.

102. David Brinkley, *David Brinkley*, 216.

103. Reuven Frank, *Out of Thin Air*, 248.

104. Val Adams, "Huntley Accuses Actors in AFTRA," *New York Times* (19 October 1967), 95.

105. "NBC News expands roles of four correspondents," *Broadcasting* (7 August 1967), 65–66.

106. Howard Prouty, ed., *Variety TV Reviews*, IX:1966–1969 (30 August 1967).

107. William Whitworth, "Profiles," 58.

108. William Whitworth, "Profiles," 58–59.

109. Fred Ferretti, "Chet Gets Ready … ," D-13.

110. Howard Prouty, ed. *Variety TV Reviews*, IX:1966–1969 (15 November 1967).

111. "There Comes a Time: American Revolution '63," NBC Television Network documentary (2 September 1963).

112. Robert Kintner, "Television and the Real World," *Harper's* (magazine) 230:6 (June 1965), 94.

113. "There Comes a Time: American Revolution '63."

114. Robert Kintner, "Television and the Real World," 94–95; David Brinkley as quoted in Robert Kintner, "Television and the Real World," 94.

115. Francis Valeo, *Mike Mansfield Majority Leader* (Armonk, N.Y.: M. E. Sharpe, 1999), 58, 58–59, 75

116. Terry Anderson, *The Sixties* (New York: Longman, 1999), 109.

117. Edward Epstein, *News from Nowhere: Television and the News* (New York: Random House, 1973), 23–24. This excerpt reprinted by permission of Sterling Lord Literistic, Inc., ©1973 by Edward Epstein, all rights reserved. Hereafter: *News from Nowhere*.

118. David Brinkley, "The Huntley-Brinkley Report," (7 June 1968).

119. David Hallin, *The Uncensored War*, 4, 5.

120. Edward Epstein, *News from Nowhere*, 10.

121. Joe Derby, letter to Tippy Huntley (29 October [1974?]). Original in Chet Huntley Collection.

122. Jack Smith, interview with Chet Huntley (Smith Features) (22 February 1974), 4.

123. Martin Carr, "Shame is Still the Harvest," *New York Times* (12 July 1970), D-13.

124. Fred Ferretti, "TV: Plight of the Migrant Worker," *New York Times* (17 July 1970), 63.

125. Fred Ferretti, "Coca-Cola Denies Link to Farm Ills," *New York Times* (17 July 1970), 63.

126. William Porter, *Assault on the Media*, 8–9.

127. Dick Hawkins, "Whatever Happened to Chet Huntley?" KATU-TV, Portland, Ore. (December 1973).

128. John Coyne, Jr., *The Impudent Snobs — Agnew vs. The Intellectual Establishment* (New Rochelle, N.Y.: Arlington House, 1972), 16.

129. James Keogh, *President Nixon and the Press* (New York: Funk and Wagnalls, 1972), 93.

130. "The Huntley-Brinkley Report" (20 October 1969).

131. James Keogh, *President Nixon and the Press*, 93.

132. Richard Nixon, *The Memoirs of Richard Nixon* (New York: Touchstone Books, 1978, 1990), 411. Reprinted by permission of Warner Books, rights owner, ©1978, all rights reserved. Nixon did not name newscasters in his autobiography. Theodore Lippman, Jr. in his book, *Spiro Agnew's America*, 189, said Nixon did not see Agnew's "text in advance." Lippman stated Nixon's influence on the text was "indirect." William Porter stated in his book, *Assault on the Media*, p. 49, that Nixon had nothing to do with the speech.

133. Herbert Parmet, *Richard Nixon and His America* (New York: Konecky and Konecky, 1990), 585.

134. "Transcript of Address by Spiro Agnew Criticizing Television on Its Coverage of the News," *New York Times* (14 November 1969), 24.

135. Reuven Frank, *Out of Thin Air*, 297.

136. Theodore Lippman, Jr., *Spiro Agnew's America*, 194–195.

137. Richard Salant in Michael Beaubien and John Wyeth, Jr., eds., *Views on the News: The Media and Public Opinion*, 16–17.

138. Richard Nixon, *The Memoirs of Richard Nixon*, 412.

139. MacPherson cartoon, *New York Times* (23 November 1969), section 4, page 13.

140. Thomas Brady, "Dispute Over Agnew's Speech Keeps on Boiling," *New York Times* (16 November 1969), 78.

141. Liz Trotta, *Fighting for Air*, 188.

142. Richard Salant in Michael Beaubein and John Wyeth Jr., eds., *Views on the News*, 17. An excellent study on this issue can be found in this chapter by Mr. Salant.

143. Goodman was quoted in Richard Nixon, *The Memoirs of Richard Nixon*, 412.

144. Lawrence Van Gelder, "Huntley Defends Journalists' Acts," *New York Times* (25 March 1970), 95; Les Strobel, ed., *Facts on File Yearbook 1970* (16–22 April 1970), XXX:273.

145. Thomas Thompson, "Chet Heads for the Hills," 36.

146. Chet Huntley, "Good Night, All!" 11. This excerpt reprinted by permission from TV Guide Magazine Group, Inc., © 1970, renewed 1998, all rights reserved.

147. Fred Ferretti, "Chet Gets Ready … ," D-13.

148. "A Look at Chet Huntley," *Bozeman Daily Chronicle* (21 March 1974), 2.

149. "Huntley to be Missed," *Bozeman Daily Chronicle* (21 March 1974), 4.

150. David Schoenbrun, *On and Off the Air*, 189–190.

151. Barbara Ryan, "Chet Huntley Reports Everything Fine in Montana," *Denver* [Col.] *Post* (2 May 1971), 23:8. By permission of *Denver Post,* ©1971, renewed 1999, all rights reserved.

152. Thomas Thompson, "Chet Heads for the Hills," 36.

153. Chet Huntley, "Letters to the Editor," *Life* (17 August 1970), 17.

154. "Huntley denies some harsh words," *Broadcasting* (27 July 1970), 61. Hereafter: "Huntley denies some harsh words."

155. Thomas Thompson, "Letters to the Editor, *Life* (22 July 1970), 17.

156. James Keogh, *President Nixon and the Press*, 131.

157. "Newsmakers," *Newsweek* (17 August 1970), 52.

158. "Chet Embarrassed, He Writes Nixon," *Billings Gazette* (7 August 1970).

159. James Naughton, "White House Papers Outline Pressure on Networks, *The New York Times* (2 November 1973), 24.

160. "Huntley denies some harsh words," 62.

161. Memo (16 July 1970), quoted in Michael Beaubein and John Wyeth, Jr., eds., *Views on the News*, 23–24.

162. Quoted in William Porter, *Assault on the News*, 271.

163. H. R. Haldeman, *The Haldeman Diaries* (New York: G. P. Putnam's Sons [Penguin Putnam] 1994) (14 July 1970, 25 July 1970), 182, 185. Reprinted by permission of Penguin Putnam, Inc., ©1994, all rights reserved; in checking books by John Dean and Henry Kissinger, no entries were found concerning Nixon's and/or Agnew's media problem.

164. "Huntley denies some harsh words," 62. See also Joseph Spears, *Presidents and the Press* (Cambridge, Mass.: MIT Press, 1984), 144–145. Reprinted by permission of MIT Press, ©1984, all rights reserved.

165. "Chet Huntley has his say — at last," *Broadcasting* (20 July 1970), 52.

166. William Buckley, ed. (editorial), *National Review*, XXII:29 (28 July 1970), 268. Reprinted by permission of *National Review*, ©1970, renewed 1998, all rights reserved.

167. Chris Cosgriffe, "Chatting About Chet," *Billings Gazette* (July 1970).

168. In a postscript, this writer noticed that Walter Cronkite and Barry Goldwater wrote several pages in their biographies that mirrored what Chet said in a couple of sentences: Barry Goldwater, *Goldwater* (New York: Doubleday and Co., 1988), 255–258; Walter

Cronkite, *A Reporter's Life* (New York: Alfred A. Knopf, 1996), 221, 224–225, 227–228. Francis Valeo in *Mike Mansfield Majority Leader* (p. 223) stated that Senator Mansfield saw President Nixon as "personally insecure." This writer also checked several Nixon biographies and mention of the media was not part of them, except as noted above.

169. "A Look at Chet Huntley" (21 March 1974), 2.

170. "Huntley denies some harsh words," 72.

171. "Brinkley Announces Huntley's Departure from N.B.C. August 1," *New York Times* (17 February 1970), 87.

172. David Brinkley, *David Brinkley*, 218.

173. S Matloff, "The Saco Kid," *Newsweek* (7 October 1968), 114.

174. Fred Ferretti, "Chet Huntley is Expected to Leave N.B.C. Next Year," *New York Times* (17 October 1969), 95.

175. Reuven Frank, *Out of Thin Air*, 314.

176. Reuven Frank, *Out of Thin Air*, 314.

177. "Brinkley Announces Huntley's Departure from N. B. C. August 1," 87.

178. Thomas Thompson, "Chet Heads for the Hills," 36.

179. "More legwork in NBC's new news," *Broadcasting* (3 August 1970), 42.

180. Lawrence Laurent, "Chet Huntley's Goodbye," C-8.

181. Bob Williams, "Chet gets NBC Horse and heads Out West," *New York Post* (1 August 1970), 2.

182. "The Huntley-Brinkley Report" (31 July 1970).

183. "CBS Evening News with Walter Cronkite" (31 July 1970), by permission of CBS News, New York, a division of CBS Broadcasting, Inc., ©1970, renewed 1998, all rights reserved.

184. "ABC Evening News" (31 July 1970). Reprinted by permission of ABC News, New York, ©1970, renewed 1998, all rights reserved.

185. Michael Beaubein and John Wyeth, Jr., eds., *Views on the News*, xiii.

186. Liz Trotta, *Fighting for Air*, 204–205.

187. "Good Night to All That," *Newsweek* (17 August 1970), 60.

VII. Tippy

1. John Garraty and Mark Carnes, "Chet Huntley," *American National Biography*, II:549.

2. Bill Ewald, "First Team," 57.

3. Grace Kenfield, "Chet Has Interesting Career," 1; J. Liston, "At Home with Chet Huntley," 17.

4. Tippy Huntley, letter to Ron Berler (3 May 1974). Original in Chet Huntley Collection.

5. "Chet Huntley Weds Miss Tipton Stringer," *New York Times* (8 March 1959), I:95.

6. Grace Kenfield, "Chet Has Interesting Career," 1.

7. Vernon Scott, "Chet Huntley: Barnyard Still in His Blood," *Billings Gazette* (22 September 1963), 10.

8. J. Liston, "At Home with Chet Huntley," 82.

9. Florence Trout, "Tippy Today," *Bozeman Daily Chronicle* (7 August 1977), 1.

VIII. Other Events

1. Grace Kenfield, "Chet Huntley Has Interesting Career," 1.

2. J. Liston, "At Home with Chet Huntley," 82.

3. "Chet Huntley Has Farm Relaxation," *Big Timber Pioneer* (10 November 1963), 10; Jay Gould, "Huntley says Vandalism Ruined Farm," *New York Times* (9 August 1967), 78.

4. Edith Efron, "The Travels of Chet Huntley," 7. This excerpt reprinted from *TV Guide* (magazine), Inc., ©1965, renewed 1993, all rights reserved.

5. Harold Gal, "F.C.C. Rebukes N.B.C.," *New York Times* (14 September 1968), 63.

6. "Huntley Drops Name from Beef Brand," *Great Falls Tribune* (1 April 1964), 23. This excerpt © 1964, and all related articles below reprinted by permission of *Great Falls Tribune*, © various, all rights reserved; Harold Gal, "F.C.C. Rebukes N.B.C.," 63.

7. Edith Efron, "The Travels of Chet Huntley," 8. This excerpt reprinted by permission from TV Guide Magazine Group, Inc., © 1965, all rights reserved.

8. "Chet Huntley Dies of Cancer in Resort Home," (Nashville) *Tennessean* (21 March 1974), 6.

9. Harold Gal, "F.C.C. Rebukes N.B.C.," 63.

10. "Backers of Meat Acts Granted Air Time to Answer Huntley," *New York Times* (12 June 1968), 28.

11. Harold Gal, "F.C.C. Rebukes N.B.C.," 63.

12. "N.B.C. News Staff Must Bare Finances," *New York Times* (28 October 1968), 95.

13. "N.B.C. News Staff Must Bare Finances," 95.

14. John Kuglin, "Steam Plant Dedicated," *Great Falls Tribune* (23 September 1968), 2.

15. "N.B.C. News Staff Must Bare Finances," 95.

16. Fred Ferretti, "Chet Gets Ready…," D-13.

17. Harold Gal, "F.C.C. Rebukes N.B.C.," 63; Jay Gould, "Huntley Says Vandalism Ruined Farm," 78.

18. "Chet Huntley Has Farm Relaxation," 10; "Mayor Denied Chet Wronged," *Independent-Record* (Helena, Mont.) (11 August 1967). This excerpt © 1967 and all related articles below reprinted by permission of the *Independent-Record*, © various, all rights reserved; Jay Gould, "Huntley Says Vandalism Ruined Farm," 78.

19. Fred Ferretti, Chet Gets Ready…," D-13.

20. Harold Gal, "F.C.C. Rebukes N.B.C.," 63; William Whitworth, "Profiles," 36.

21. William Whitworth, "Profiles," 36.

22. Donald Freeman, "Chet Huntley's Eye on the Past," B-7.

23. "New Books," *New York Times* (30 September 1968), 44.

24. S. Matloff, "The Saco Kid," 112.

25. "Chet Huntley — The Generous Years" (ad), *New York Times* (6 October 1968), 25.

26. *New York Times Review of Books* (19 December 1968), 20.

27. "Books of the Times," *New York Times* (19 October 1968), 35.

28. *New York Times Book Review* (17 November 1968), VII:44.

29. Phyllis White, "New of Fawcett-Crest Books" (news release) (12 January 1970). This excerpt reprinted by permission of Fawcett-Crest, a division of Random House, ©1970, renewed 1998, all rights reserved.

30. Donald Freeman, "Chet Huntley's Eye on the Past," B-7.

31. Chet Huntley, *Generous Years*, 194.

IX. Big Sky

1. Carlos Schwantes, *Pacific Northwest — An Interpretative History* (Lincoln, Neb.: University of Nebraska, 1989, 1996), 314–315. Reprinted by permission of University of Nebraska Press, ©1989, 1996, all rights reserved.

2. Michael Malone, Richard Roeder and William Lang, *Montana A History of Two Centuries*, 393–397, passim.

3. Fred Ferretti, "Chet Huntley Is Expected to Leave NBC Next Year," *New York Times* (17 October 1969), 95.

4. Janet Cronin and Dorothy Vick, *Montana's Gallatin Canyon* (Missoula, Mont.: Mountain Press Publishing Co., 1992), 232. Reprinted by permission of Mountain Press Publishing Co., ©1992, all rights reserved.

5. "Gallatin Canyon Development Traced," *Bozeman Daily Chronicle* (15 February 1970, etc.) (a three-part series).

6. Janet Cronin and Dorothy Vick, *Montana's Gallatin Canyon*, 73, 128, 141, 200–201, 229, 230, 231.

7. Lee Cades, "Montana's Recreation Potential Enormous," 12.

8. Chuck Rightmire, "Chet 'Had to Find an Angel,'" *Billings Gazette*, date unknown, in Chet Huntley file, Montana Historical Society Library, Helena, Mt.

9. "Famous Skier Checks Lone Mountain Site," *Bozeman Daily Chronicle* (11 February 1970), 1. Carol Bradley, "Big Sky — Ski resort eclipses developer's down-to-earth dream," *Great Falls* [Mont.] *Tribune* (12 December 1999), 1A; Rick and Susie Graetz, *Big Sky* (no publisher mentioned, ca. 2000), 10. Reprinted by permission of Rick Graetz. Graetz' booklet is the best short history this writer found on the Big Sky Resort.

10. Hugh Van Swearingen, "Chet Huntley Eyes State Resources," *Independent-Record* (Helena, Mont.) (8 August 1969), 1.

11. "Newsmakers," *Newsweek* (27 October 1969), 67. See also quoted in Fred Ferretti, "Chet Huntley Is Expected To Leave NBC Next Year," 95.

12. E. W. Kenworthy, "Chet Huntley, in Montana, Likes Not Living by Clock," *New York Times* (16 May 1971), 66.

13. Press release, Chrysler Corporation (16 February 1970), 1-2.

14. Ron Peterson, "Palmer and Killy Enter Development Picture," *Bozeman Daily Chronicle* (19 February 1970), 1.

15. Rick and Susie Graetz, *Big Sky*, 10–11.

16. A. B. Guthrie, Jr., letter to Chet Huntley (17 July 1970). Original in Chet Huntley Collection.

17. Don Schanche, "Good Night NBC … HELLO MONTANA!" *Today's Health* (May 1972), 56.

18. "Chet Speaks His Mind," *National Wildlife* (June-July 1972), 35.

19. "Huntley-Chrysler Verify Resort Project Plans, *Bozeman Daily Chronicle* (16 February 1970), 1, 10; Bill Brewster, "Big Sky of Montana Complex is Revealed," *Billings Gazette* (16 February 1970), 1, 6; J. D. Holmes, "Chet Huntley Unveiled Plans for 'Big Sky of Montana,'" *Great Falls Tribune* (17 February 1970), 1A.

20. "Big Sky Firm Picks Director," *Billings Gazette* (30 June 1970).

21. Florence Trout, "Tippy Today," 1.

22. Thomas Thompson, "Chet Heads for the Hills," 36.

23. E. W. Kenworth, "Resort Plan Sparks Montana Controversy," *New York Times* (31 May 1971), 6.

24. "Chrysler's Magic?" (letter to the editor), *Billings Gazette* (3 March 1970), 2.

25. Harvey Griffin, quoted in Anthony Ripley, "Chet and the Big Sky Issue," *Billings Gazette* (25 April 1970); Harvey Griffin, "Big Sky Isn't Set Yet," *Billings Gazette* (16 July 1970), 2.

26. Both Berg and Keightley are quoted in Anthony Ripley, "Huntley's Resort Meets Protest," *New York Times* (25 April 1970), II:60.

27. Anthony Ripley, "Huntley's Resort Meets Protest," II:60

28. Robert Smith, "The Big Sky Development," *American West* (September 1975), XII:5 62–63.

29. Anthony Ripley, "Huntley's Resort Meets Protest," II:31

30. "Federation Says Chet Misinformed," *Billings Gazette* (13 June 1970).

31. E. W. Kenworthy, "Resort Plan Sparks Controversy," 6; Robert Smith, "The Big Sky Development," 62.

32. Gary Svee, "Chet: I'll Quit Big Sky if it Hurts Environment," *Billings Gazette* (14 June 1971).

33. Richard Balough, "Good Knight, Chet," *Chicago Daily News* (5 September 1972), III:27.

34. "Huntley Denies Report," *Bozeman Daily Chronicle* (28 August 1973), 1.

35. Jonathan Wiesel, "Big Sky," *Montana* (magazine) (November-December 2000), 48–49. Reprinted by permission of the author, Jonathan Wiesel, ©2000, all rights reserved.

36. Robert Smith, "The Big Sky Development," XII:5; 62.

37. Bill Brewster, "Big Sky Permit May Stir Criticism," *Billings Gazette* (11 May 1970), 1.

38. Ron Peterson, "Palmer and Killy Enter Development Picture," 1.

39. Ron Peterson, "Palmer and Killy Enter Development Picture," 1.

40. E. W. Kenworthy, "Environmental Chief Silent on 2 U. S. Plans," *New York Times* (14 August 1971), 21.

41. James Naughton, "Dean Ends Testimony Story Unshaken; Senators Hint They Want Nixon to Reply," *New York Times* (30 June 1973), 15; E. W. Kenworthy, "Ecology Unit Sends Dean Data to Court," *New York Times* (5 July 1973), 17.

42. E. W. Kenworthy, "Resort Plan Sparks Montana Controversy," 6; Dennis Curran, "Big Sky," *Billings Gazette* (12 September 1971), 1; E. W. Kenworthy, "Trade of Forest Land for Montana Resort," *New York Times* (22 April 1972), 66; E. W. Kenworthy, "Ecology Unit Sends Dean Data to Court," 17.

43. Dennis Curran, "Big Sky," 1.

44. James Clarity, "Notes on People," *New York Times* (15 September 1973), 21.

45. Arthur Hutchinson, "Federal Funds Are Sought for Road Into Big Sky Resort," *Independent-Record* (Helena, Mont.) (4 May 1971).

46. "U. S. Funds Barred for Road to Montana Resort," *New York Times* (13 December 1972), 44.

47. "U. S. Funds Barred for Road to Montana Resort," 44.

48. "U. S. Funds Barred for Road to Montana Resort," 44.

49. Robert Smith, "The Big Sky Development," 63.

50. "Huntley Project Hits Stretch of Rough Sledding," *Great Falls Tribune* (30 June 1970), C-4.

51. Bill Brewster, "MSU to Study Big Sky," *Billings Gazette* (1 July 1970), 8.

52. Dennis Curran, "Big Sky," 5.

53. E. W. Kenworthy, "Resort Plan Sparks Controversy," 6.

54. Dennis Curran, "Big Sky, 1.

55. Dennis Curran, "Big Sky," 1.

56. George Beebe, "Pollution in the Big Sky," *Miami Herald* (2 June 1970).

57. Richard Balough, "Good Knight, Chet," 27.

58. Dennis Curran, "Big Sky," 5.

59. Dennis Curran, "Big Sky," 1.

60. "Big Sky Dedication Scheduled Saturday," *Bozeman Daily Chronicle* (22 March 1974), 1, 2.

61. Gary Svee, "Chet: I'll quit Big Sky if it Hurts the Environment."

62. Gary Svee, "Chet: I'll quit Big Sky if it Hurts the Environment."

63. "MSU Students Back Big Sky," *Billings Gazette* (3 March 1970).

64. Bill Brewster, "Chamber Supports Chet's Project," *Bozeman Daily Chronicle* (13 March 1970), 7; Anthony Ripley, "Huntley's Resort Meets Protest," II:31.

65. William Merrick, interview with author, Bozeman, Montana (10 July 2001).

66. "Exponent sports editor makes good," *Exponent* (newspaper of Montana State University), Bozeman, Mont. (27 May 1970), 5. This excerpt reprinted by permission of the *Exponent,* ©1970, renewed 1998. All rights reserved.

67. "Welcome to the Big Sky Country" (editorial), *Bozeman Daily Chronicle* (2 August 1970), 4.

68. "Don't Criticize Chet Huntley, Look in your Own Mirror RE: Big Sky Mont. Criticism," *Park County News* (Livingston, Mont.) (12 March 1970).

69. "Fish and Game Back the Big Sky Complex," *Billings Gazette* (13 March 1970), 7.

70. Rob Barnes, "Mike Likes Chet's Big Sky Idea," *Billings Gazette* (29 March 1970), 3.

71. E. W. Kenworthy, "Chet Huntley, in Montana, Likes Not Living by Clock," *New York Times* (16 May 1971), 66.

72. E. W. Kenworthy, "Chet Huntley, in Montana, Likes Not Living by Clock," 66.

73. E. W. Kenworthy, "Chet Huntley, in Montana, Likes Not Living by Clock," 66.

74. Don Schanche, "Good Night, NBC ... HELLO MONTANA!" 54, 57, 58.

75. E. W. Kenworthy, "Chet Huntley, in Montana, Likes Not Living by Clock," 66.

76. E. W. Kenworthy, "Chet Huntley, in Montana, Likes Not Living by Clock," 66.

77. Carol Bradley, "Big Sky — Ski resort eclipses developer's down-to-earth dream," 6A.

78. James Sterba, "Resort Opens 3 Days After Huntley's Death," *New York Times* (25 March 1974), 20.

79. Carol Bradley, "Big Sky — Ski resort eclipses developer's down-to-earth dream," 6A.

80. "Chet Huntley Speaks His Mind," 35.

81. James Sterba, "Resort Opens 3 Days After Huntley's Death," 20.

82. Bill Brewster, "Big Sky Dedicated," *Bozeman Daily Chronicle* (24 March 1974), 1.

83. James Sterba, "Resort Opens 3 Days After Huntley's Death," 20.

84. James Sterba, "Resort Opens 3 Days After Huntley's Death," 20.

X. Other Interests/Honors

1. "Huntley Scheduled to Broadcast Again," *Independent-Record* (Helena, Mont.) (18 May 1970).

2. William "Bill" Merrick, Bozeman, Mont., interview with author (10 July 2001).

3. Fred Ferretti, "Chet Gets Ready...," 95.

4. William Whitworth, "Profiles," 60.

5. Hugh Van Swearingen, "Chet Huntley Eyes State Resources," 1.

6. "Chet says Politics are Out," *Independent-Record* (8 December 1970), 12.

7. Robert Sanford, "Two Parties Courted Huntley," *St. Louis Post-Dispatch* (19 November 1971), 15A.

8. E. W. Kenworth, "Chet Huntley, in Montana, Likes Living by Clock," 66.

9. William Small, *Political Power and the Press* (New York: W. W. Norton and Co., Inc., 1972), 306. Reprinted by permission of W. W. Norton and Co., Inc., ©1972, all rights reserved.

10. William Small, *Political Power and the Press*, 338.

11. Barbara Ryan, "Chet Huntley Reports Everything Fine in Montana," 23.

12. Philip Dougherty, "Advertising: Newsweek Shifts Executives," *New York Times* (23 March 1972), 73.

13. Michael Beaubein and John Wyeth, Jr., *Views on the News*, xi.

14. Michael Beaubein and John Wyeth, Jr., *Views on the News*, xi.

15. Michael Beaubein and John Wyeth, Jr., *Views on the News*, xi.

16. Don Schanche, "Good Night, NBC ... HELLO MONTANA!" 57.

17. "Good Bye, Chet," *Newsweek* (10 April 1972), 57.

18. Alan Kriegsman, "The Incredible Peddlers," *Washington Post* (16 March 1972), K-13. This excerpt © 1972 the *Washington Post*, reprinted with permission, all rights reserved.

19. Don Schanche, "Good Night, NBC ... HELLO MONTANA!" 57.

20. Copies in Chet Huntley Collection; Phillip Dougherty, "Advertising: Chet is Airline's Spokesman," *New York Times* (6 March 1972), 48.

21. Howard Thompson, "TV: N.B.C. Offers Samplings in a Trio of Specials," *New York Times* (21 October 1972), 67.

22. "Good Bye, Chet," *Newsweek*, 57.

23. Thomas Thompson, "Chet Heads for the Hills," 36.

24. Chet Huntley, "Represent the Best of the Democratic Tradition," Delivered before the National School Board Convention, April 7, 1973. Original speech in Chet Huntley Collection.

XI. Death

1. Don Schanche, "Good Night, NBC ... HELLO MONTANA!" 58.
2. "Chet Huntley Listed as Satisfactory," *Bozeman Daily Chronicle* (18 January 1974), 3; "Notes on People," *New York Times* (19 January 1974), 23.
3. Jack Smith, telephone interview with Chet Huntley, Smith Features (22 February 1974).
4. "Chet Huntley Dead at 62," *Bozeman Daily Chronicle* (21 March 1974), 1.
5. "A Look at Chet Huntley," *Bozeman Daily Chronicle* (21 March 1974), 3.
6. Tippy Huntley, letter to James Farley, [ca May 1974]. Original in Chet Huntley Collection.
7. "Chet Huntley Dead at 62," 1.
8. Cemetery Records, Bozeman, Mont., City Hall.
9. Chet Huntley Dies of Cancer in Resort Home," (Nashville) *Tennessean* (21 March 1974), 6.
10. "Chet Huntley Dead at 62," 1, 2.
11. "Chet Huntley dies; former TV newsman," (Phoenix) *Arizona Republic* (21 March 1974), A16.
12. "CBS News with Walter Cronkite" (20 March 1974).
13. Richard Nixon, letter to Tippy Huntley (21 March 1974). Original in Chet Huntley Collection. Reprinted by permission of K. Ross Toole Archives, Richard Nixon Presidential Papers Staff, Bethseda, Md., and Richard Nixon Library, Yorba Linda, Cal.
14. Hubert Humphrey, letter to Tippy Huntley (21 March 1974). Original in Chet Huntley Collection.
15. Henry Jackson, letter to Tippy Huntley (22 March 1974). Original in Chet Huntley Collection. Used by permission of Mrs. Helen Jackson.
16. "Anchorman" (editorial), *New York Times* (24 March 1974), 4.
17. "Huntley Eulogized," *Bozeman Daily Chronicle* (27 March 1974), 4.
18. Michael Beaubein and John Wyeth, Jr., *Views on the News*, 10–11.
19. "Huntley Estate Valued," *Bozeman Daily Chronicle* (20 September 1974), 4.

Epilogue

1. Carol Bradley, "Big Sky — Ski resort eclipses developer's down-to-earth dream," 1A; Rick and Susie Graetz, *Big Sky*, 27.
2. Carol Bradley, "Big Sky — Ski resort eclipses developer's down-to-earth dream," 1A, 6A.
3. Carol Bradley, "Big Sky — Ski resort eclipses developer's down-to-earth dream," 1A, 6A.
4. Rick and Susie Graetz, *Big Sky*, 28, 31.
5. Pat Simmons' summary, "Save the Gallatin Coalition," in *Gallatin Wildlife Association* (newsletter) (January 2000).
6. Nick Gevock, "Big Sky voters face decision on sewer bond issue," *Bozeman Daily Chronicle* (5 March 2002); "Voters pass bond election," *Lone Mountain Lookout* (a subsidiary of the *Bozeman Daily Chronicle*) (8 May 2002).

7. "The Company: Big Sky, A Boyne USA," on Big Sky Resort web site.

8. "25th Anniversary Season a Success," Big Sky press release (21 April 1999), on Big Sky web site.

9. "United Airlines Announces New Flights to Big Sky," Big Sky Resort press release (23 June 2000), Big Sky web site.

10. Florence Trout, "Tippy Today," B-1.

11. C. Howard MacDonald, *Voices in the Sky*, 79.

12. "Nine To Be Honored," *River Press* (Ft. Benton, Mont.), 3 January 1975.

13. Chet Huntley, *Chet Huntley's News Analysis*, 122.

Appendix A. Documentaries and Awards

1. Jeff Kisseloff, *The Box — An Oral History of Television — 1920–1961*, 379.

2. Reuven Frank, *Out of Thin Air*, 91–95.

3. Robert Kintner, "Television and the Real World, *Harper's* (magazine) (June 1965), 94.

4. Beverly Keever, Carolyn Martindale, Mary Ann Weston, eds., *US News Coverage of Racial Minorities — A Sourcebook, 1934–1996* (Westport, Ct.: Greenwood Press, 1997).

5. *Variety Television Reviews*, "Second Agony of Atlanta," New York: Garland Publishing, Inc., 1989, VI:1957–1959 (4 February 1959); *Variety Television Reviews*, "Followup Comment — Chet Huntley," VI:1957–1959 (11 February 1959), used by permission of *Variety* (magazine), copyright owners, © 1957–1959, all rights reserved; Jay Gould, "Television: Controversial Viewpoint of Integration," *New York Times* (2 February 1959), 49; Robert Kintner, "Mailbag: A Defense," *New York Times* (1 March 1959), section 2:13; Reuven Frank, *Out of Thin Air*, 143.

6. Howard Bigart, "Capetown Irked TV Talk Here," *New York Times* (22 April 1960), 9.

7. *Variety Television Reviews*, VII:1960–1961 (22 November 1961).

8. Robert Dallos, "Huntley and Brinkley United — Briefly," 87.

9. C. Howard MacDonald, *Voices in the Big Sky*, 119.

10. James Strauss, executive editor, "100 Montanans of the Twentieth Century," *Great Falls Tribune* (19 December 1999), 29.

11. Richard Stolley, ed., *Our Century in Pictures* (Boston: Little, Brown and Co., ca. 1999), 261.

Appendix B. Selected Speeches and Radio Commentaries

1. CBS Radio Network (6 December 1942). Used by permission of CBS Broadcasting, Inc., © 1942, renewed 1970, 1998, all rights reserved.

2. ABC Radio Network (3 January 1955). Used by permission of ABC News, © 1955, renewed, all rights reserved.

3. Original in Chet Huntley Collection.

4. "Perspective," NBC Radio Network (7 March 1969). Used by permission of National Broadcasting Company, Inc. (NBC), © 1969, renewed 1997, all rights reserved.

5. *New York Times* (3 November 1970). Used by permission of the *New York Times*, © 1970, renewed 1998, all rights reserved.

6. Original in Chet Huntley Collection.

7. Original in Chet Huntley Collection.

8. Original in Chet Huntley Collection.

Bibliography

"About Time," *New Republic*, 130 (25 January 1954), 4:3–4.

Ad for *The Generous Years* by Random House, in *New York Review of Books* (19 December 1968), 20.

Ad, "Now One Full Hour of News on 4." *New York Times* (9 September 1963).

Adams, Van. "Huntley Accuses Actors in AFTRA." *New York Times* (19 October 1967), 95.

Ads in *Broadcasting* (13 July 1964), 16–17; (27 July 1964), 16–17; (19 August 1968), 13–14.

Advertisement for Big Sky Resort — beautiful 5-page color spread, *Ski* (magazine) (December 1973).

Allison, Callie. "A Tribute to Chet Huntley." *Jefferson Valley News* (Whitehall, Mont.) (28 March 1974), 8.

Alpert, Hollis. "TV's Unique Tandem: Huntley-Brinkley." *Coronet* (February 1961), 162–169.

Altschuler, Glenn, and David Grossvogel. *Changing Channels: America in TV Guide.* Urbana: University of Illinois Press, 1992.

Ambrose, Stephen. *Eisenhower.* 2 vols. New York: Simon and Schuster, 1983, 1984.

"Anchorman." *New York Times* (editorial) (24 March 1974), Section I:6.

"Anderson Recalls Huntley." *Bozeman Daily Chronicle* (21 March 1974), 4.

Anderson, Terry H. *The Sixties.* New York: Longman, 1999.

"As We See It" (editorial). *Bozeman Daily Chronicle* (15 February 1970), 4.

"Backer of Meat Act Is Granted Air Time to Answer Huntley." *New York Times* (12 June 1968), 28.

Bailey, Charles A. *The Vietnam War According to Chet, David, Walter, Harry, Peter, Bob, Howard and Frank: A Content Analysis of Journalistic Performance by the Network Television Evening News Anchorsmen 1965–1970.* Ph.D. dissertation, Madison : University of Wisconsin, 1973.

Baker, Russell. "Observer: Further Words on the Chet Huntley Affair." *New York Times* (4 August 1970), 30.

Balough, Richard. "Good Knight, Chet." *Chicago Daily News* (5 September 1972), Section III:25, 27.

Barnouw, Erik. *The Golden Web — A History of Broadcasting in the United States.* Volume II —1933–1953. (Three volumes.) New York: Oxford University Press, 1968.

_____. *The Image Empire — A History of Broadcasting in the United States.* Volume III — from 1953. (Three volumes.) New York: Oxford University Press, 1970.

Barrett, B. "Chet Huntley: The Fatherly Rebel." *Biographical News* (1 April 1974), 416.

Barrett, David, ed. *Lyndon B. Johnson's Vietnam Papers.* College Station, Tex.: Texas A & M University Press, 1997.

Beaubien, Michael, and John Wyeth, Jr., eds. *Views on the News: The Media and Public Opinion.* New York: New York University Press, 1994.

Beebe, George. "Pollution in the Big Sky." *Miami* [Fla.] *Herald* (2 June 1970).

"Big Developments for Our Economy." *Billings Gazette* (2 March 1970), 4.

Big Sky Chamber of Commerce brochure on Internet.

"Big Sky Dedication Scheduled Saturday." *Bozeman Daily Chronicle* (22 March 1974), 1, 2.

"Big Sky dream take shape." *Exponent* (newspaper of Montana State University, Bozeman, Mont.) (27 May 1970), 5.

"Big Sky Firm Picks Director." *Billings Gazette* (23 June 1970), 1.

"Big Sky Opens." *Ski* (magazine) (September 1973), 72–75.

Big Sky Resort.com., computer Internet website.

Bigart, Homer. "Capetown Irked by TV Talk Here." *New York Times* (22 April 1960), 9.

Bishop, Jim. *The Day Kennedy was Shot.* New York: Funk & Wagnalls, 1968.

Blair, Gwenda. *Almost Golden: Jessica Savitch and the Selling of Television News.* New York: Simon and Schuster, 1988.

Blair, William. "New Federal Standards on Meat Packing and Processing Lead to the Shutdown of 40 to 50 Plants." *New York Times* (18 June 1968), 25.

Bliss, Edward, Jr. *Now The News: The Story of Broadcast Journalism.* New York: Columbia University Press, 1991.

Boorstin, Daniel. *The Landmark History of the American People.* 2 vols. New York: Random House, 1987, revised edition.

Bowman, Lynn. *Los Angeles: Epic of a City.* Berkeley, Cal.: Howell-North Books, 1974.

Bradley, Carol. "Big Sky — Ski resort eclipses developer's down-to-Earth dream." *Great Falls* [Mont.] *Tribune* (12 December 1999), A1, A6.

Brady, Thomas. "Dispute Over Agnew's Speech Keeps on Boiling." *New York Times* (16 November 1969), 78.

Braestrup, Peter. *Big Story: How the American Press and Television Reported and Interpreted the Crisis of Tet 1968 in Vietnam and Washington.* Volume one. Boulder, Col.: Westview Press, 1977.

Brewster, Bill. "Big Sky Dedicated." *Bozeman Daily Chronicle* (24 March 1974), 1, 6.

_____. "'Big Sky of Montana' Complex is Revealed." *Billings Gazette* (16 February 1970), 1, 6.

_____. "Big Sky Permit May Stir Criticism." *Billings Gazette* (11 May 1970), 1.

_____. "Chamber Supports Chet's Project." *Billings Gazette* (13 March 1970), 7.

_____. "Fish and Game Backs the Big Sky Complex." *Billings Gazette* (13 March 1970), 7.

_____. "MSU to Study Big Sky Impact." *Billings Gazette* (1 July 1970), 8.

_____. "Speaker Had 'Distinct Superiority.'" *Billings Gazette* (19 February 1970).

Brinkley, David. *David Brinkley.* New York: Alfred A. Knopf, 1995.

Brinkley, David, and Chet Huntley. "How They Survived 10 years of TV — And Each Other." *New York Times* (23 October 1966), Section II:19.

"Brinkley Announces Huntley's Departure From N.B.C. Aug. 1." *New York Times* (17 February 1970), 87.

Brown, Robert. *Manipulating The Ether: The Power of Broadcast Radio in Thirties America,* Jefferson, N.C.: McFarland and Co., Inc., 1998.

Burner, David. *Making Peace with the 60s.* Princeton, N. J.: Princeton University Press, 1996.

Burnes, Rob. "Mike Likes Chet's Big Sky Idea." *Billings Gazette* (29 March 1970), 3.

Buzenberg, Susan, and Bill Buzenberg. *Salant, CBS, and the Battle for the Soul of Broadcast Journalism.* Boulder, Col.: Westview Press, 1999.

Byers, Paul, ed. *Encyclopedia of World Biography.* Detroit, Mich.: Gale Research, 1998, 8:49–51, "Chet Huntley," "The Huntley-Brinkley Report."

Cades, Lee. "Montana's Recreation Potential Enormous." *Montana Farmer-Stockman* (Whitehall, Mont.) (3 May 1973), 12, 13, 14, 15.

"Calm Controversialist." *Newsweek,* XLIII (19 April 1954), 54.

"Cancer Claims Chet, Who Swapped TV for Big Sky." *Des Moines Register* (21 March 1974), 2.

Carpenter, Ted. *The Captive Press.* Washington, D.C.: Cato Institute, 1995.

Carr, Martin. "Shame is Still the Harvest." *New York Times* (12 July 1970), D-13.

Cartoon by MacPherson, "Brinkley and Bluntly." *New York Times* (23 November 1969), Section IV:13.

"CBS and NBC: Walter vs. Chet and Dave." *Newsweek* (23 September 1963), 62–65.

Chaffe, Oscar. "Big Sky resort work will start soon." *Billings Gazette* (18 April 1971), 55.

Chancellor, John, and Walter Mears. *The News Business.* New York: Harper and Row, 1983.

Chase, Harold, and Allan Lerman, eds. *Kennedy and the Press — the News Conferences.* New York: Thomas Crowell Co., 1965, 487–488.

"Chester Robert Huntley." Montana State University Alumni Association biography (c1957).

"Chet-David: reunion in Chicago." *Broadcasting* (10 April 1967), 74–75.

"Chet denies political rumor." *Billings Gazette* (20 November 1971), 14.

"Chet Embarrassed, He Writes Nixon." *Billings Gazette* (7 August 1970).

"Chet Huntley." (Ad) for *The Generous Years. New York Times Book Review* (6 October 1968), 24–25.

"Chet Huntley." In: *Current Biography Yearbook 1956.* New York: H. W. Wilson Co., 1957, 290–291.

"Chet Huntley." In: Eleanore Schoenebaum, ed. *Political Profiles: The Kennedy Years.* New York: Facts on File, Inc., 1976, 242–243.

"Chet Huntley." NBC News release (8 August 1968), 1–2.

"Chet Huntley Addresses Montana Centennial Dinner at Washington D.C." *Jefferson Valley News* (Whitehall, Mont.) (7 July 1964), 7.

"Chet Huntley Dead at 62." *Bozeman Daily Chronicle* (20 March 1974), 1, 2.

"Chet Huntley dies; former TV newsman." *Arizona Republic* (Phoenix) (21 March 1974), A1, A16.

"Chet Huntley Dies of Cancer in Resort Home." *The* (Nashville) *Tennessean* (21 March 1974), 6.

"Chet Huntley Eulogizes the Three Astronauts." NBC Special Report (31 January 1967), 3–3:30 P.M.

"Chet Huntley Has Farm Relaxation." *Big Timber* [Mont.] *Pioneer* (10 October 1963), 6.

"Chet Huntley has his last say — at last." *Broadcasting* (20 July 1970), 52.

"Chet Huntley: He has risen high in the radio world." *Great Falls Tribune,* August 1943, quoted in *Jefferson Valley News,* Whitehall, Mont. (19 August 1943).

"Chet Huntley Obituary: transcript from NBC Nightly News, March 20, 1974. Congressional Record, CXX (20 March 1974), 8921–8922.

"Chet Huntley recognized as outstanding newscaster." *San Mateo* [Cal.] *Times,* July 1951, quoted in *Jefferson Valley News,* Whitehall, Mont. (12 July 1951).

"Chet Huntley sells farm, blames vandals." untitled newspaper article (9 August 1967), in Chet Huntley File, Montana Historical Society library, Helena.

"Chet Huntley Speaks His Mind — An Interview." *National Wildlife* (June 1972), X:34–35.

"Chet Huntley — The Generous Years" (ad). *New York Times* (3 October 1968), 45.

"Chet Huntley to Tell All in Helena." *Independent Record* (Helena, Mont.) (2 February 1970), 5.

"Chet Huntley Weds Miss Tipton Stringer." *New York Times* (8 March 1959), Section 1:95.

"Chet Huntley Will Receive Doctors Degree." *Belgrade* [Mont.] *Journal* (23 May 1968), 7.

"Chet Says Politics Are Out." *Independent Record* (Helena, Mont.) (8 December 1970), 12.

Clarke, Norm. "Big Sky course 'one of a kind,'— Palmer." *Billings Gazette* (16 July 1971).

Close, Harold, and Allan Lerman, eds. *Kennedy and the Press— The News Conferences.* New York: Thomas Crowell Co., 1965.

Cogley, John. "Report on Blacklisting," in *Blacklisting— Two Key Documents.* New York: Arno Press, 1971. Also in *New York Times*, 1971.

Collier, Peter, and David Horowitz. *The Kennedys: An American Drama.* New York: Summit Books, 1984.

"Commentators Deny Networks Are Irresponsible." *New York Times* (15 November 1969), 21.

Corwin, Miles. "William Conrad; Star of 'Cannon,' 'Fatman.'" *Los Angeles Times* (12 February 1994), A24.

Cosgriffe, Chris. "Chatting About Chet." *Billings Gazette* (July 1970).

"County Zoning Said Possible." *Billings Gazette* (3 May 1970), 1.

Coyne, John, Jr. *The Impudent Snobs— Agnew vs. The Intellectual Establishment.* New Rochelle, N.Y.: Arlington House, 1972.

Cronin, Janet, and Dorothy Vick. *Montana's Gallatin Canyon.* Missoula, Mont.: Mountain Press Publishing Co., 1992.

"Cronkite out, Trout, Mudd in." *Broadcasting* (3 August 1964), 62.

Cronkite, Walter. *A Reporter's Life.* New York: Alfred A. Knopf, 1996.

_____. Phone interview with author (15 March 2002).

Curran, Dennis. "Big Sky." *Billings Gazette* (13 September 1971), 1, 5.

_____. "Environmentalists rap Big Sky Highway." *Billings Gazette* (14 April 1972), 16.

Dallek, Robert. *Flawed Giant: Lyndon Johnson and His Times.* New York: Oxford University Press, 1998.

Dallos, Robert. "AFTRA Walks Out of Talks, Calls Networks' Offer 'Insulting.'" *New York Times* (3 April 1967).

_____. "Executives on Air in TV-Radio Strike." *New York Times* (30 March 1967), 1, 47.

_____. "Radio-TV Strike Ends in New Pact." *New York Times* (11 April 1967), 1, 95.

_____. "Rusk Planning to Honor Picket Line in TV Strike." *New York Times* (31 March 1967), 75.

"David Brinkley." Press release, biography from NBC (6 August 1968), 1–2.

"Deaths: William Conrad." *Broadcasting* (21 February 1994), 79.

Derby, Joe. "The Huntley-Brinkley Bandwagon." *Electronic Age* (Summer 1970), 29:3; 22–28.

_____. Letter to Tippy Huntley (29 October [1974]). Original in Chet Huntley Collection.

Diamond, Edwin. *The Last Days of Television,* Cambridge, Mass.: MIT Press, 1982.

"Don't Criticize Chet Huntley, Look in Your Own Mirror RE: Big Sky Mont. Criticism" (editorial). *Park County News* (Livingston, Mont.) (12 March 1970).

Dougherty, Philip H. "Advertising: Broadcast Credit Association." *New York Times* (18 February 1971), 56. (American Airlines sponsors Bicentennial program.)

_____. "Advertising: Chet Is Airline's Spokesman." *New York Times* (6 March 1972), 48.

_____. "Advertising: Newsweek Shifts Executives." *New York Times* (23 March 1972), 73. (Huntley joins Levine, Huntley Ad agency.)

Downing, Lyle. "Ed Wren, Chet Huntley in Farm Battle." *Independent Record* (Helena, Mont.) (21 December 1961), 1, 6.

Dunning, John. *Tune in Yesterday: The Ultimate Encyclopedia of Old-Time Radio— 1925–1976.* Englewood Cliffs, N.J.: Prentice-Hall, Inc., 1976.

Edmerson, Estelle. "A Descriptive Study of the American Negro in United States Professional Radio, 1922–1953." Master's thesis, University of California, Los Angeles, 1954.

Efron, Edith. "The Travels of Chet Huntley." *TV Guide* (19 June 1965), XIII:6–8.

Emery, Edwin. *The Press and America: An Interpretative History of the Mass Media.* 3rd ed. Englewood Cliffs, N.J.: Prentice-Hall, Inc., 1972.

Epstein, Edward. *News from Nowhere: Television and the News.* New York: Random House, 1973.

"The Evening Duet." *Time* (19 October 1959), 92.

Ewald, Bill. "First Team." *Newsweek* (13 March 1961), cover, 53–57.

"Exponent sports editor makes good." *Exponent* (newspaper of Montana State University, Bozeman, Mont.) (27 May 1970), 5.

Fabricant, Florence. "Big ranch in Big Sky is a winter wonderland for cross country skiers." *New York Times* (26 December 1996).

"A Family Affair." *Wisconsin Then and Now* (January 1971) (Madison,Wis.: Wisconsin Historical Society Press), 6.

"Famous Skier Checks Lone Mountain Site." *Bozeman Daily Chronicle* (11 February 1970), 1.

Fang, Irving. *Those Radio Commentators!* Ames, Ia: Iowa State University Press, 1977.

Farber, David, ed. *The Sixties: From Memory to History*. Chapel Hill, N.C.: University of North Carolina Press, 1994.

"F.C.C. Gives Networks 20 Days to Reply to Chicago Complaints." *New York Times* (14 September 1968), 61.

"F.C.C. Questioning of News Coverage Disputed by N.B.C." *New York Times* (29 October 1968), 94.

"Federation Says Chet Misinformed." *Billings Gazette* (13 June 1970), 1.

Fensch, Thomas, ed. *Television News Anchors*. Jefferson, N.C.: McFarland and Co., 1993.

Ferretti, Fred. "Chet Gets Ready to say, 'Goodby[e], David.'" *New York Times* (5 July 1970), Television section, D-13.

_____. "Chet Huntley Is Expected to Leave N.B.C. Next Year." *New York Times* (17 October 1969), 95.

_____. "Coca-Cola Denies Link to Farm Ills." *New York Times* (17 July 1970), 63.

_____. "TV: Plight of the Migrant Worker." *New York Times* (17 July 1970), 63.

_____. "Who Is Chet Huntley?" *New York Times*, 1970 (rewrite of above article).

Fixx, James. "An Anniversary Talk with Huntley and Brinkley." *McCall's*, XCIV:1 (October 1966), 56, 59, 176.

_____. *The Mass Media and Politics*. New York: Arno Press, 1972. Also in *New York Times*, 1972.

Frank, Reuven. *Out of Thin Air: the Brief Wonderful Life of Network News*. New York: Simon and Schuster, 1991.

Freeman, Donald. "Chet Huntley's Eye on the Past." *San Diego Union* (27 December 1968), B7.

Freeman, Paul. "Huntley's Big Sky ecologically ok." *Billings Gazette* (6 May 1971).

Frost, David. *The Americans*. New York: Stein and Day, 1970, 185–188.

Gal, Harold. "F.C.C. Rebukes N.B.C. in Huntley-Livestock Case." *New York Times* (14 September 1968), 63.

Gallagher, Susan. "Montana's Big Sky quickly filling up." *Arizona Republic* (Phoenix) (2 January 1998), E1, E2.

"Gallatin Canyon Development Traced." (Three-part history.) *Bozeman Daily Chronicle* (15, 16, 17 February 1970), 1–2.

Gardner, Paul. "Anniversary Time for a Top Team." *New York Times* (15 August 1965), X13.

Garraty, John, and Mark Carnes. "Chet Huntley." In *American National Biography*. New York: Oxford University Press, 1999, 11:548–549.

Garrett, Wilbur, ed. *Historical Atlas of the United States*. Washington, D.C.: National Geographic Society, 1988.

Gates, Gary. *Air Time*. New York: Harper and Row, 1978.

Gevock, Nick. "Big Sky voters face decision on sewer bond issue." *Bozeman Daily Chronicle* (5 March 2002).

Gitlin, Todd. *The Sixties — Years of Hope — Days of Rage*. New York: Bantam Books, 1987.

Godbout, Oscar. "Hollywood: People on TV." *New York Times* (18 December 1955), Section II:13.

Goldberg, Robert, and Gerald Goldberg. *Anchors: Brokaw, Jennings, Rather and the Evening News*. New York: Birch Lane Press, 1990.

Goldwater, Barry. *Goldwater*. New York: Doubleday, 1988.

_____. Letter to Chet Huntley (10 January 1973). Original in Chet Huntley Collection.

_____. *With No Apologies*. New York: William Morrow and Co., 1979.

"Good Buy, Chet." *Newsweek* (10 April 1972), 57.

Gould, Jay. "Huntley Says Vandalism Ruined Farm." *New York Times* (9 August 1967), 78.

_____. "N.B.C. News Ending Anchor-Teams Era." *New York Times* (19 July 1971), 1, 51.

_____. "N.B.C. News Staff Must Bare Finances." *New York Times* (28 October 1968), 95.

_____. "Radio: Emphasis on Meat." *New York Times* (20 March 1964), 67.

_____. "Television: Controversial Viewpoint on Integration." *New York Times* (2 February 1959), 49.

_____. "TV: Chet Huntley vs. Industrial Union." *New York Times* (31 March 1967), L75.

_____. "TV: Hour of Huntley and Brinkley." *New York Times* (10 September 1963), 79.

_____. "TV: Nonpolitical Rivalry." *New York Times* (11 July 1960), 55.

_____. "TV: Spotlight on News." *New York Times* (30 October 1956), 75.

_____. "TV: Strike and Ratings." *New York Times* (1 April 1967), 43.

_____. "TV: Witty Observers." *New York Times* (15 July 1960), 49.

Graetz, Rick, and Susie Graetz. *Big Sky — From Indian Trails to the Tram*. No publisher, 2000.

Grant, H. Roger. *Living in the Depot — the Two-Story Railroad Station*. Iowa City: University of Iowa Press, 1993.

Grant, H. Roger, and Charles Bohi. *The Country Railroad Station in America*. Boulder, Col.: Pruett Publishing Co., 1978.

Green, Maury. *Television News: Anatomy and Process*. Belmont Cal.: Wadsworth Publishing Co., Inc., 1969.

Griffin, Harvey. "Big Sky Isn't Set Yet." *Billings Gazette* (16 July 1970), 4.

Gunther, Marc. *The House that Roone Built*. New York: Little, Brown and Co., 1994

Guthrie, A.B., Jr. Letter to Chet Huntley (20 July 1970). Original in Chet Huntley Collection.

Halberstam, David. *The Powers That Be*. New York: Alfred Knopf, 1979.

Halderman, H. R. *The Halderman Diaries*. New York: G. P. Putnam's Sons, 1994.

Hallin, Daniel. *The Uncensored War: The Media and Vietnam*. New York: Oxford University Press, 1986.

Hanson, Patricia. *American Film Institute Catalog of Motion Pictures produced in the United States*. 2 volumes. Berkeley, Cal.: University of California Press, 1999.

Hawkins, Dick. "Whatever Happened to Chet Huntley?" December 1973 broadcast on KATU, Channel 2, Portland, Ore.

Hehn, Erhardt. "Welcome Back Chet." *Exponent* (newspaper of the Montana State University, Bozeman, Mont.) (27 May 1970), 5.

Hickey, Neil. "Television in Turmoil." *TV Guide* (February 8, 1969).

Holmes, J.D. "Chet Huntley Unveils Plans for 'Big Sky of Montana.'" *Great Falls Tribune* (17 February 1970), 84:1

"How deep the scars in Chicago?" *Broadcasting* (2 September 1968), 17–26.

Hoyt, Kendall, and Frances Leighton. *Drunk Before Noon: The Behind the Scenes Story of the Washington Press Corps*. Englewood Cliffs, N.J.: Prentice Hall, Inc., 1979.

Humphrey, Hubert. Note to Tippy Huntley (22 March 1974). Original in Chet Huntley Collection.

"Hungarian Fund to Give Awards to 5 at Dinner." *New York Times* (3 April 1970), 49.

"Huntley, at Luncheon, Cited As 'Broadcaster of Year.'" *New York Times* (21 May 1970), 44.

"Huntley: Better Results with Petitions, Not Riots." Untitled, undated newspaper article in Chet Huntley file, Montana Historical Society Library, Helena, Mont.

"Huntley Bids Brinkley and N.B.C. Last 'Good Night.'" *New York Times* (1 August 1970), 47.

"Huntley-Brinkley Chronicle." (Advertisement section) *New York Times* (4 August 1968), section 11.

"The Huntley-Brinkley Report," NBC News tapes, copies in University of Wisconsin, Madison, Wisconsin; NBC World Headquarters, Rockefeller Center, New York; Vanderbilt University Archives, Nashville, Tenn.

"Huntley case moves Hart to recommend disclosure." *Broadcasting* (15 July 1968), 48–49.

Huntley, Chet. "A Word for the War." CBS radio broadcast (6 December 1942). Copy in Chet Huntley Collection.

_____. "Bourguiba: 'Moderate Revolutionary.'" *New York Times Magazine* (23 February 1958), 19, 72.

_____. *Chet Huntley's News Analysis.* New York: Pocket Books, 1966.

_____. "Collection and Papers." In K. Ross Toole Archives, Maureen and Mike Mansfield Library, University of Montana, Missoula, Mont.

_____. *The Generous Years: Remembrances of a Frontier Childhood.* New York: Random House, 1968.

_____. "Good Night All." *TV Guide*, XVIII (1 August 1970), 8–11.

_____. "Hatred." Commentary on Martin Luther King assassination, NBC News (4 April, 1968). Copy in Chet Huntley Collection.

_____. "In the Huntley Matter." *New York Times* (3 May 1964), television/radio, 12.

_____. Letter to Dr./Mrs. L. R. Packard, in *Jefferson Valley News* (Whitehall, Mont.) (30 March 1939).

_____. "The News in 1959." In Harry Skornia and Jack Kitson, eds. *Problems and Controversies in Radio and Television: Basic Readings*, Palo Alto, Cal.: Pacific Books, 1968, 358–363.

_____. "Perspective — Harmony." NBC Radio (7 March 1969).

_____. Radio piece: "Regarding American Youth." (20 March 1974), 74:60. Original in Chet Huntley Collection.

_____. "Resolved That — ." *Reporter* (magazine), 12 (27 January 1955), 2:4.

_____. "So This Is Retirement." *Modern Maturity* (April-May 1971), 45–46.

_____. Speech at Rochester Institute of Technology (3 June 1967). Original in Chet Huntley Collection.

_____. "Squares." Radio Broadcast (week of 21 February 1972). Original in Chet Huntley Collection.

_____. Telegram to friend Ronald (no last name) (17 June 1924). Original in Chet Huntley Collection.

_____. "The Silent Majority," *The New York Times* (5 November 1970), 47.

_____. "Tourism." Speech delivered in San Diego, Cal., date unknown. Original in Chet Huntley Collection.

_____. "What's Happened to Spellbinders?" *TV Guide*, IV (20 October 1956), 10–11.

_____. "The World Is His Beat." *TV Guide*, VI (23 August 1958), 17–19.

Huntley, Chet, and David Brinkley. "How to Watch a Convention." *New York Times* (11 July 1960), 54.

Huntley, Tippy. Letter to Bob Helmer (1 September 1977). Original in Chet Huntley Collection.

_____. Letter to James Farley (May 1974). Original in Chet Huntley Collection.

_____. Letter to Ron Berler (3 May 1974). Original in Chet Huntley Collection.

"Huntley-Chrysler Verify Resort Project Plans." *Bozeman Daily Chronicle* (16 February 1970), 1, 10.

"Huntley Denies Quotation in Life About the President." *New York Times* (21 July 1970), 13.

"Huntley Denies Report." *Billings Gazette* (28 August 1973), 1.

"Huntley denies some harsh words." *Broadcasting* (27 July 1970), 61–62.

"Huntley Drops Name From Beef Brand." *Great Falls Tribune* (1 April 1964), 23.

"Huntley Eulogized." *Bozeman Daily Chronicle* (27 March 1974), 4.

"Huntley gets award in New York, Brinkley his in Washington." *Broadcasting* (26 October 1964), 62.

"Huntley Is Hopeful Despite Opposition." *Billings Gazette* (14 January 1971).

"Huntley Memorial Services Scheduled Sunday at 6 p.m." *Bozeman Daily Chronicle* (22 March 1974), 1.

"Huntley Project Hits Stretch of Rough Sledding." *Great Falls Tribune* (30 June 1970), C-4.

"Huntley Says He Dropped Idea of Race for Senate." *New York Times* (6 August 1969), 79.

"Huntley Scheduled to Broadcast Again." *Independent Record* (Helena, Mont.) (18 May 1970).

"Huntley to Be Missed." *Bozeman Daily Chronicle* (21 March 1974), 4.

"Huntley to Make Home in Montana." *Bozeman Daily Chronicle* (16 February 1970), 1, 10.

"Huntley Will Speak to Graduating Class." *Gallatin County Tribune/Belgrade* (Mont.) *Journal* (28 May 1970), 3.

"Huntley's Estate Valued." *Bozeman Daily Chronicle* (20 September 1974), 4.

Hutchinson, Arthur. "Federal Funds Are Sought for Road Into Big Sky Resort." *Independent Record* (Helena, Mont.) (4 May 1971), 1.

_____. "Forrest Eyes Federal Funds for Big Sky." *Billings Gazette* (4 May 1971).

Illson, Murray. "Books of the Times—'End Papers'—*The Generous Years*." (Book review.) *New York Times* (19 October 1968), 35.

"In the Cow Palace: 'Toads' and 'Brinklies.'" *Newsweek* (27 July 1964), 50–51.

Ingets, Don. "Big Sky Big League." *Montana West* (Fall 1971), 11–14.

"It All Added Up" (ad). *New York Times* (9 August 1968), 70.

Jackaway, Gwenyth. *Media at War: Radio's Challenge to the Newspapers, 1924–1939.* Westport, Ct.: Praeger Publishers, 1995.

Jackson, Henry. Letter to Tippy Huntley (22 March 1974). Original in Chet Huntley Collection.

Johnson, Lyndon. *The Vantage Point.* New York: Holt, Rinehart and Winston, 1971.

Kahin, George. *Intervention — How America Became Involved in Vietnam.* New York: Alfred A. Knopf, 1986.

Karabell, Zachary. *The Rise and Fall of the Televised Political Conventions.* Cambridge, Mass.: Harvard University Press, 1998.

Kaufman, Michael. "Chet Huntley, 62, Is Dead." *New York Times* (21 March 1974), 44.

Keever, Beverly, Carolyne Martindale and Mary Ann Weston, ed. *U. S. News Coverage of Racial Minorities — A Sourcebook — 1934–1996.* Westport, Ct.: Greenwood Press, 1997.

Kenfield, Grace. "Chet Huntley Has Interesting Career." *Big Timber* [Mont.] *Pioneer* (7 July 1960), 1.

Kenworth, E. W. "Chet Huntley, in Montana, Likes Not Living by Clock." *New York Times* (16 May 1971), 66.

_____. "Ecology Unit Sends Dean Data to Court." *New York Times* (5 July 1973), 17.

_____. "Environmental Chief Silent on 2 U.S. Plans." *New York Times* (14 August 1971), 21.

_____. "Resort Plan Sparks Montana Controversy." *New York Times* (31 May 1971), 6.

_____. "Two Environmental Suits Filed Against Montana Resort Project." *New York Times* (14 May 1971), 21.

_____. "Trade of Forest Land for Montana Resort Approved." *New York Times* (22 April 1972), 66.

_____. "Volpe Disputed on Use of Montana Environmental Report in Clearing Aid to 'Big Sky' Road." *New York Times* (27 March 1972), 25.

Keogh, James. *President Nixon and the Press.* New York: Funk and Wagnall's, 1972.

Kintner, Robert. "Broadcasting and the News." *Harper's* (magazine), 230:4 (April 1965), 49–55.

_____. "Mailbox: A Defense — N.B.C. President Discusses Huntley's Remarks on Segregation Issue." *New York Times* (1 March 1959), Section II:13.

_____. "Television and the Real World." *Harper's* (magazine), 230:6 (June 1965), 94–96, 98.

Kisselhoff, Jeff. *The Box — An Oral History of Television, 1920–1961.* New York: Viking Press, 1995.

Kriegsman, Alan. "The Incredible Peddlers." *Washington Post* (16 March 1972), K13.
Kuglin, John. "Steam Plant Dedicated." *Great Falls Tribune* (23 September 1968), 1, 2.
"Lady from Altoona." *Nation*, 178 (16 January 1954), 3:3.
Laurent, Lawrence. "Chet Huntley's Goodbye." *Washington Post* (31 July 1970), C8.
Letofsky, Irv. "Good-by, Chet." *Minneapolis Tribune — TV Week* (14–20 Dec. 1969), 7.
"Letters to the editor." *Life* (17 August 1970), 17.
Lichty, Lawrence, and Malachi Topping. *American Broadcasting*. New York: Hastings House, Publishers, 1975.
Lipman, Theo, Jr. *Spiro Agnew's America*. New York: W. W. Norton & Co., Inc., 1972.
Liston, J. "At Home with Huntley." *American Home* (September 1961), 12, 17, 82.
"Live from Space." *Newsweek* (14 June 1965), 72.
"Lone Mountain Looms Over Site of Big Sky Complex." *Gallatin County Tribune and Belgrade Journal* (Mont.) (17 February 1970).
"A Look at Chet Huntley." *Bozeman* (Mont.) *Daily Chronicle* (21 March 1974), 2.
MacDonald, C. Howard. *Voices in the Big Sky*. Bozeman, Mont.: Big M Broadcast Service, 1992.
MacDonald, J. Fred. *Don't Touch that Dial*. Chicago: Nelson-Hall Press, 1979.
_____. *Television and the Red Menace — The Video Road to Vietnam*. New York: Praeger Publishers, 1985.
MacNeil, Robert. *The People Machine — The Influence of Television on American Politics*. New York: Harper & Row, Publishers, 1968.
"Magazine Says Huntley's Wrong About Quotes." *Independent Record* (Helena, Mont.) (23 July 1970), 15.
Malone, Michael, Richard Roeder, and William Lang. *Montana: A History of Two Centuries*. Seattle, Wash.: University of Washington Press, 1976, 1991.
Manchester, William. *The Death of a President: November 20–November 25 1963*. New York: Harper & Row, 1967.
Marchand, B. *The Emergence of Los Angeles: Population and Housing in the City of Dreams — 1940–1970*. London, Eng.: Pion Limited, 1986.
Mason, Phil. "Huntley Calls for Ideas in Government." *Billings Gazette* (23 September 1968).
Matloff, S. "The Saco Kid." *Newsweek* (7 October 1968), 112, 114.
Matusow, Allen. *The Unraveling of America: A History of Liberalism in the 1960's*. New York: Harper and Row, 1984.
Matusow, Barbara. *The Evening Stars*. Boston: Houghton-Mifflin Co., 1983, 69, 70–103, 202.
Mau Mau (review). *New York Times Film Review* (14 July 1955), 19:1.
"Mayor Denied Chet Wronged." *Independent Record* (Helena, Mont.) (11 August 1968).
McGraw, Pat. "Huntley Cites Role of Media." *Denver Post* (18 February 1972), 4.
McPherson cartoon. *New York Times* (23 November 1969), 4:13.
Merrick, William. Interview with author (10 July 2001), Bozeman, Mont.
Mickelson, Sig. *The Decade That Shaped Television News (CBS in the 1950s)*. Westport Ct.: Praeger Publishers, 1998.
Millegan, Roy. "Chet Huntley — Radio, TV Newsman." Parts I and II. *Whitehall* [Mont.] *Ledger* (29 October and 5 November 1986), both on page 2.
_____. Letter to author (20 March 2001).
"Montana Aroused By Plan for Road." *The New York Times* (13 June 1971), 58.
"Montana-Born Chet Huntley Rapped as Pro-Red." *Yellowstone News* (Billings, Mont.) (31 August 1961), 2.
Moore, Steve. "No Opposition Voiced on Big Sky Complex." *Bozeman Daily Chronicle* (17 February 1970), 1, 3.
"More legwork on NBC's new news." *Broadcasting* (3 August 1970), 42.
"More Union Problems on the Way." *Broadcasting* (17 April 1967), 44.
Morgan, Thomas. "Crisis, Conflict and Change in TV News." *Look* (magazine) (7 November 1961), 23:48–62.
Mosby, Aline. "Aline Talks to Chet." *Billings Gazette* (1 January 1967), 29.

"Most Influential People." *New York Post*.com Reader Poll, September 1999, website on internet.

"The Most Intimate Medium." *Time* (14 October 1966), 56–58, 63–64.

"MSU Students Back Big Sky." *Billings Gazette* (2 March 1970).

"Mudtrout on the Hook." *Newsweek* (7 September 1964), 77–78.

Murray, Michael, and Don Godfrey, eds. *Television in America*. Ames, Ia.: Iowa State University Press, 1997.

Nash, J. Robert, and Stanley Ross. *Motion Picture Guide*. Chicago: Cinebooks, 1985, 10 volumes.

_____. *Motion Picture Guide Index*. Evanston, Ill: Cinebooks, Inc., 1987, 2 volumes.

Naughton, James. "Dean Ends Testimony Story Unshaken, 3 Senators Hint They Want Nixon Reply." *New York Times* (30 June 1973), 1, 15.

_____. "White House Papers Outline Pressure on Network." *New York Times* (2 November 1973), 24.

"NBC News Election Year '68" (ad.) *Broadcasting* (9 September 1968), 32–33.

"NBC News expands roles of four correspondents." *Broadcasting* (7 August 1967), 65–66.

"N.B.C. News to Tell It in Color Every Day, Starting in the Fall." *New York Times* (16 August 1965), 49.

"Networks take on AFTRA Strike." *Broadcasting* (3 April 1967), 92–93.

"New Books." *New York Times* (30 September 1968), 44.

"New Displays Include Huntley Memorabilia." *News and Views* (brochure), Bozeman, Mont.: Museum of the Rockies (Winter, 1980).

News briefs on Chet Huntley. *Jefferson Valley News*, Whitehall, Mont. (19 November 1931, 13 October 1932, 31 May 1934, 8 November 1934).

"News chiefs would do it all over again." *Broadcasting* (9 September 1968), 48.

"Newsmakers." *Newsweek* (27 October 1969), 67.

News Release, Chrysler Corporation Press Information Service (16 February 1970), 1–2.

Newton, Eric, ed. *Crusaders, Scoundrels, Journalists*. New York: Times Books, 1999.

"Nine to Be Honored." *River Press* (Fort Benton, Mont.) (3 January 1975).

"Nixon As President 'Frightens' Huntley." *New York Times* (13 July 1970), 23.

Nixon, Richard. Letter to Chet Huntley (18 January 1969). Original in Chet Huntley Collection.

_____. *The Memoirs of Richard Nixon*. New York: Touchstone Books, 1978, 1990.

_____. Note to Tippy Huntley (21 March 1974). Original in Chet Huntley Collection.

"Notes on People." *New York Times* (2 September 1972), 14; (15 September 1973), 21; (19 January 1974), 23.

Oberdorfer, Don. *Tet!* Garden City, N.Y.: Doubleday and Co., Inc., 1971.

"Outburst by Hecklers Silence Senator Fulbright at Peace Luncheon Here." *The New York Times* (6 March 1969) 16.

"Palace Warfare." *Newsweek* (6 July 1964), 48.

Pallot, James. *The Movie Guide*. New York: The Berkley Publishing Group (A Pedigree book), 1995.

Parmet, Herbert. *Richard Nixon and His America*. New York: Konecky and Konecky, 1990.

"Peabodys of 1954." *Newsweek* (19 April 1954), 54.

Peterson, John. "Hello Chet: He's Out West, Now, But He's No Country Squire." *National Observer* (25 September 1971), 10.

Peterson, Ron. "Palmer and Killy Enter Development Picture." *Bozeman Daily Chronicle* (19 February 1970), 1, 8.

Phillips, Annabelle. "Big Sky Highway Won't Affect County Projects." *Bozeman Daily Chronicle* (19 February 1970), 1.

Poindexter, Ray. *Golden Throats and Silver Tongues: The Radio Announcers*. Conway, Ark.: River Road Press, 1978.

Polier, R. "His Co-Workers Respected Huntley." *Biographical News* (April 1974), 416.

Porter, William. *Assault on the Media: The Nixon Years*. Ann Arbor: University of Michigan Press, 1976.

Proceedings, Helena Convention on the Northern Pacific [Railroad] *Land Grant.* Helena, Mont., 1888, 14–15.

Prouty, Howard, ed. "NBC News" (31 October 1956); "Second Agony of Atlanta" (4 February 1959); "Tele Followup — Chet Huntley" (11 February 1959); "Chet Huntley Reporting" (28 September 1960); "Huntley-Brinkley Report" (11 September 1963); "Tele Followup Comment — Huntley-Brinkley" (17 November 1965); "Huntley-Brinkley & 4 Horsemen" (30 August 1967); "Just a Year to Go" (15 November 1967); "S'Long David, G'Bye Walter" (5 August 1970). *Variety Television Reviews.* New York: Garland Publishing, Inc., 1989, no pages, dates only.

Redfield, D. P. "Letters to the Editor." *Bozeman Daily Chronicle* (17 March 1970), 4.

Renz, Louis. *The History of the Northern Pacific Railroad.* Fairfield, Wash.: Ye Ole Galleon Press, 1980.

"Resolution Backing Big Sky Opposed." *Billings Gazette* (8 January 1971).

Reston, James. "Washington: Are You an Agnewstic." *New York Times* (23 November 1969), Section IV:12.

Ring, Ray. "Big Sky, big mess in Montana." *High Country News* (Panonia, Col.) (31 March 1997).

_____. "How Huntley sold Big Sky to Montana." *High Country News* (Panonia, Col.) (31 March 1997).

Ripley, Anthony. "Chet and the Big Ski Issue." *Billings Gazette* (25 April 1970), 1, 4.

_____. "Huntley's Resort Meets Protest." *New York Times* (25 April 1970), 31, 60.

"The Rugged Anchor Man." *Time* (1 April 1974), 44.

Ryan, Barbara. "Chet Huntley Reports Everything Fine in Montana." *Denver Post* (2 May 1971), 23.

Sanford, Robert. "Two Parties Courted Huntley." *St. Louis Post-Dispatch* (19 November 1971), 15A.

Savage, Barbara. *Broadcasting Freedom — Radio, War, and the Politics of Race, 1938–1948.* Chapel Hill: University of North Carolina Press, 1999.

Saxton, Berma. "Huntley Raps U.S. Foreign Policy Critics." *Billings Gazette* (15 June 1965), II:13.

Schanche, Don. "Good Night, NBC ... HELLO, MONTANA." *Today's Health,* 50 (May 1972), 5:54–58.

Scheibel, Kenneth. "'Stick with Brinkley', His Advice." *Billings Gazette* (7 April 1967), 1.

Schoenbrun, David. *On and Off the Air.* New York: E. P. Dutton, 1989.

Schwantes, Carlos. *Pacific Northwest: An Interpretative History.* Lincoln: University of Nebraska Press, 1989, 1996.

Scott, Vernon. "Chet Huntley, Barnyard Still in His Blood?" *Billings Gazette* (22 September 1963), 10.

Seventeen, editors of. "Chet Huntley." In: *In My Opinion.* New York: Macmillan, 1966, 121–124.

Shalit, Gene, and Lawrence Grossman. *Sometimes It Works.* New York: Doubleday and Co., 1965.

Sharp, U[lysses] S.G., and William Westmoreland. *Report On the War in Vietnam.* Washington, D.C.: Government Printing Office, 1969.

Shayon, Robert. "Mileage in Morality." *Saturday Review* (28 December 1957), 24.

Shepard, Richard. "News As a Main Course on TV." *New York Times* (25 August 1963), Section II:15.

Simmons, Jean. "Big Sky Builds Paradise Retreat in Mountain Air." *Dallas Morning News* (28 July 1974), C8.

Simmons, Pat. "Save the Gallatin Coalition." *Gallatin Wildlife Association* (newsletter) (January 2000).

"Six Straight" (ad). *New York Times* (30 August 1968), 68.

Skornia, Harry, and Jack Kitson, eds. *Problems and Controversies in Television and Radio.* Palo Alto, Cal.: Pacific Books, Publishers, 1968.

Small, William. *Political Power and the Press*. New York: W. W. Norton and Co., Inc., 1972.
_____. *"To Kill a Messenger" (Television News and the Real World)*. New York: Hastings House, 1970.
Smith, Jack. Telephone interview of Chet Huntley, Smith Features (22 February 1974). Original in Chet Huntley Collection.
Smith, Robert. "The Big Sky Development: A Lesson for the Future." *American West*, XII (September 1975), 5:46–47, 62–63.
Southworth, James. "Letter to the Editor." *Billings Gazette* (2 March, 1970, 3 May 1970), 4.
Spears, Joseph. *Presidents and the Press*. Cambridge Mass.: MIT Press, 1984.
Sperber, A. M. *Murrow: His Life and Times*. New York: Freundlich Books, 1986.
"Sportsmen knock report on Huntley's Big Sky." *Billings Gazette* (18 April 1971), 1.
Sprague, Marshall. "Growing Up in Montana — *The Generous Years*" (book review). *New York Times Book Reviews*. (17 November 1968), Section II:44.
Spritzer, Don. *Roadside History of Montana*. Missoula, Mont.: Mountain Press Publishing Co., 1999.
"Statement by N.B.C. Official." *New York Times* (22 April 1960), 9.
Steigerwald, David. *The Sixties and the End of Modern America*. New York: St. Martin's Press, 1995.
Sterba, James. "Big Sky of Montana: Chet Huntley's Controversial Legacy." *New York Times* (31 March 1974), Section 10:1, 17.
_____. "Big Sky reports open officially despite opponents." *Billings Gazette* (25 March 1974), 15.
_____. "Resort Opens 3 days After Huntley's Death." *New York Times* (25 March 1974), 20.
Stobel, Les, ed. "TV-Radio Strike" (13–19 April 1967), XXVII:124–125; "Chet Huntley Speaking" (16–22 April 1970), XXX:273; "Chet denies" (6–12 August 1970), XXX:584. *Facts on File*. New York: Facts on File.
Svee, Gary. "I'll quit Big Sky if it hurts environment." *Billings Gazette* (14 June 1971).
_____. "Little white school at Saco is part of Montana's history." *Billings Gazette* (19 June 1962), 3.
"Television — The Viewers' Choice." *Time* (25 July 1960), 42.
Thompson, Howard. "TV: N.B.C. Offers Samplings in a Trio of Specials." *New York Times* (21 October 1972), 67.
Thompson, Tommy. "Chet Heads for the Hills." *Life* (16 July 1970), 33–36.
Torre, Marie. "Interview with Chet." *New York Herald-Tribune* (29 March 1956.)
Trail, 1927 and 1929. (Yearbooks, Whitehall [Montana] High School.)
"Died: Chet Huntley." *Newsweek* (1 April 1974), 49.
"Tribute: Man of Substance — William Conrad's gruff oversize presence was a perfect fit for Cannon and Jake and the Fatman." *People* (magazine) (28 February 1994).
Trotta, Liz. *Fighting for Air*. Columbia, Mo.: University of Missouri Press, 1991, 1994.
Trout, Florence. "Tippy Today." *Bozeman Daily Chronicle* (7 August 1977), B1, 21–22.
Turner, Kathleen J. *Lyndon Johnson's Dual War: Vietnam and the Press*. Chicago: University of Chicago Press, 1985.
"U. S. Funds Barred for Road to Montana Resort." *New York Times* (31 December 1972), 44.
Van Gelder, Lawrence. "Huntley Defends Journalists' Acts." *New York Times* (25 March 1970), 95.
Van Swearingen, Hugh. "Chet Huntley Eyes State Resources." *Independent Record* (Helena, Mont.) (4 August 1969), 1.
Weintraub, B. "Chet Huntley: He Changed TV News." *Biographical News* (April 1974), 415.
Weisel, Jonathan. "Big Sky." *Montana* (magazine) (November/December 2000), 44–48, 51–54.
"Welcome to the Big Sky Country." *Bozeman Daily Chronicle* (2 August 1970), 4.
Westin, Av. *"Newswatch": How TV Decides the News*. New York: Simon and Schuster, 1982.

White, Phyllis. "News of Fawcett Crest Books." Fawcett World Library news release (12 January 1970), 1.

White, Theodore. *America In Search of Itself : The Making of the President 1956–1980.* New York: Harper and Row, 1982.

_____. *The Making of the President: 1964.* New York: Atheneum Publishers, 1965.

"Whitehall Graduates to Hear Huntley." *Independent Record* (Helena, Mont.) (6 February 1970), 16.

Whitworth, William. "Profiles: An Accident of Casting." *New Yorker* (3 August 1968), 34–42, 44–60.

Wicker, Tom. "Miller Suggests Secret Service Provide a Guard for Goldwater." *New York Times* (12 August 1964), 18.

Williams, Bob. "Chet Gets NBC Horse and Heads Out West." *New York Post* (1 August 1970), 2.

Workers of the Writers' Project. *Washington — A Guide of the Evergreen State* Revised edition. (American Guide Series.) Portland, Ore: Binfords & Mort, 1950.

_____. *Oregon — End of the Trail.* (American Guide Series.) Portland Ore.: Binfords & Mort, 1940.

Wren, Christopher. "Beyond the Black Diamonds." *New York Times* (11 November 2001), Section 5: 10, 16.

Index

Numbers in *italics* indicate photographs